# ESOTERIC GUIDE
## to New York

### By SCOTT HARNEY

Susan —
I hope you
enjoy this!

D0869506

ESOTERIC GUIDES

Copyright (C) Esoteric Guides
Author: Scott Harney
Published by Esoteric Guides
www.esotericguides.com
Esotericnewyork@esotericguides.com
Cover artwork by: Stedroy Cleghorne
Design and layout: Kenneth Harney
Cover model: Lea Kraemer, Prana Mandir Yoga Studio
Printed in the United States of America
First Edition ISBN 0-9745224-0-6

# ESOTERIC GUIDE
## to New York

## *Contents*

# Introduction

I was born with a caul on my face and my grandfather was the seventh son of a seventh son. In some cultures this may have marked me as potentially "gifted," or even a candidate for shamanic training.

But growing up in Irish-Catholic Boston, I was always just considered a bit "odd," with strange sensibilities. I gravitated toward the mystical and unusual.

Moving to New York was an obvious choice, the mythical city of possibility and personal freedom, the archetype of all cities. To me, New York was the home of witches, yoga adepts, spiritual gurus, tantric priestesses and spiritual explorers. New York remains a place where you can reinvent yourself, and more importantly, transform yourself.

I fell in love with New York City rather quickly and the flames of passion have never subsided; it is a city of many different subcultures, where diverse worlds exist simultaneously on one city block. If you don't believe in time travel, all you have to do is take a stroll down Mulberry Street on a Saturday afternoon, where old souls rooted in the consciousness of ancient China stroll next to hip yogis, whose vibrations resonate with the new "Aquarian consciousness."

This guide reflects this new Aquarian consciousness, as we move out of the consciousness of the Piscean age. The Age of Aquarius is all about one's personal, unique spiritual path, while the Piscean age was all about hierarchy and organized religion. The Aquarian vision is a planetary vision, one that transcends ethnic and religious differences and views the whole world as one family.

Manhattan is a big rock, granite to be exact, interwoven with billions of quartz crystals. The island itself descends down into the molten, core of the Earth. Manhattan is a fiery, passionate spiritual amplifier. What happens in Manhattan happens to the world. Many believe that Manhattan plays a crucial role in the spiritual balance of the planet. Some even say that the island of Manhattan was part of the lost continent of Atlantis, and that an ancient "solar temple" is located right near the Statue of Liberty, in the waters off lower Manhattan. New York City may be known as the financial capital of the world; it is also the esoteric center of the world. Nearly every esoteric group in the 20th century got its start in New York.

This guide is dedicated to the far-out spiritual explorers who still call New York their home, the psychics, yogis, occultists and mystics. In pursuing their unique vision, they are pursuing the American dream. New York has become the living example of the spiritual freedom that our Founding Fathers had envisioned, where man can "worship any deity he pleases, in any way he pleases" without fear of arrest or persecution. I have tried to make this guide as complete as possible. I will be updating it periodically, so please contact me if you would like to be included in the next edition. Use this guide as a reference for your own spiritual growth, or as simply entertainment. New York - what a great, mystic city.

**Scott Harney**
**New York City, 2003**

# Yoga: Fitness of the Future

No one does yoga like New Yorkers do. New York is the "yoga capital" of the world. There is an apocryphal story of a New York yogi who saved up all his money and traveled to India so he could study at the feet of the masters. On the way from the airport, the Indian taxi driver - upon learning his fare was a New Yorker - excitedly said: "I wish someday to travel to New York where I can learn yoga!"

New York City has more than 100 yoga studios. The city offers everything from traditional hatha, to sweat-producing Vinyasa (a constant movement from pose to pose), to traditional Mysore-style Ashtanga (an intense, aerobic-style yoga that uses a specific, *ujjayi* breathing).

I have included only studios in the guide, though New York also has plenty of outstanding teachers who will come to your home and give a private session. Nearly every health club in the city also has a yoga class.

Yoga is an ancient science, but it truly is the "fitness of the future." It differs from aerobic exercise because yoga poses combine movement with breath. Breath - or *prana* - is the source of our life. When we come into contact with the source of our being, profound changes can occur. Yoga truly is an esoteric practice in motion.

I developed this listing to help myself find a yoga class in any neighborhood of the city. Like so many New Yorkers, I have a busy schedule, and try to fit in a yoga class whenever I can. The New York yoga scene is vibrant and just waiting to be explored.

## UPPER WEST SIDE/HARLEM
### BABY OM
*212-615-6935*
*www.Babyom.com*
Young mothers Laura Staton and Sarah Perron began Baby Om in 1999 in order to continue practicing yoga, while bonding with their babies at the same time. Their idea has caught on - Baby Om is a hit. They added Prenatal Om and Mommy Om classes in 2003. Classes are held throughout the city, including Peggy Levine Fitness, Karma Yoga and the Jewish Community Center on the Upper West Side, The Shala in Greenwich Village and Yoga People in Brooklyn. Baby Om classes stress "regaining alignment, toning the pelvic floor and regaining strength" - all while holding one's baby. Classes are heavily influenced by the Iyengar style, but Baby Om promises an aerobic workout as well.

## BATEMAN INSTITUTE
*175 West 72nd Street between Columbus Avenue
and Broadway*
*212-243-2311*
*Closest subway: 1/9/2/3 to 72nd Street*
In late fall, 2002, the famed Bateman Institute
closed its Chelsea studio after legendary yogi Alan
Bateman decided to concentrate on finishing several
of his book projects. Bateman, however, still teaches
a full schedule of classes out of his spacious Upper
West Side apartment. Bateman has been practicing
yoga for more than 50 years and teaching professionally for nearly 35 years. A former opera singer,
performer and dancer, Bateman developed his
unique system in 1963, after he was severely injured
in a car accident. The Bateman System combines traditional hatha yoga with chi kung exercises. In the
Saturday morning class I took in his living room,
Bateman began by demonstrating a series of chi
kung arm movements. The class was not a class in
the traditional sense - students worked at their own
pace and Bateman, along with his girlfriend Kathy,
worked with students one-on-one. In a little more
than two hours, my understanding of yoga was
changed. Bateman clearly doesn't like the way yoga
is taught in the United States. "Yoga was designed
for the bodies of Indians, not Westerners," says
Bateman, a bearded, muscular man in his 60s. "I do
what works. Nothing should be forced in yoga." For
instance, straight-legged plough pose is forbidden in
the class - the legs must remain bent. Headstands?
Forget about doing them against the wall. The Cobra
pose? No hands allowed. Bateman points out that his
classes are deceptively difficult. "Sometimes the
least movement can be the most difficult," he says.
The class ended with a 15-minute "chi" workout, that
consisted of a flowing chi kung routine. Bateman still
offers a teacher training program, which qualifies
graduates to become a Bateman Health System
yoga therapist. Bateman said that he prefers teaching smaller classes, so you need to call ahead to
reserve a space.

## BIKRAM YOGA
*West 72nd Street between Broadway and
West End Avenue, second floor*
*212-724-7303*
*www.bikamyoganyc.com*
*Drop in class: $20*
*Closest Subway: 1/9, 2/3 72nd Street*
This Bikram studio is one of four Manhattan studios

owned by Donna Rubin and Jennifer Lobo. The Upper West Side studio began with a few students in a room in a chiropractic studio, but has mushroomed into two rooms, full with sweaty and steamy students. Bikram Yoga can be addictive. The heated room "sometimes as hot as 104 degrees" creates a profound relaxation, once you get used to it. Bikram yoga also does the same 26 poses every class, so that after a while the poses became ingrained into the body. This is not a style that will force you "inside" yourself. All poses are done with eyes open, in a bright room, facing a mirror. Students tend to be in shape and attractive, sometimes wearing only the scantiest clothing, which creates a very steamy environment indeed. It is a fantastic workout, fun and physically challenging.

## CHILDREN OF LIGHT CENTER FOR PERSONAL HEALING
*2672 Broadway at 102nd Street*
*212-932-9433*
*www.childrenoflight.com*
*Drop-in class: $13*
*Closest subway: 1/9 to 103rd Street*
The Children of Light Center offers a full selection of yoga classes, in addition to its regular, channeling sessions. The schedule is eclectic, from traditional hatha and Kundalini yoga to tai chi, NIA and Yoga in a Healing Vibration classes. The space itself is very soothing. Classes are held in the center's plush, blue carpeted main room, which is decorated with ancient Egyptian artwork. Center directors Ron Baker and Robert Baker are known for their psychotherapy and channeling work; Robert has been channeling the archangel Gabriel since 1990, he says. The center offers channeling sessions every Sunday evening.

## INTEGRAL YOGA UPTOWN CENTER
*200 West 72nd Street between Broadway and West End Avenue, 4th floor*
*www.integralyogaofnewyork.org*
*Drop in class: $13*
*Closest subway stop: 2/3/1/9 to 72nd Street*
*212-721-4000*
The uptown branch of Integral Yoga offers gentle, yet invigorating hatha yoga classes in a bright, cheerful room that overlooks Broadway. Integral Uptown faithfully follows the philosophy of the late Swami Satchidananda, who founded the Integral system. All classes include traditional hatha poses,

deep breathing and meditation, with an emphasis
on yogic philosophy. In the Integral system, lifestyle
is part of yoga. They advocate vegetarianism and
incorporating non-violence into one's lifestyle. The
uptown center also offers a well-respected teacher
training program.

### KARMA YOGA
*37 West 65th Street between Columbus*
*and Central Park West, 4th floor*
*212-769-YOGA*
*Drop-in class: $15*
*www.karmayoganyc.com*
*Closest subway stop: 1/9 to 66th Street*
Karma Yoga is one of New York's newest and most
stylish studios. The yoga rooms and changing areas
are sleek, with a great attention to detail. Even the
yoga rental mats smell nice - like peppermint. It
came as no surprise to me when I found out that the
studio is owned by Alexis Stewart, the daughter of
Beautiful Living doyenne Martha Stewart. Stewart
opened the studio in early 2003, offering primarily
Astanga and Vinyasa classes, along with Pilates and
Kundalini sessions. For a brief time, Karma Yoga was
known as Jai Yoga, however the studio changed the
name after Jai Yoga in California complained that
they owned the rights to the name.

### LIFE IN MOTION
*2726 Broadway at West 104th Street, second floor*
*212-666-0877*
*www.lifeinmotion.com*
*Drop in class: $14*
*Closest subway: 1/9 to 103rd Street*
Energetic healers Bruce and Elizabeth Andes Bell
created the Life in Motion system of transformative
movement as a healing modality using yoga asana
and dance. Their Upper West Side studio offers
healing, massage, along with a full, day-long schedule of yoga classes. They offer daily classes in
Vinyasa, hatha and Jivamukti styles of yoga. They
also have classes as late as 8 pm for those who
work late.

### LITTLE YOGA SPACE
*102 West 85th Street between Amsterdam and*
*Columbus, apt. 1B*
*212-501-8010*
Robin Janis teaches Iyengar-style yoga at this cozy,
but beautiful studio in the Upper West Side. Janis
teaches all classes and the space has the feel of a

family; she gives individual attention to each student and the classes are small and intimate. Janis - who is on the faculty of the Iyengar Institute of New York - emphasizes proper alignment and breathing. Call to get the daily schedule. Evening classes are held at 6 pm on most weekday evenings.

## MAHAYOGI MISSION
*New York Buddhist Church*
*331 Riverside Drive between 105th and 106th Streets212-281-8648*
*www.mahayogiyogamission.org*
*Drop in class: $20*
*Closest subway: 1/9 to 103rd Street*
Every Monday night from 6:30-8:30pm, the folks from the Mahayogi Mission hold an open yoga and meditation class. The yoga classes are based upon the teachings Sri Sadguru Mahayogi Paramahansa, a Japanese yoga master who spends part of the year living in New York City. Mahayogi's students claim that he "spontaneously entered samadhi" when he was eight years old, "awakening to true reality." The classes include basic asanas, primarily done on the floor, and each pose is held for several minutes. It is a very meditative experience. The Mahayogi Mission also gives classes in Tribeca, at Sufi Books.

## NEXT GENERATION YOGA FOR KIDS
*200 West 72nd Street between Broadway and West End Avenue*
*212-595-9306*
*www.nextgenerationyoga.com*
*Drop in class: $20 for kids and teen classes;*
*$25 for Daddy/Mommy and Me, $35 for My Baby and Me (check for space)*
Jodi Beth Komitor, the author of the Complete Idiot's Guide to Yoga with Kids, founded Next Generation Yoga in 1998 as a yoga studio specifically for children. Inspired by the Wizard of Oz, the multi-color yoga studio features a "yellow brick road," and is decorated with butterflies, flowers and rainbow curtains. Komitor is a professional teacher and spent six year as an elementary school teacher for children with special needs. She developed a passion for "kid's yoga" after studying with her first yoga teacher, Sonia Sumar, who developed Yoga for the Special Child. Classes at her studio are grouped according to the ages of the students, ranging from "2-4 year olds" to "teens." Komitor also offers Mommy/Daddy and Me classes as well as Yoga Therapy for Children with Special Needs. Komitor

# The New Life Expo:
# Bringing New Age to the city

Twice a year, in October and March, the Hotel New Yorker becomes a "New Age scene." Thousands of spiritual seekers, New Agers, UFO enthusiasts and holistic health practitioners gather together for a three-day celebration of alternative ideas and cutting-edge spiritual science.

Considered to be the best New Age conference and exhibition in the country, the New Life Expo is the brainchild of Mark Becker, a long-time New York yogi and holistic health practitioner.

"The New Life expo is a smorgasbord of new ideas and new products," says Becker, who began the New Life Expo in 1990. "I want to open people up to all possibilities."

Becker's own spiritual journey began in the 1960s. A native New Yorker, Becker moved to California "on a spiritual quest" when he was a teenager.

"I was a 60s child. Growing up in Brooklyn, I always knew that there was a bigger world out there," says Becker. "I originally moved to California for the music and the counter-culture scene, but I ended up learning yoga."

Becker eventually moved back to New York City in 1974 and began teaching yoga at New York Health Club - one of the first such classes in the city. Becker eventually opened his own yoga studio and health food store on the Upper East Side.

Becker was the first in the city to introduce such alternative health products such as wheatgrass, Bach Flower remedies, and macrobiotic products. His store offered bulk herbs, tinctures and supplements.

During this time, Becker began hosting cutting-edge healers

---

says that children's yoga is "extremely playful" and is an important way for children to become active, given the fact that many children now spend hours sitting in front of the television set. Proponents of kid's yoga say that the classes "inspire creativity, build self-esteem, teach environmental awareness and create a relaxed state of mind."

## OM SHAKTI YOGA
*Harlem, USA*
*212-831-1886*
*Walk-in class: $12*
*www.omshaktiyoga.com*
Yoga changed Cathleen Lewis' life and now she wants to share her knowledge and transformation with others in her Harlem neighborhood. Lewis is an accomplished artist and educator who discovered yoga five years ago. She says that she originally

like live food guru Ann Wigmore, sound healer Steve Halpern and macrobiotic expert Michel Abhesera, along with old pioneers like iridologist Bernard Jensen, herbologist Dr. Christopher and food healer Hana Kroeger. They would stay with Becker and give workshops at his store.

As the workshops grew in popularity, Becker expanded the vision and began co-producing the New York "Diet Expo" in the 1970s. The idea for the New Life Expo came to Becker after he opened his magazine *New Life*.

The New Life Expo draws some of the most interesting and eclectic guest speakers in the New Age community. Recent participants have included Ram Dass, Dannion Brinkley, Deepak Chopra, John Gray, and the current audience favorite, Sean David Morton. The expo was the first to introduce healing magnets, the Q-Link pendent, and crystal healing.

The Expo has also created some much-anticipated underground side events. For instance, photographer Nancy Burson throws an unofficial "New Life Expo" party at her Soho photo gallery/loft. The party I attended included such eclectic guests as Lama Kunzang Dorje, psychic Sean David Morton, healer Starr Fuentes, master teacher Lewis Harrison, healer J.P. Farrell, and *A Better World TV* host Mitchell Rabin, along with an assorted group of psychics and healers. The highlights of the evening included Morton singing *American Pie*, while a group of models were on the floor receiving "energy healings" from several healers.

Becker has since expanded the expo to Miami and Ft. Lauderdale; however his focus remains on New York. "My intention is all about education and teaching people to be open, so they can reach their maximum potential," says Becker.

*The website for the twice-yearly expo is www.newlifeexpo.com*

took the Sivananda Yoga Teacher Training program to only deepen her practice, but from the course, she developed a love of teaching. "It was at Sivananda that yoga became much more than a physical exercise for me, it became a lifestyle. I became much more aware of the spiritual dimension of yoga," she says. Her yoga journey took her to Eddie Stern's Patanjali Yoga Studio, where she continues to study Ashtanga yoga. She also recently spent four months in India, studying with Ashtanga yoga guru Pattabhi Jois. Lewis teaches out of her home, which is near 126th Street, as well at several community schools in Harlem. She says that her classes are for "people who love yoga," noting that her biggest challenge in her neighborhood is "competing with the gym culture" there. Class times vary so it is best to contact Lewis prior to attending class. "I decided to give something back, to share

**YOGA** | ESOTERIC GROUPS | WITCHCRAFT | OCCULT UNDERGROUND | BOOKS | UFOS | BOTANICAS | TANTRA | ASTROLOGERS & PSYCHICS |

the art of yoga with the public," says Lewis. "It is like you have something magical to tell people. You just need to share it."

## PRACTICE YOGA
*140 West 83rd Street between Columbus and Amsterdam*
*212-724-4884*
*www.practiceyoga.com*
*Drop in class: $15*
*Closest subway stop: 1/9 to 86th Street*
Jennifer Walker opened Practice Yoga in 2001 to give residents in her Upper West Side neighborhood an opportunity to study various styles of hatha yoga. Walker recruited an eclectic group of teachers who specialize in Vinyasa, power yoga, Ashtanga yoga and Pilates. During the Vinyasa class I took, the teacher - Michael V. - began the class by asking if any student had "any wisdom to share." He peppered the lively class with quotes from Aristotle and Plato. The class moved smoothly, yet was challenging. It was also hard not to stare at the two hand-painted murals of nature scenes and grass-covered mountains that cover the walls and give the first floor space a clean, refreshing feel. Practice Yoga offers more than 12 types of yoga - including a Yoga and High Tea Social event that it holds every Tuesday for expectant mothers, who take a gentle 75-minute prenatal class, and then head over to the nearby Alice's Tea Cup restaurant for some "yogic fellowship."

## PRENATAL YOGA CENTER
*251 West 72nd Street between Broadway and West End Avenue, suite 2F*
*212-362-2985*
*www.prenatalyogacenter.com*
*Closest subway stop: 1/9/2/3 to 72nd Street*
Yoga is considered one of the best exercises to pre-pare a woman for childbirth and the Prenatal Yoga Center offers a full-range of classes for pregnant and new mothers. The center also offers workshops and education for women to prepare for the birth experience. Director Debra Flashenberg opened the center in 2000 as a "resource community center" for expecting mothers. "This center is for body, mind and baby," says Flashenberg, who is a certified teacher in both Bikram and Vinyasa yoga. "We begin all our classes with a circle, so that expectant moth-ers can discuss how their pregnancy is going, as well as the anxieties they may be feeling about this pro-found life change." Flashenberg is a graduate of the

Boston Conservatory of Music, and has studied yoga with well-known prenatal yoga teacher Colette Crawford, as well as with California yogi Shiva Rea. In addition to yoga classes, the center also offers workshops on preparing for childbirth.

## RASA YOGA CENTER
*246 West 80th Street between Broadway and West End Avenue, fourth floor*
*212-875-0475*
*www.rasayoga.com*
*Drop in classes: $15*
*Closest subway stop: 1/9 to 79th Street*
Rasa Yoga is a unique yoga style that uses humming and chants, along with gentle hatha movements. Rasa Yoga Center has been a West Side secret for the past ten years, since it has only recently begun advertising. Charismatic teacher Ketul developed the Rasa style after spending a number years living at the Kripalu Yoga Center in Lenox, Mass. The classes are conducted with very subdued lighting and students are instructed to keep their eyes closed to facilitate a meditative state. The humming deepens the relaxation, according one teacher. The majority of poses are conducted on a soft floor mat; the results are often consciousness-altering. During the class I took, I found myself drifting in and out of the hypnogogic zone, that magical state of consciousness just before sleep. The classes are great for those who prefer a more meditative experience over that of a brightly-lit yoga workout.

## TA LIFE
*71 West 128th Street between 5th and Lenox Avenues*
*212-289-6363*
*www.ta-life.com*
*Drop in class: $15*
*Closest subway: 2/3 to 125th Street*
Teresa Kay-Aba Kennedy opened the Ta Life Yoga Studio in 2002 after leaving a "high stress corporate job." Kennedy grew up in an environment where her mother practiced and taught her yoga. However, after earning an MBA from Harvard University, Kennedy forgot her yogic roots and ended up with an ulcerated digestive system. "I decided to return to the path that my mother had taught me and I left the corporate world," says Kennedy, who earned her teacher training from Integral Yoga. Kennedy says that she decided to open a studio in Harlem because, at the time, there were no other yoga

studios in the neighborhood. "Part of my mission
is to bring positive, healthy living to this area," she
says. Kennedy has also developed a unique self-
improvement program called Power Living, which
trains people in the "principles and practices of
healthy and successful living." The studio offers
nutrition and cooking classes, in addition to a
full selection of yoga classes, ranging from power
yoga to gentle hatha.

## WORLD YOGA CENTER
*265 West 72nd Street between Broadway and*
*West End Avenue, second floor*
*212-787-4908*
*www.worldyogacenter.com*
*Drop in classes: $15*
*Closest subway stop: 1/9/2/3/ to 72nd Street*
World Yoga is a traditional yoga studio, which has
been giving classes in the Upper West Side since
1972. Director Rama Patella and founder Rudrani
Farbman Brown both have an impressive knowledge
of yoga and teach from a spiritual point of view.
Rudrani and Rama were both disciples of Swami
Muktananda, the founder of Siddha Yoga. Since the
mid-1990s, World Yoga has been offering classes in
Anusara yoga, the spiritually-focused style of John
Friend. Rudrani also heads the school's well-regard-
ed teacher training program and is the author of the
NYC Teacher Training Manual, based upon her nearly 40 years of experience. World Yoga still maintains
the idealistic feeling of the early 1970s, when yoga
first became popular in the United States. Their
classes remain focused on spiritual growth, while
still providing a good workout. Both teachers also
spend a great deal of time during the class giving
hands-on corrections and tailoring each class to
the yoga skills and "energy" of the students.

## YOGA DEN
*236 West 75th Street between Broadway and*
*West End Avenue*
*212-874-8701; 212-795-8885*
*Drop in classes: $14*
*Closest subway: 1/9/2/3 to 72nd Street*
The Yoga Den - formerly known as "Sat Nam Garden"
- is located in the basement of the Ruhani Satsang
Ashram. The studio offers a style that incorporates
hatha, Ashtanga and japa yoga in a soothing room
that overlooks a garden. The primary yoga teacher,
Tahji, is a student of the late Kirpal Singh, who
founded the Satsang Divine Science of the Soul,

**| YOGA** | ESOTERIC GROUPS | WITCHCRAFT | OCCULT UNDERGROUND | BOOKS | UFOS | BOTANICAS | TANTRA | ASTROLOGERS & PSYCHICS |

a meditation technique that focuses on the "inner light and sound." She guides the class with a lilting, sing-song voice. Every class begins with a spiritual reading from Singh, then pranayama, before the asana practice. Yoga Den offers classes on Tuesday, Thursday and Friday at 6 pm and Saturday at 2 pm and 4:30 pm. The ashram also has a weekly meditation, open to initiates of Satsang.

## *UPPER EAST SIDE*
### GOODSON PARKER WELLNESS CENTER
*30 East 76th Street between Madison and Park Avenues*
*212-717-5273*
*www.goodsonparker.com*
*Closest subway: 6 to 77th Street*
The Goodson Parker Wellness Center is far more than just a yoga studio; yoga is only one of the services that the center provides. Dr. DeAnsin Goodson Parker - a clinical psychologist - founded the center in the late 1990s as a center to "heal the body and mind." Dr. Parker is a certified yoga instructor and developed the Yogababy program for parents and babies. In addition to yoga, the center also offers massage, Pilates, acupuncture, psychotherapy, nutritional counseling and even dream analysis. "This is not a spa," says Rachel, an employee. "This is a center for holistic healing of the entire person." Yoga classes are limited to 15 students, so you need to reserve a space. "Many people like to combine modalities," says Rachel. "They may take a yoga class and then finish their workout with a massage."

### JIVAMUKTI UPTOWN YOGA CENTER
*853 Lexington Avenue between 64th and 65th Street, second floor*
*212-396-4200*
*www.jivamuktiyoga.com*
*Drop in class: $17*
*Closest subway: 6 to 68th Street*
The "uptown" branch of the Jivamukti Yoga Center has all the edgy energy of the downtown center - and the same exhilarating workout. The studio itself "evokes a feeling of serenity" with its lavender walls, dark wooden floors, and an altar featuring the Indian deity Ganesh. The center has the feel of an Indian temple. The Jivamukti style was developed by accomplished yogis David Life and Sharon Gannon in 1984. While many yoga studios have attempted to divorce yoga asana practice from its spiritual

roots, Jivamukti celebrates yoga's Vedic roots. The yoga classes are vigorous, sweat-producing, yet always mindful of the ultimate goal of yoga - which is liberation (Jivamukti).

## NEW YORK YOGA
*1629 York Avenue at 86th Street*
*212-717-9642*
*www.newyorkyoga.com*
*Drop in class: $20*
*Closest subway: 4/5/6 to 86th Street*
New York Yoga is the most extreme example of yoga gone corporate in the city. The studio itself has the dour atmosphere of a real estate office. When I jokingly commented on the steep price of their classes, a "marketing representative" suggested I come back for the weekly "community class," for people who can't afford a regular yoga session. Its website brags that the studio was designed by the same guy who designed the "MGM Grand Spa and the Caesars Palace Hotel and Casino." For those too lazy to leave their apartments, New York Yoga also offers "live internet classes" for $1.20 a day.

## OPEN SKIES YOGA
*1321 Madison Avenue between 93rd and*
*94th Streets*
*212-369-5001*
*www.openskiesyoga.com*
*Walk-in Class: $25*
*Closest subway: 6 to 96th Street*
Open Skies Yoga is dedicated to "open hearts and open minds." Sarah Deharenond and her husband Joe Fowler decided to open their yoga studio to give their Upper East Side neighborhood a space for high-quality yoga. Deharenond describes the style taught at Open Skies as "eclectic." "There are so many styles of yoga, that we wanted to take the best of the styles," says Deharenond. "We are not married to any one style." She says that her own influences are Ashtanga and Anusara styles of yoga and that most of the classes are Vinyasa-based flow classes. The classes at Open Skies tend to be smaller and "intimate." "This is a great place for a beginner to learn, because our teachers give so much one-on-one instruction," says Deharenond. "We really stress working individually with the student and give a lot of hands-on adjustments."

## YOGILATES
*1-877-964-4528*

www.yogilates.com
New Yorker Jonathan Urla developed Yogilates in 1997 to join the "unifying essence of yoga and the powerful therapeutic value of Pilates." Yogilates is a registered trademark class and there around 30 certified teachers, most of which are on the East Coast. Yogilates is taught in the Equinox Health Clubs, MangOh Yoga Studio, Sports Club/LA and Practice Yoga. Urla, who has published several books and video tapes on Yogilates, spends much of his time traveling the country giving workshops and training Yogilates teachers. The Yogilates class that I took combined traditional hatha yoga poses with some killer Pilates abdominal work. The class moved like a Vinyasa class, unlike the static poses of a traditional Pilates class. Urla has elegantly updated the Pilates regime to fit into the active life of the average New Yorker.

### MIDTOWN WEST
### BIKRAM YOGA COLLEGE OF INDIA
*797 8th Avenue between 48th and 49th Street, fourth floor*
*212-245-2525*
*www.bikramyoganyc.com*
Hell's Kitchen just got hotter with the addition of the midtown branch of Donna Rubin and Jennifer Lobo's Bikram yoga empire. In addition to sweaty yoga, the midtown branch also has a massage studio that offers Hot Stone Massage, Shamanic Healing and Head/Neck/Shoulder Massage. The midtown studio also offers first-time Bikram students a beginners class every Monday and Wednesday evening at 6:30 pm. This individualized class is limited to 10 people and is a great way to learn the 26-pose system, as well as get acclimated to the heated room.

### HEALING YOGA CENTER
*400 West 37th Street between 9th and 10th Avenues, suite 7N*
*212-239-0951*
*Drop in class: $15*
*www.healingyoga.com*
*Closest subway: 2/3/1/9 to 34th Street*
Amita Puri teaches traditional hatha yoga the "way it was originally taught thousands of years ago." "Yoga is not just a physical practice, but primarily a spiritual practice and way of life," says Puri. "In every class we discuss yogic philosophy and lifestyle, in

addition to our asana practice." Puri moved to New York City in the summer of 2003 from Washington, D.C., where she grew up. She has been teaching yoga since 1997, after graduating from the Vivekananda Kendra Yoga Institute in Bangalore, India. Puri teaches several group classes a week in various locations in Manhattan and also has a healing practice out of her Manhattan office. She uses asanas and "yogic kriyas" to heal diseases such as hypertension, depression and chronic fatigue. Puri says that her group classes are gentle and she has students hold each pose for up to three minutes, which facilitates internal cleansing. She says that many fast-paced Vinyasa classes miss the point of yoga, since they don't hold poses long enough to reap the benefits of the asana. "Most of the people who come to my classes are professionals and executives with high-stress jobs," says Puri. "They don't want a fast-paced class, they come because they want a place to relax."

## INDO-AMERICAN YOGA VEDANTA SOCIETY
*Swami Bua*
*330 West 58th Street between 8th and*
*9th Avenues, apt. 11J*
*212-265-7719*
*Drop in class: $20 donation*
*Closest subway: 1/9/A/C/B/D to 59th Street*
Sick of "spandex yoga" done in a health club? Then why not study with Swami Bua, a genuine 116-year-old yoga master, who still teaches yoga to a small group of students out of his Hell's Kitchen apartment. Bua has lived in New York since 1972 and has been the "guru" to countless yogis in the city. Walking into his one-bedroom apartment is like walking into an Indian ashram; Bua sits shirtless on a sofa, wearing an orange sari, his white beard flows over the many religious prayer beads around his neck. He begins each class by blowing on a conch shell, which fills his living room with a deep, resonant vibration. Bua's classes are as much about philosophy as about physical movement. He sprinkles his instructions with advice like "you don't do yoga for you - you do it for your children." He says that all sickness is the result of "sin" and one of the biggest sins in his book is meat-eating. For Bua, yoga done without observance of the yamas and niyamas is not yoga - it is merely physical exercise. Bua stresses precision and awareness of the body; his classes are challenging and include many body twists to massage the inner organs. Bua's classes are unlike any

other yoga classes in the city. He has taken his more than 100 years of experience and distilled them into an hour-long session that he says gently "awakens the body's glandular system" for healing. Bua generally teaches every weekday at 1 p.m. and 6 p.m. and, on Saturday and Sunday, he teaches a 4 p.m. class. Says Swami Bua: "If you spend three months with me, I'll have you as flexible as a rattlesnake."

### SONIC YOGA

*754 9th Avenue at 51st Street, second floor*
*212-397-6344*
*www.sonicyoga.com*
*Walk-in class: $14*
*Closest subway station: 1/9 to 50th Street*
Sonic Yoga lives up to its name. Think Uktanasana done to the music of Led Zeppelin. Former lawyer-turned-yogi Jonathan Fields has developed a "yoga on steroids" workout that combines Vinyasa, a heated room "80 degrees - not as hot as Bikram yoga" and rock music. Fields trained under Boston "power yoga" guru Baron Baptiste, along with Rodney Yee. Fields opened the Hell's Kitchen studio in December 2001, and it has already developed a huge following. The beginner's class I attended one evening was packed full with an interesting and diverse group of young professionals, actors and artists. The class moved at a fast pace, flowing from one asana to another. The sleek studio has a sound system worthy of a nightclub. The class began with the ethereal music of Krishna Das, and then moved into the adrenaline-pumping music of groups like Foo Fighters, Jimi Hendrix and Stone Temple Pilots. We ended with some mellow Indian chants. Fields, a former music DJ, said that he puts a lot of effort into picking music for the classes. Fields also recently introduced a class called Theta Flow, a power yoga session with an acoustic soundtrack and synchronized lighting to promote a meditative state.

### THE PRANA STUDIO

*66 West 39th Street between 5th and 6th Avenues,*
*third floor*
*212-666-5816*
*www.thepranastudio.com*
*Walk-in class: $17*
*Closest subway stop: N/R, 2/3, 1/9 to 42nd Street*
The Prana Studio owner Danicia Ambron decided to open her midtown yoga studio in 1998, as a way to present Ashtanga yoga in an accessible way. Ashtanga is a challenging and aerobic series

of yoga movements that often includes jumping into poses. "Ashtanga yoga is such a great workout that I wanted to make it available to everyone," says Ambron, who was an athlete and pre-med student at Columbia University. Ambron says that she is the perfect example of how Ashtanga can benefit a person. She is the mother of two children and suffers from Rheumatoid Arthritis. "I was doing the full Ashtanga series when I was eight months pregnant," she says. "If I can do Asthtanga, anyone can." Unlike some of the other Ashtanga studios in the city, Ambron says that she teaches "verbal classes," in which she guides her students through the poses, often working with students individually. "I'd rather have someone do Ashtanga for their whole life, than get burned-out after only a few years," she says. The Prana Studio is clean, well-lit and ventilated. It also features a boutique that sells yoga clothing, mats and books. For those who have been intimidated by the elitism and inflexibility of the more traditional studios, The Prana Studio is the place to go and learn this wonderfully empowering form of yoga.

## *MIDTOWN EAST*
### BE YOGA
*160 East 56 Street between Lexington and 3rd Avenue, 12th floor*
*212-935-9642*
*www.beyoga.com*
*Drop in class:$20*
*Closest subway: N/R/W/4/5/6 to 59th Street; V/E/6 to 53rd Street*
Be Yoga teaches the ISHTA "Integrated Science of Hatha, Tantra and Ayurveda" style of yoga developed by Alan Finger, that combines tantric philosophy, ayurvedic healing and the physical practice of hatha. Finger formerly operated the famed Yoga Zone studios in New York and has created more than 50 yoga videotapes. In 2001, Finger closed the Yoga Zone studios and opened the four Be Yoga studios with partners Beverly and Bob Murphy and Jean Koerner. The classes are challenging and Vinyasa-flow driven. Classes tend to fill up pretty quickly, so it is best to reserve a class on the studio's website.

### BIKRAM YOGA EAST
*235 East 49th Street between 2nd and 3rd Avenues*
*212-832-1833*
*www.bikramyogaeast.com*

*Walk-in class: $18*
The slogan of Bikram Yoga East is "sweat a little, strain a little, laugh a little." This East Side studio offers daily classes during the week at 5:30 pm and weekend classes at 10 am. Bikram Yoga guru Viraj Santini teaches many of the classes. For those who have never heard of him, Santini has been recommended by Bikram Chaudhury as the best teacher in New York for advanced Bikram students to train with. Santini, however, welcomes students of all levels at his classes. Bikram Yoga East shares space with the Manhattan Children's Athletic Training School "CATS".

## DAHN YOGA CENTER
*532 Madison Avenue at 54th Street, 5th floor*
*212-935-5777*
*www.dahnyoga.com, www.healingsociety.com*
*Drop-in classes: no*
*Closest subway stop: 6 to 51st Street*
At first glance, this Madison Avenue yoga center appears more "dojo" than yoga studio. When I walked in, I was greeted by Master Tan Do, who was wearing a martial arts-type uniform. Tan Do is one of the most senior students of Ilchi Lee, the Korean-born founder of this fast-growing spiritual movement. Dahn Yoga combines hatha yoga poses with Oriental marital arts movements, to "move the energy" in the body. The classes are fun, energetic and upbeat, often with Asian music playing in the background. Do explained that students are required to sign-up for at least six months and make a commitment to attend class three times a week. There are no drop-ins allowed, because he said that it would be too "disruptive" for the closely-knit group of long-time students. After the class, many of the students sat around the Korean-style studio, sipping green tea and chatting with the Master. Many students end up going through the Dahn Yoga teacher training program, culminating with a retreat in Sedona, Arizona, so that they can also become Dahn "masters" themselves. Tan Do says that Dahn Yoga is a unique system because it concentrates on the energy systems in the body, creating physical and spiritual health.

## DHARMA YOGA CENTER
*297 Third Avenue at 23rd Street between*
*2nd and 3rd Avenues*
*212-889-8160*
*www.dharmayogacenter.com;*

www.yogaasanaposter.com
*Drop in class: $15*
*Closest subway stop: 6 to 23rd Street*
Dharma Yoga Center is one of the few yoga studios
in New York City where you can study with a true
spiritual master. Sri Dharma Mittra teaches class
at least once a day in his beautiful temple of a
yoga studio. His sinewy body contorts into asana
poses in a masterful, awe-inspiring way that most
yogis could only dream of. Mittra originally hails
from Brazil and began his yoga training more
than 40 years ago under famed Yogi Swami
Kailashananda "known in the West as Yogi Gupta".
After spending many years as a celibate renunci-
ate monk, Mittra was asked by his teacher to go
out into the world and teach. Mittra opened the
Dharma Yoga Center in 1975 and has been a fix-
ture on the New York yoga scene ever since. Most
of Mittra's students come through word of mouth,
since Dharma Yoga does not advertise. Mittra's
classes are some of the most physically challenging in the city. Mittra stresses spiritual growth
and his flyer advertises "psychic development"
as a benefit from studying with him. Mittra begins
each class with chanting and plays a traditional
Indian organ; he ends each class with chanting
and meditation on a candle. Pictures of saints and
spiritual teachers line the walls of the practice
space that Mittra calls "Kailashananda Temple."
Dharma Yoga also has a small store that sells
books, ayurvedic products, as well as his famous
poster, the Ultimate Yoga Chart of 908 Poses,
that Mittra produced in 1984. Dharma Yoga is
a gem of a studio and Sri Mittra is one of the
spiritual beacons of the New York yoga scene.

### KUNDALINI YOGA EAST
*873 Broadway between 18th and 19th Streets,*
*sixth floor*
*212-982-5959*
*www.kundaliniyogaeast.com*
*Walk-in class: $15*
*Closest subway: 4/5/6/N/R/L to Union Square*
Kundalini Yoga East founder and director Sat Jivan
Kaur Khalsa has been teaching Kundalini yoga and
meditation for more than 28 years in New York City.
She was personally trained by Yogi Bhajan and is in
demand also as a yoga therapist, numerologist and
spiritual counselor. The studio offers two classes a
day. Khalsa's classes include dynamic exercises,
breathing techniques and meditation. Khalsa says

that the practice of Kundalini yoga helps get rid of "fatigue, depression and stress." The classes taught by Khalsa feature "celestial healing and the trans-formational sound of the gong." Kundalini Yoga East also offers the only 3HO-approved teacher training in New York City.

## MANGOH YOGA STUDIO
*322 East 39th Street between 1st and 2nd Avenues*
*212-661-6655*
*www.mangohstudio.com*
*Drop in class: $15*
*Closest subway: 4/5/6/7 to 42nd Street*
MangOh Yoga studio is a welcome addition to the "yoga-starved" area around the United Nations. The studio was opened in October 2002 and offers 52 classes a week. MangOh classes are an hour long - perfect for a lunch time yoga class. The studio has classes on the hour, ranging from Pilates, Harmony Yoga, Yogilates (combining yoga and Pilates) and Gyrokinesis (combining yoga, dance, ta'i chi and gymnastics). MahgOh has the feel of an aerobics studio; it is well-lit and ventilated with hard-wood floors. The teachers seem enthusiastic and well-trained. Since it is a new studio, the classes tend to be smaller and the teachers tend to give personal attention. MangOh offers a special "lunch-time" special, with eight noon classes for only $10 each.

## PRANA MANDIR
*316 East 59th Street between 1st and 2nd Avenues*
*212-803-5446*
*www.pranamandir.com*
*Drop in class: $17 ($10 first class)*
*Closest subway stop: 5/6 to 57th Street*
Accomplished yogi Lea Kraemer opened Prana Mandir in 2002 as a center for Kundalini and Vinyasa yoga. The charismatic Kraemer is one of the rising stars of the New York Yoga scene. She has been teaching for 15 years and has training certificates in several yogic disciplines, including Kundalini yoga as taught by Yogi Bhajan. Prana Mandir feels very homey, because is it located in the top-two floors of a luxurious townhouse. The top-floor studio has a vaulted ceiling and the feel of an upscale Swiss lodge. Kraemer, who is a student of Siddha Yoga, began the Vinyasa class by having us rub our hands together to gather the energy. She then announced that she was in a good mood and wanted to treat us to a "spicy and delicious" yoga class. She didn't let us down - she even threw a few Kundalini "breath of fire"

# Swami Bua: The 116-year old Yogic Master of Manhattan

The amazing Swami Bua Maharaj may be 116-years old, but he hasn't let his age slow him down. Bua has survived childhood illness, dangerous pythons - and even ornery Manhattan landlords to become one of the most accomplished yogis in the world. One of his disciples said that Bua was very sickly as a child and reportedly "died" when he was young. When his parents put Bua's body on the cremation fire, he began moving. Everyone ran away, except for an Indian *sadu* "holy man",

who took Bua off the fire and brought him to his ashram, where Bua became his student. Learning yoga in the ashram was not easy; Bua says that he had to contend with the dangerous animals that lived in the jungles next to the ashram - including pythons which would chase him.

Bua still teaches two classes a day out of his mid-town apartment located in Hell's Kitchen, within walking distance of Central Park. He is living proof of the effectiveness of yoga for health and healing. "I didn't start doing yoga because I wanted to, I did it out of my own necessity - to regain my good health," says Bua, sitting in lotus position on a coach in his yoga studio/apartment. "I learned by watching others practice. I did yoga to get longevity and not fall prey to sickness."

Bua seems to have achieved his yogic goals; his disciples claim that he is 116-years old. However, Bua won't confirm or deny his age.

"Our Hindu Bible does not allow us to tell our age," he says. What certain, however, is that Bua is one heck of a yogi. To demonstrate his yogic abilities, Bua closes off his nose and mouth and "breathes" through his eyes. His eyes squeak, as he apparently pushes air out of his eyeball sockets. He then performs *kechari mudra*, in which he "swallows" his tongue - completely. He opens his mouth and I can see his patella, but his tongue is nowhere to be seen. According to esoteric yogic

| YOGA | ESOTERIC GROUPS | WITCHCRAFT | OCCULT UNDERGROUND | BOOKS | UFOS | BOTANICAS | TANTRA | ASTROLOGERS & PSYCHICS |

teachings, when the tongue is swallowed, higher "psychic" centers are activated.

"See if any yoga teacher in New York can do this!" he says, after regaining his composure.

Bua seems disdainful about how yoga is taught in the West. "In America, yoga is mostly taught for the sake of money," says Bua. "Others teach yoga because of self-prestige." Bua concedes that he has heard of some yoga studios in Manhattan "who do teach yoga nicely," but says he can't recall the names of the studios.

Bua's own classes are based upon "what is written in the *Vedas*." "Yoga is a science and must be practiced precisely," says Bua. "When yoga is practiced correctly, your body gets trimmed, your face becomes bright, your eyes become clear, you become disease-less, you revitalize your nervous system - and you sublimate your sex energy."

Over the years, Bua has taught countless other yogis this ancient science. He moved to New York City in the late 1960s, through the assistance of the former Shah of Iran, one of Bua's yoga students and patients; Bua reportedly cured the Shah of cancer. Bua won't list his famous students, however one photograph on his wall is telling. It shows a middle-aged Bua teaching yoga to a group of young students - one of whom is Satya Sai Baba, 14 years old at the time.

Despite his advanced age, Bua continues to teach class every day. He teaches with passion, yelling out instructions to his student from his couch, occasionally blowing his conch shell. He radiates yogic energy and guides his students with the caring of a father. Bua definitely comes from the "tough love" school of yoga, often berating his students who don't follow his instructions exactly.

For Bua, yoga is a sacred lifestyle, based upon the wisdom of Hindu *Vedic* scriptures. It includes daily ablutions, rituals, "being peaceful, silent and not entering into frivolous conversation." He is also insistent upon the yogic principle of *ahimsa*, which is non-violence. He has been a vegetarian his entire life and says that the vegetarian way is the way for all of humankind.

"If one is a human being, one must be a vegetarian," says Bua. "When you eat meat, you are eating a dead corpse. The human was not meant to eat corpses. It is man's duty to safeguard and protect the animals."

When asked why he continues to teach at an age when most would be retired, Bua seems a bit taken aback.

"What else would I do with my time if I didn't teach, sit idly?" asks the yoga master. We work because we love our work, but we also must feed the belly."

After each class, Bua's students sit around him as he answers questions and shares his own experiences. As his class is ending, he always gives the same advice and perhaps a clue to his own longevity.

"Begin the day with love, fill the day with love, spend the day in love and end the day with love," he says. "This is the true way to God."

rounds into the mix. We ended the class with part-ner-assisted back bends. Prana Mandir offers a full-schedule of Kundalini, Vinyasa and Anusara classes, as well as workshops like the Ta Ke Ti Na Rhythm workshop, which uses "voice, stepping patterns and clapping" to revitalize the nervous system. The studio also offers an advanced Agni teacher training program that includes in-depth yogic studies. "My intention in opening the studio is to work with people heart-to-heart," says Kraemer. "I wanted to create a community center where teachers and students can share yoga with individuals who otherwise would not have been exposed to this ancient system."

### SAL ANTHONY'S MOVEMENT STUDIO
*190 Third Avenue between 17th and 18th Streets*
*212-420-7242*
*www.movementsalon.com*
In addition to being a great restaurateur, Anthony Macagnone, owner of Sal Anthony's Movement Studio (and restaurant of the same name), is also a fitness enthusiast. Macagnone is black belt in Tae Kwon Do, as well as a Gyrotonics instructor. His passion for fitness has paid off in his movement salon. The salon offers yoga, Pilates and Gyrotonic classes in a historic Third Avenue building. The yoga classes are held in the second floor studio, in an airy, sun-light-filled room with a vaulted ceiling and exposed brick walls. The class I attended was taught by a teacher name Alison, who was trained at the Om Yoga Center. She began the class with chanting and put the class through a challenging Vinyasa-style session. By the end, the room was steamy and I was covered in sweat. The class was full and made up of mostly of fit women. Although I was a bit hesitant to take a yoga class at a studio that shares the same name as an Italian restaurant, my fears were quickly dispelled. Sal Anthony's just may become the next craze in fitness centers - workouts with a New Age twist.

### THE HARD AND SOFT ASHTANGA YOGA INSTITUTE
*Held at Exhale Spa*
*980 Madison Avenue between 77th and*
*76th Street*
*212-661-2895*
*www.power-yoga.com*
Beryl Bender Birch"s Power Yoga has found a new home in Manhattan at the Exhale Spa on Madison Avenue. Birch also teaches at Om Yoga, as well as

her primary studio in East Hampton. Birch originally founded the Hard and Soft Ashtanga Yoga Institute in Colorado way back in 1975, before moving to New York City in 1980. She began teaching at the New York Road Runners Club and became a national figure in 1995 with the publication of her book Power Yoga. Birch's style is energetic and challenging, drawing upon the Ashtanga yoga of Pattabhi Jois, along with the precision of the Iyengar and Desikachar styles of yoga. Birch and her husband Thom were one of the first to train yoga instructors in the West, as well as the first to popularize Ashtanga yoga. Their style of yoga is "both a workout for the body, as well as the mind," she says. Registration is required prior to taking the classes at Exhale.

### YOGA MOVES
*1026 Sixth Avenue between 38th and 39th Streets*
*212-278-8330*
*www.yogamovesgyro.com*
*Closest subway stop: N/R/1/2/3/9/A/C/E to*
*42nd Street*
Yoga Moves is dedicated completely to the Gyrotonic exercise, the "yoga for dancers" system developed by former ballet dancer Juliu Horvath. Horvath - who also competed in gymnastics and swimming - defected to the United States from Hungary in the 1960s, and took up yoga in an attempt to heal himself from his own chronic pain and injuries. Center co-directors Luisa Laurie and Si-Hwa Noh both studied with, and were certified by Horvath. The patented system uses a machine for a combination of stretching and strengthening exercises. The Gyrontonic system has been described as a "spiraling, circular system" as opposed to the more "linear" Pilates system. Sessions at Yoga Moves are $65 and you work one-on-one with a trainer. For those who already know the system, you can work by yourself on a machine for $25.

## CHELSEA
### ANANDA MARGA YOGA
*1182 Broadway between 28th and 29th Street,*
*suite 802*
*718-898-1603*
*www.yogainnewyork.org*
*Drop-in class:$11*
*Closest subway: 1/9/N/R to 28th Street*
Every Wednesday evening, the folks from the

Ananda Marga ashram in Queens trek out to the
Dharmakaya Center in Manhattan for a yoga class,
followed by a meditation given by one of their funky,
orange-robed monks. The 5:30 pm yoga class is
advertised as a "preparation for meditation," based
on the teachings of the late Shrii Shrii Anandamurti.
The class I took consisted of traditional asanas
held for eight seconds, or done eight times "for
mystical reasons, it was explained to me". The class
was definitely not sweat-producing, but did loosen
my hips to prepare for lotus posture. At 7 pm, Dada
Rainjitananda, an Ananda monk, showed up and gave
a meditation and talk on Shiva's Tantric teachings.
According to Rainjitananda, tantra has nothing to do
with sex and, for the most part, is misunderstood in
the West. Turns out, tantra is all about chanting and
"internal spiritual techniques" - the "true" bliss, he says.

## BE YOGA DOWNTOWN
*138 Fifth Avenue between 18th and 19th Streets,
fourth floor*
*212-647-9642*
*www.beyoga.com*
*Drop in class: $20*
*Closest subway: N/R/W to 23rd Street*
Be Yoga was founded by Alan Finger, a second-gen-
eration yoga master who developed the ISHTA
"Integrated Science of Hatha, Tantra and Ayurveda"
system. Classes are energetic and challenging. Be
Yoga evolved from Finger's "Yoga Zone" studios in
2001, with partners Beverly and Bob Murphy and Jean
Koerner. The downtown branch of Be Yoga offers a full
range of classes, from restorative to advanced level.

## BIKRAM YOGA CHELSEA
*250 West 26th Street between 7th and 8th Avenues*
*212-929-9052*
*www.bikramyogachelsea.com*
*Drop in class: $18*
*Closest subway: N/R/1/9 to 28th Street*
The motto of Bikram Yoga Chelsea is "inspiration,
freedom and community." Studio owner John
Golterman opened the center in 2001, after finishing the grueling Bikram yoga teacher training course
in California. Golterman led a colorful life before
devoting all his energies to yoga; the former actor
wrote and performed a one-man play about his
experiences as a commercial fisherman in Alaska.
He also has worked as a model in Japan, where he
also toured with a pop music group. Golterman's
classes are "motivational" and the center has creat-

ed a "supportive environment" in which to learn the challenging 26-pose, heated yoga routine.

### BIKRAM YOGA NYC
*182 5th Avenue between 22nd and 23rd Streets, third floor*
*212-206-9400*
*www.bikramyoganyc.com*
*Drop in class: $20*
*Closest subway stop: 1/9/N/R to 23rd Street*
Classes are top-notch at this "hot yoga" studio run by Donna Rubin and Jennifer Lobo. The room is heated to over 100 degrees as classes are brought through the 26-pose Bikram yoga regimen. Be sure to wear shorts or bathing trunks, and bring a towel for the sweat. The Bikram experience is profoundly relaxing, energizing and cleansing. But be warned, the classes can be challenging if you are not used to the heat. Bikram proponents claim that doing Bikram at least three times a week can reduce the symptoms of many chronic diseases, such as arthritis, diabetes and thyroid disorders.

### DAHN YOGA CENTER
*830 6th Avenue between 28th and 29th Streets, third floor*
*212-725-3262*
*www.dahnyogany.com; www.healingsociety.org*
All Dahn Yoga classes consist of three parts: fitness, "chakra breathwork" and chi energy meditation. Practitioners wear martial-arts-type outfits and say that the practice helps clear them of negative emotions and "troubling thoughts." Many students train and eventually become Dahn masters. The classes are more tai chi than yoga; nearly all poses are standing and include calisthenics, deep stretching and breathing techniques that makes the practitioner more "sensitive to the chi "life energy"." Dahn offers special introductory classes, but you have to make a six-month commitment to join a class. Korean spiritual teacher Ilchi Lee "rediscovered" the Asian Dahnak teachings 25 years ago, after his students say he reached enlightenment.

### DHARMAKAYA
*1182 Broadway between 28th and 29th Streets, room 802*
*212-306-0534*
*www.dharmakaya.com*
*Drop in class: $10*

YOGA | ESOTERIC GROUPS | WITCHCRAFT | OCCULT UNDERGROUND | BOOKS | UFOS | BOTANICAS | TANTRA | ASTROLOGERS & PSYCHICS |

*Closest subway: N/R to 28th Street*
The Dharmakaya Center is a small, but very intimate yoga and meditation space used by various yoga teachers. With a soothing, Asian motif, the studio has a feel of a chic home. Dora Tarver, a student of the late teacher Rama (Frederick Lenz), founded the center in 1999 for "students who want to learn the ancient arts of mediation and healing."

"I wanted to create a comfortable space that felt very personal and not institutional," says Tarver, who has her own computer consulting company. Tarver teaches a meditation class every Thursday evening, based upon the teachings of Rama, who died in 1998. She says that her meditation style is very Western, designed for the typical, busy New Yorker. Teachers from Ananda Marga offer yoga and meditation classes on Wednesday evenings. Other classes include Harmonic Yoga, which combines asana with chi kung forms, and twice a week Vinyasa classes taught by Gail Greenwald. The center also offers Thai Yoga Massage sessions for those who want to "deepen their yoga practice."

Tarver says that she would like to someday expand the center to include other modalities - including computer training. "Rama said that career success is a reflection of your inner practice," Tarver says. "The mental discipline of computer science is very similar to the mental discipline that monks would undergo years ago in Eastern monasteries. Yoga isn't just practiced on the mat."

### HOT NUDE YOGA
*Private loft in Chelsea*
www.hotnudeyoga.com
For many in New York, nude yoga seems to be the next progression from the sweaty, scantily-clad "Bikram" yoga craze. Accomplished yogi Aaron Star apparently thinks so as well. Star has organized an enormously popular bi-weekly Nude Yoga class in a private Chelsea loft. The class is made up of predominantly gay men who shed their clothes for a two-hour session that combines Vinyasa flow with a "tantric" feel, in a heated room. Star screens every yoga participant. You generally have to be fit and serious about yoga - no gawkers allowed. There is no sexual contact allowed in the class, but some of the poses include "sensual" partner-assisted asanas. The nude yoga craze is spreading - there are also similar groups now in Boston, Ft. Lauderdale and San Diego. Word has it that a documentary and

video are also on tap. Star also organizes regular nude yoga retreats in Hawaii and upstate New York.

## IYENGAR YOGA INSTITUTE OF NEW YORK

*27 West 24th Street between 5th and*
*6th Avenues, suite 800*
*212-691-9642*
*www.Iyengarnyc.org*
*Drop in class: $16*
*Closest subway: 1/9/F/Q/N to 23rd Street*
Iyengar Yoga is the "ballet" of the yoga world, and the Chelsea institute remains true to the teachings of its founder, the living yoga master B.K.S. Iyengar. Its classes are elegant, precise and disciplined. In the class I took, the teacher Brooke Myers stressed alignment, yogic posture and flexibility. Iyengar teachers tend to be purists when it comes to yoga. Students at Iyengar generally need to start at Level I class and work their way up to the general level, which requires at least six-months of experience. Each day, the Chelsea center offers classes for nearly every level. Iyengar himself dedicated the New York center in 1993. The teaching staff includes such notables as Mary Dunn, Robin Janis and James Murphy.

## JOYOUS LIFE ENERGY CENTER

*119 West 23 Street, suite 700*
*212-352-9910*
*www.joyouslifeenergycenter.com*
*Drop in class: $10*
*Closest subway: 1/9 to 23rd Street*
The Joyous Life Energy Center is more than just a yoga studio. Director Simone Lillian has put together an ambitious program of classes in yoga, ta'i chi, NIA (Neuromuscular Integrative Action), Pilates - and even comedy. The studio is spacious and light-filled. Friday nights are "a cappella and acoustic music" nights and Saturday's are the "comedy improv" nights, featuring various comedy and improvisation troupes. The studio hosts numerous workshops like Shamanic Drumming, Yoga for Musicians and Manifesting your Inner Power. In addition, Kripalu Yoga of New York now calls Joyous Life its home and meets there every Friday at 6:30 pm for a two-hour Kripalu class.

## KARMA KIDS YOGA

*104 West 14th Street between 6th and*
*7th Avenues, second floor*
*646-638-1444*
*www.karmakidsyoga.com*

Karma Kids Yoga offers what its title promises - yoga for kids of all ages. Jeannene Levison and Shari Vilchez-Blatt opened Karma Kids in 2003 to "encourage an early practice of yoga that will grow with children into adulthood." The 500-square-foot studio is brightly decorated with flower murals, green foam flooring and "a rainbow of colors." Classes are designed specifically for various age groups - anywhere from three years old to teens. Karma Yoga makes yoga fun for children, having them "play yoga by imitating animals and nature and by using creative expression, games, music and storytelling." The center also has Yoga for Moms, as well as Family Yoga. And for the completely enlightened family, there is the Yoga Birthday Package, which includes an hour of yoga - followed by a party with pizza and refreshments.

## MOVEMENTS AFOOT
*151 West 30 Street between 6th and 7th Avenues, room 201*
*212-904-1399*
*www.movementsafoot.com*
Founded by Leslie Powell in 1993, Movements Afoot specializes in "neuromuscular re-training," which is psycho-physical exercises that bring relaxation, better flexibility and posture. Some of the cutting-edge fitness classes include the Physio Ball class "a Pilates-style class using a big, inflated ball", the Tower class (a Pilates-style class with a small "tower" that you grab onto), Pilates Mat (you know what that is) and yoga. Yoga classes are held several times a week and are primarily Iyengar-style classes. The studio also offers private and semi-private classes, along with physical therapy using Pilates, Myofascial Release Technique and electrical stimulation.

## OM YOGA
*826 Broadway between 14ths and 13th Streets, sixth floor*
*212-254-yoga*
*www.omyoga.com*
*Drop in class: $16*
*Closest subway: 4/5/6/L to 14th Street*
Cindy Lee's Om Yoga is one of the friendliest yoga studios in the city. Walking into the new Om space on Broadway is like walking into an art gallery. Om displays and sells "spiritual art" by talented New Yorkers. Its yoga rooms beckon you to come in, with names like Forest and Rain. The flowing, Vinyasa style is challenging, but the teachers allow enough rest

between poses so that you aren't exhausted after the class. Om also hasn't divorced the spiritual from the workout. Lee's practice comes from a very spiritual place. She has been a yoga teacher for more than 20 years and is also a student of Tibetan Buddhism. Om has one of the most popular teacher training programs in the area - and its graduates have become some of the best yoga teachers in the country. Doing yoga at Om is a pleasurable experience. The locker rooms are big and clean and the practice spaces are well-lit, nicely decorated and ventilated. The studio also has a small bookstore, which offers such items as Cindy Lee's Om Yoga in a Box cards, yoga clothing, videos and books. Om Yoga is a class act and one of my favorite studios in the city.

### RUFF YOGA
*Yoga for dogs*
*212-993-0355*
*www.crunch.com*
Suzie Teitelman, the yoga director of Crunch Fitness Center, was doing yoga at her home one day when her dog "Coali" came on the mat with her. "He saw me doing yoga and it looked as though he wanted to practice as well," says Teitelman. The result was Ruff Yoga, yoga for dogs. Teitelman began teaching "doga," as she calls it, in the summer of 2003 in both group and private classes. During the summer, Teitelman teaches in various outdoor parks in Chelsea and during the cold weather, the classes are brought indoors. Teitelman says that the primary style she teaches dogs is Iyengar, since it "seems to work well with them." During classes, dog owners guide their animal companions into various hatha poses. "As a yoga class, it is not the most vigorous," says Teitelman. "Even if the dog does not want to get into a pose, as long as the dog is breathing and centered, the dog will get benefits." Group classes meet once a week.

### SHAMBHALA MEDITATION CENTER OF NEW YORK
*118 West 22 Street between 6th and 7th Avenues, sixth floor*
*212-675-6544*
*www.vajrayoga.com*
Jill Satterfield's "Vajra Yoga" is the closest you will get in New York to Tibetan yoga. Satterfield teaches her unique style of yoga on Mondays, Tuesdays and Thursdays at the Shambhala Center. Although trained as a classical Iyengar teacher, Satterfield

incorporated a much more meditative practice when she became the student of Tibetan Buddhist Master Tsoknyi Rinpoche. The result was Vajra Yoga. The class I took with her started with a half-hour of meditation and "body scanning." She then put us through our paces with a Vinyasa-style workout, with an emphasis on proper alignment. Satterfield says that the Tibetan hatha yoga system is "very secretive," and students must go on a three-year retreat just to be accepted by the teacher. Satterfield has her own teacher-training program that she begins twice a year.

### SIVANANDA YOGA VEDANTA CENTER
*243 West 24th Street between*
*7th and 8th Streets*
*212-255-4560*
*www.sivananda.org*
*Drop in class: $12; first class free*
*Closest subway: 1/9 to 23rd Street*
The Sivananda Center in Chelsea feels more like an ashram, than a yoga studio. Sivananda offers traditional, "old school" yoga-like sun salutations, headstands, cobra poses and pranayama. The teachers at Sivananda don't get paid, they teach as part of the "karma yoga" service to the center. The class that I took was meditative, gentle and extremely well-paced. Sivandanda aims at changing the consciousness of the student. The center has a "community" feel to it, and a vegetarian dinner is served every evening at 7:30 pm. The wall of the satsang room is covered with a mural of the spiritual founder of the center, Swami Sivananda (1883-1963) and his advice for a spiritual life. Sivananda remains wonderfully dedicated to the true spirit of yoga - right lifestyle leading to the expansion of consciousness.

### STRETCH
*601 West 26th Street at 11th Avenue, suite 1635-b*
*212-366-1003*
*www.stretchnyc.com*
*Drop in class: $15*
*Closest subway: 1/9 to 28th Street*
Located in the historic Starrett-Lehigh building in Chelsea, Stretch is a "light-filled 5,700 square foot studio" overlooking the city and the Hudson River. Although primarily a Pilates and Gyrotonic studio, Stretch also offers a decent selection of yoga classes. Stretch has a really cool vibe to it and has a great atmosphere to practice yoga; after

class you can even grab a bite to eat at Nectar, a cafe that shares space with the studio. Daily yoga classes include traditional hatha, Vinyasa flow and Anusara styles.

## UNIVERSAL FORCE YOGA

*7 West 24th Street between 5th and 6th Streets*
*917-606-9005*
*www.universalforceyoga.com*
*Drop-in class: $17; mat rental: $1*
*Closest subway: 1/9 to 23rd Street*

Gurunam (Joseph Michael Levry) founded the Universal Force Yoga Center in 2001 as a non-profit center for healing and spirituality. Levry touts himself as a "master Kabbalist," as well as master of Kundalini yoga. Originally from the Ivory Coast, Levry spent several years as Kundalini yoga founder Yogi Bhajan's personal assistant. Levry certainly is charismatic, a sort of Bobby McFerrin with a turban. During the class I took with him, he walked in like a celebrity, to the hugs of his many attractive students. He began the class by saying he was jet-lagged from a recent trip to India. He explained to his wide-eyed students that his physical body had arrived in New York, but his "etheric body was still in India," which was causing him some discomfort. His Kundalini class was extremely challenging. Levry banged his fist on the ground, and goaded his students into doing just one more "frog pose." Levry also teaches classes on the Kabballah. He charges $120 for a two-hour group Kabbalah class, making him one of the most expensive teachers in the city. He published a book, Lifting the Veil, in 2002, which combines Kabbalistic philosphy with Kundalini yoga cosmology. The center also offers classes by other Kundalini yoga notables such as Ravi Singh and Ravi Hari, along with classes in Pilates, Vinyasa, Astanga and Iyengar styles of yoga. The healing center offers a wide selection of massages, including an energy healing system that Levry developed called Harmonyum, which "raises the vibrational frequency of the astral body."

## GREENWICH VILLAGE
## AMRITA YOGA CENTER

*125 Fourth Avenue between 12th and 13th Streets*
*212-614-6993*
*www.amritayoga.net*
*Drop in class: $16*
*Closest subway: L/N/R/4/5/6 to 14th Street*

Amrita Yoga offers intimate classes in a "very warm, welcoming space," just outside Union Square. Owner Jodi Rufty says that she and Jon Keller opened the studio to offer high-quality Vinyasa flow classes, featuring top-notch teachers. Both Rufty and Keller have studied with yoga notables Rodney Yee and John Friend. "The studio integrates many different styles of yoga," says Rufty, who opened the studio in October 2002. "Our classes also tend to be small, so that students receive individual attention from the teachers. The students are well taken care of." The studio offers a variety of classes ranging from challenging to gentle classes, in a studio that overlooks a garden.

## BIKRAM YOGA UNION SQUARE

*841 Broadway between 13th and 14th Streets, suite 608*
*212-929-8926*
*www.bikramyogaunionsquare.com*
*Drop in class: $18*
*Closest subway: 4/5/6/N/R/L to 14th Street*
When Otto Cedeno first tried Bikram yoga, he never imagined that his chronic asthma condition would disappear. Cedeno, however, ended up throwing his asthma medicine away, and then flying to California to take the Bikram Yoga College of India teacher training program. Cedena has now given up his acting career to concentrate all his energy into running his Union Square studio. Cedeno, who witnessed the World Trade Center tragedy, said that it was no coincidence that he opened his studio overlooking Union Square Park, where many of the 9-11 vigils were held. "Bikram Yoga is a healing practice," says Cedeno. The studio teaches the heated, 26-pose system with enthusiasm and skill.

## HIMALAYA INSTITUTE

*78 5th Avenue at 14th Street*
*212-243-5995www.himalyanyoga.org*
*Drop in classes: $15*
*Closest subway stop: 1/9, 2/3 to 14th Street;*
*5/6/N/R to Union Square*
For more than 25 years, the Himalaya Institute has offered high-quality yoga and meditation classes. Located over East-West Books, the Institute is one of the flagship centers of the non-profit organization founded by the spiritual master Sri Swami Rama, who passed away in 1996. Rama was an orphan who was raised by Himalayan spiritual master Bengali Baba Swamiji. He spent many years

studying with masters in the Himalayas before coming to the United States in 1969, and founded the Himalayan Institute in 1971. New York center director Nishit Patel now oversees a full schedule of hatha yoga, meditation and pranayama classes that stress the "inner practice." Most of the classes are geared toward floor asanas and meditative poses. During the class that I attended, Patel worked closely with students to ensure they were breathing correctly. "The breath is incredibly powerful," says Patel, who studied directly under Swami Rama. "If you breathe incorrectly, you can injure yourself." Himalayan classes are geared toward the yogic fitness level of the students, with the goal of preparing students for meditation. After a class, head to the bookstore down below, which has one of the best spiritual book, incense and yoga supply collections in the city.

## INTEGRAL YOGA

*227 West 13th Street between 7th and 8th Avenues*
*212-929-0585*
*www.integralyogany.org*
*Drop in classes: $14*
*Closest subway stop: 1/9, 2/3 to 14th Street*
The late Sri Swami Satchidananda gained overnight fame in the late 1960s when he gave the opening meditation at the famed Woodstock concert. Yet now he is most known for the gentle, elegant yoga system that he developed. The New York Integral Yoga Center is one of Satchidananda's oldest and most distinguished centers. The center boasts of four floors of classrooms and classes on the hour. It is a pleasure to do yoga at Integral; the studio has one of the best changing rooms of any yoga studio in New York, completely with free lockers. Don't expect to sweat much during a class there, however. Unlike some of the newer, "power yoga" studios, Integral is refreshingly "old school," concentrating on chanting, gentle hatha and pranayama. For those more interested in yoga for spiritual growth, Integral is perfect, and has a dedicated spiritual community. On the first floor of the center, Integral operates a bookstore that sells health and yoga books, incense and videotapes. Next door, Integral operates a health-food store. Integral Yoga offers plenty of workshops on subjects like Creating More Peace in Your Life and Vegetarian Cooking. The entire Integral experience has a decidedly "counter-culture" feel to it, like going back to the innocent time before yoga became big business.

## LAUGHING LOTUS YOGA CENTER
*55 Christopher Street between West 10th
and Grove Streets
212-414-2903
www.laughinglotus.com
Drop in classes: $14
Closest subway stop: 1/9 Christopher Street*
Festive and pink are the two words that come to
mind when entering the bright and cheery Laughing
Lotus Yoga Center. The pink walls, lights and festive
decorations, like the androgynous Laughing Lotus
nymph statue that sits on a fireplace mantel, give
the studio a "Mardi Gras meets Mahabarata" atmosphere. Directors Dan Flynn and Jasmine Tarkeshi
created the studio to share their fun and intimate
approach to yoga studies. The center offers primarily Vinyasa-style classes in the unique Lotus style.
In the basic class I took, the teacher - Tovah - began
with a short talk on self-study and gave a reading
from a Jack Kornfeld book. During the Sarvasana,
she came over to me and rubbed Lavender oil on
my third eye chakra - a first in any yoga class I
have taken. During July, Laughing Lotus gives its
popular Sunset Rooftop Yoga classes every Tuesday
evening on top of the Greenwich House, located
at 27 Barrow Street.

## THE SHALA YOGA HOUSE
*815 Broadway between 11th and 12th Avenues,
second floor
212-979-9988
www.theshala.com
Drop in class: $15
Closest subway: N/R, 5/6, 2/3/1/9 to
14th Street*
The Shala Yoga House is the one of the city's
newest and freshest studios. Founded in 2002
by Jivamukti-trained yogis Kristin Leigh and Barbara
Verrochi, the studio exudes warmth and old-world
charm, with its pastel colored walls and violet,
gauzy curtains. The Shala is faithful to the Jivamukti
style, which incorporates a great deal of Vedic spirituality. Its Vinyasa classes include plenty of chanting and many of the teachers play the Indian organ
during the chanting sessions. The basic class that
I took had only two people in it "including myself".
The teacher, Lisa Yi, took her time to work with
each of us, guiding us in each pose with her hands.
She went the extra distance to make sure that
our alignment was right. The Vinyasa class is
much more challenging and crowded and is recom-

mended only for people who have been practicing regularly for at least six months. The Shala has two practice rooms and decent changing spaces for men women.

## *SOHO*
### ATMANANDA
*525 Broadway between Spring and Prince Streets, third floor*
*212-625-6935*
*www.atmananda.com*
*Drop in classes: $16*
*Closest subway stop: 5/6 to Spring Street; R to Prince.*
Stunning is the only word that came to mind when I first walked into the Atmandanda Yoga Center in Soho. The Oriental motif of the studio blends bamboo, luxurious Indian wall hangings, and a gurgling fountain, to create a sensuous ambience. The classes at Atmananda are a unique blend of Vinyasa, Astanga and meditative hatha poses. Atmananda's director, Jhonn Tamayo, has created a robust style and teacher training program - a perfect blend of sweat and spirit. The open class I took, taught by Jill, began with chanting and meditation, then moved into sun salutation variations and a Vinyasa flow. Atmandana is partnered with the Ayurvedic Holistic Center next door to it. The center offers massage, meditation, facials and boasts of being the only center to offer "aura readings." With a juice bar, small bookstore and yoga classes held every half-hour, Atmananda is a true holistic center for the New Age.

### SOHO SANCTUARY
*119 Mercer Street between Spring and Prince Streets, third floor*
*212-334-5550*
*www.sohosanctuary.com*
*Walk in class: $22*
*Closest subway: R to Prince; 6 to Spring*
Soho Sanctuary is part of the "womens only" trend (i.e. keeping women away from guys like me). So, unfortunately, I was unable to take a class here. From what I'm told, it is a beautiful space to do yoga. Located in a landmark Soho loft, the space is a "tranquil retreat," with hardwood floors, plants and large windows. The Sanctuary is both a spa and studio for women who "want to restore health, beauty, and vitality within them." Its locker rooms have a "chi-balanced eucalyptus steam bath," and the spa offers massage, body treatments and

facials. In addition to yoga, the center teaches
Pilates and Gyrotonic classes.

## VIRAYOGA

*580 Broadway between Houston and Prince Streets*
*212-334-9960*
*www.virayoga.com*
*Drop-in classes: $16*
*Closest Subway stop: 6 to Bleecker; R to Prince*
Virayoga is one of my favorite yoga studios in the
city - and the reason is owner Elena Brower. Brower
earned her teaching certificate from Om Yoga and
studies now with Anusara yoga founder John Friend.
Brower's classes at Virayoga are packed full; Brower
has an intensity and powerful energy about her.
She strides through class, adjusting students with
the focus of a drill sergeant and the wisdom of a
Buddha. Brower is the real deal; she lives her yoga.
Her classes begin with a short talk. In the class
I took, she discussed the tantric philosophy of
Anusara - that yoga is practiced in everywhere,
not just on the mat. She included elements of
Vinyasa flow in the class, focusing also on alignment
and the "inner spiral." It was a sweat-drenching workout. Another benefit: Virayoga tends to attract the
beautiful people in Soho - models, actors and
artists. Virayoga is definitely one of the hottest
studios in town.

## YOGA MANDALI

*502 LaGuardia Place between Bleecker and*
*Houston, second floor*
*212-473-9001*
*www.yogamandali.com*
*Drop in class: $16*
*Closest subway stop: 1/9 to Houston Street; 6 to*
*Bleecker Street; A/B/C to East Fourth*
Yoga Mandali devotes itself entirely to the practice
of Anusara Yoga, the yoga system developed by John
Friend. Long-time yogi Phil Di Pietro took over the
studio in January 2003 and has created a strong
yoga program. Di Pietro studied Iyengar yoga for a
number of years and switched over to Anusara, which
he considers a more "heart centered yoga." Anusara
is less concerned with alignment, than it is with the
unique development of each student. The class I took
concentrated on "softening the heart area" and did
some unique twists, focusing on the "inner spiral." The
studio offers numerous Anusara workshops and has
an excellent teaching staff that includes Cari
Friedman, Yashushi Tanaka and Kelly Bragger.

## YOGA UNION@BROOME CORNER STUDIO

*425 Broome Street between Grand and*
*Spring Streets, number 4R*
*212-889-8643*
*www.yogaunion.com*
*Drop in class: $15*
*Closest subway: N/R to Prince Street;*
*6 to Spring Street*

Alison West teaches an elegant fusion of Iyengar, Ashtanga and Sivananda styles of yoga in the space that she shares with the Broome Corner Studio. West, an art historian and expert in European sculpture of the 18th and 19th century, began studying yoga in Munich in 1983. The daughter of United States Foreign Service Officers, she was born in Paris and lived in various locations in the world. Her yoga journey took her back to New York, where she studies at the Sivananda Yoga Center, then with several Iyengar teachers including Kevin Gardiner and Mary Dunn. She eventually went to Mysore, India to study with Ashtanga yoga founder Sri Pattabhi Jois. Every July, West also runs her acclaimed teacher training program, a four-week intensive course.

## YUM YOGA

*www.yumyoga.com*
*917-359-6807*
*Drop in class: $12; $7 for lunch yoga*

"Yum" is the tantric mantra for the heart chakra and Dages Keates and Sarah Ward have created a very heart-centered and passionate studio. They opened Yum Yoga in May 2003, offering lunchtime yoga classes at 577 Broadway, Suite 2E, as well classes at the Caravan of Dreams restaurant and the Dharmakaya meditation center. Keates studied at the 7 Centers Yoga Arts in Arizona and specialized in tantric hatha, while Ward was certified by Integral Yoga. "In Tantric Hatha, you feel and notice everything around you more passionately," says Keates. "Tantra accepts all experiences as paths to spiritual growth." The lunchtime classes are only 45 minutes, which is perfect for a lunch break yoga session.

## *EAST VILLAGE*
## ASHTANGA YOGA SHALA

*295 East 8th Street between Avenues A and B*
*212-353-7718*
*www.ashtangayogashala.net*
*Drop in classes: monthly membership only, at $190*

*for full membership (6 classes a week) and*
*$150 for half-membership (3 classes a week)*
*Closest subway: 6 to Astor Place; L to 1st Avenue;*
*F to 2nd Avenue*
Located in the heart of the East Village, the
Ashtanga Yoga Shala offers "genuine" Ashtanga
yoga as taught by Sri Pattabhi Jois. Studio director
Guy Donahaye first met Jois 12 years ago, when
Donahaye traveled to India to study yoga. He has
been going back at least once a year ever since.
"Ashtanga yoga is a very ancient system. It is scientific, it works," says Donahaye. "Ashtanga goes much
deeper than some of the other styles of yoga. It is
all about breath." Donahaye says that he has tried to
make his studio as faithful to the Mysore style as
possible, though he says that he is less focused on
Hindu devotional practices than some of the other
studios in the city. In the Mysore style, every one
does their own "self-practice," according to their
own level and ability, with the instructor coming
around to work with each student individually.
Students sign up for at least one month at a time
and are encouraged to take at least three classes a
week. The studio offers four Mysore style classes a
day during the week and a "led primary series" on
Saturdays at noon, which is open to drop-ins who
are interested in learning more about Ashtanga.

### INTERFAITH YOGA
*25 First Avenue between 1st and 2nd Streets*
*212-473-0370*
*Drop in class: $11*
*Closest subway stop: F to 2 Avenue (Houston St)*
Interfaith Yoga is truly a sanctuary in the East
Village. The folks who run Interfaith Yoga were former monks under the International Society for
Krishna Consciousness (ISKON), who broke away
and formed their own organization. The yoga studio
is on the third floor of the five-story building - which
is completely owned by the Interfaith group. A beautiful Krishna Temple occupies the second floor. The
class I took was a Vinyasa style class taught by
Stephanie, who was very stringent on alignment.
The studio provides free lockers, mats and the feel
of someone's home. In addition to yoga, the center
offers twice-a-day kirtan and chanting. Next door,
the center runs a wonderful vegetarian restaurant
called The Sanctury. After class, I went to the
restaurant and ordered a "curried Tempeh" sandwich
- a perfect way to celebrate the yogic principle of
ahimsa "non-violence".

## JIVAMUKTI

*404 Lafayette Street between Astor Place and*
*7th Street, third floor*
*www.jivamuktiyoga.com*
*Drop in classes: $17*
*Closet Subway stop: 5/6 to Astor Place;*
*N/R to 8th Street*

Jivamukti is THE New York Yoga studio. What more can be said? Former punk rock artists David Life and Sharon Gannon opened the studio in 1989, after having life-transforming experiences through yoga, trading the electric guitar for the Indian organ. They channeled their avant-garde sensibilities into creating a uniquely American fusion of East and West known as Jivamukti Yoga. In my opinion, Jivamukti is the most influential yoga studio in the country, proving that yoga can be a great workout, and at the same time offer a path to spiritual enlightenment. Life and Gannon were the first to popularize the more aerobic style of yoga known as Vinyasa, influencing a generation of yoga instructors in the process. Jivamukti offers classes in Sanskrit, as well as Monday night Kirtan, devotional hymn singing, and one of the best teacher training programs in the country. Life and Gannon are also vegans and promote animal rights as part of the yogic path of ahimsa. They are sincere and passionate; their bookstore has an eclectic and thoughtful selection of yoga, spiritual and cruelty-free lifestyle titles. The studio draws many models, actors and artists to its classes, giving each class an air of glamour. The class I attended was perfectly paced - it began with meditation, chanting and pranayama. We slowly warmed up to an energetic and powerful Vinyasa/Ashtanga flow of poses. Just as the beads of sweat began to form on my forehead, the music was cranked up and lights turned up for a deep, soul-cleansing workout. Throughout the class, the teacher told us how we were all the "creative principles" of our own lives - that we could be anything we wanted to be. It was a perfect blend of sweat and spirit and, in the meaning of jivamukti - soul liberating.

## KUON MOTION

*336 East 5th Street between 1st and 2nd Avenues*
*917-577-1202*
*Walk-in class: $25*
*Closest subway: 5/6 to Astor Place;*
*N/R to 8th Street*

Kuon Motion creator Charles Kalish predicts that his

new fitness system will become the "next big thing" in the yoga world. Kalish - a former professional dancer - has been working on the system for the past 20 years. Kuon stands for Kinetic Undulating Overlapping Neuromuscular; Kuon also is the Buddhist term meaning "time without beginning". "This is a cutting-edge system ahead of its time," says Kalish. "It is designed work on a therapeutic level, balance the energy of the body and provide an Olympic-level workout." Kuon motion classes have been described as watching a choreographed dance. The hour and a half workout combines elements of ta'i chi, yoga, swimming, ballet, modern dance, chi kung and gymnastics. Practitioners claim that the constantly moving workout "makes Vinyasa work-outs look stagnant." Kalish only recently began teaching his system publicly and is already planning a video and book series. Classes are kept small, so call to reserve a space.

## LOWER EAST SIDE/DOWNTOWN
### EDDIE STERN'S PATANJALI YOGA SHALA
*430 Broome Street at Crosby*
*212-431-3738*
*Drop in class: no way*
*Closest subway: J/M to Bowery*
Eddie Stern was one of the first Westerners to study with Ashtanga yoga guru Sri Pattabhi Jois in India. Stern's Yoga Shala is definitely "old school"; you have to sign up for a minimum of three months and attend class on a regular basis. Stern doesn't advertise, doesn't do interviews and says he isn't interested in having big classes. And why should he? His students have reportedly included actress Gwyneth Paltrow, singer Madonna and model Christy Turlington. The studio has a feel of devotion and exclusivity to it; a large Ganesh statue sits prominently on an altar that Stern regularly con-ducts a puja to. Word has it that whenever Jois visits New York, he stays with Stern. The classes at the center are hard-core Ashtanga - a continuous flow of movements using synchronized ujjayi breathing, producing heat and sweat in the body. Adherents believe that Ashtanga - rediscovered by Jois - is the original asana practice as intended by Patanjali. This studio is definitely not for the masses.

### KULA YOGA PROJECT
*28 Warren Street between Church Street*
*and Broadway, fourth floor*

*212-945-4460*
*www.kulayoga.com*
*Drop-in class: $14*
*Closest subway: 1/2/A/C to Chambers Street; N/R*
*to City Hall; J/M/Z/4/5/6 to Brooklyn Bridge*
Kula means "a group coming together of its own free will," and at the Kula Yoga Project, yogis from around Manhattan have been flocking to the downtown for "vigorous, challenging, yet restorative" yoga classes. Studio director Schulyer Grant has combined her "love for the flow of Ashtanga with the precision of Iyengar" to create a yoga style she calls Freestyle Vinyasa. The studio opened in 2002, giving a much-needed boost to the World Trade Center neighborhood. Grant may look familiar to some - she is also a successful actress. Grant, the grand-niece of the late Katherine Hepburn, played "Camile Hawkins" on the soap All My Children, and "Callie" on Law and Order. Grant has temporarily traded the camera for the yoga mat, much to the pleasure of her students.

## MAHAYOGI YOGA MISSION@SUFI BOOKS

*227 West Broadway between Franklin and*
*White Streets*
*212-807-8903*
*www.mahayogiyogamission.org*
*Drop in class: $20, $23 if Mahayogi is there*
*Closest subway: 1/9 to Franklin; A/C/E/N/R/6*
*to Canal Street*
Every Sunday at 6 pm and Tuesday at 7 pm, disciples of Japanese yoga master Sri Mahayogi Paramahansa hold a two-hour hatha yoga class at the Sufi Bookstore. And if you are lucky, Mahayogi himself may show up. He usually spends the summer in New York. Mahayogi is an honest-to-God realized master who, amazingly, still teaches small yoga classes to the public. During the class I took, everyone stood when Mahayogi walked in the room. Thin, with a wispy black beard and long black hair, Mahayogi bristles with spiritual energy. He began the class by meditating and looking into the eyes of each of the roughly 15 students present. During the class, he - along with four orange-clad female disciples - walked around adjusting students. The yoga style is traditional hatha, most of which was done on the floor. Each asana is also held for several minutes - far longer than any other class that I attended in the city - with several minutes of savasana in between each pose. Mahayogi spends half the year in his homeland of Japan, and lives on Bleecker Street for the rest of the year. Once a month - when he is

in New York - he holds a satsang, where the public can ask him spiritual questions.

## SHIVA YOGA SHALA
*1 Rivington Place at the Bowery*
*212-254-6602*
*www.shivayogashala.com*
*Drop in class: $20*
*Closest subway: F to Delancey Street;*
*J/M/Z to Essex Street*
If you want to study directly from one of the sources of Ashtanga yoga, Shiva Yoga Shala is the studio to do so. Manju Jois - the eldest son of Ashtanga yoga founder Sri Pattabhi Jois - runs the school. Jois - who is considered the most qualified Ashtanga yoga teacher in the world next to his father - regularly teaches classes and workshops, and spends much of the year in New York City. "We are unique because our school is run by Manju Jois, who has been practicing Ashtanga for 50 years," says owner Patti Perez. Daily Mysore style Ashtanga classes are offered, both mornings and evenings, including "led Ashtanga" classes for beginners. Perez says that drop-ins are welcome, but she suggests that beginners take the Ashtanga Yoga Beginners Weekend Workshop, which is offered at least once a month. Jois is also offering an Ashtanga Teacher Training Course, which covers Vedic chanting, philosophy, pranayama and the first and second Ashtanga Yoga Series.

## WHITE STREET CENTER FOR MOVEMENT AND BODYWORK
*43 White Street between Broadway and*
*Church Street*
*212-966-9005*
*Drop in class: $14; mats included*
*Closest subway: 1/9 Franklin Street;*
*5/6, N/R City Hall*
The White Street Center began primarily as massage and chiropractic center, but now offers aerobic, ballet, ta'i chi, belly dance and yoga classes. The yoga classes are held daily from 1-2:15 p.m. The teachers vary; Keith Borden teaches the Thursday Vinyasa style class.

## YOGA CONNECTION
*145 Chambers Street between West Broadway*
*and Greenwich Street*
*212-945-9642*
*www.yogaconnectionnyc.com*

*Drop in class: $18*
*Closest subway: 2/3/1/9 to Chambers*
Yoga Connection was one of the first studios in New York City to offer Bikram "heated room" yoga, the rigorous style of yoga that consists of a 26-posture series done in a hot "104 degree" room. Sarah Margolis and Marilyn Barnett opened the Tribeca studio in 1996. The studio includes a decent-size yoga room, as well as changing and massage rooms. The teaching staff is top- notch and Bikram-trained teachers. And since every Bikram class is the same - you know what to expect. Margolis and Barnett have developed their own unique teaching style base on Innermotion, which they describe as "a way of exploring the mind-body connection from the inside out."

## BROOKLYN
### AREA YOGA
*275 Smith Street between Degraw and Douglass Streets*
*718-522-1906*
*www.areabrooklyn.com*
*Walk-in class: $15*
*Closest subway: F to Carroll Street*
Area Yoga is like an oasis in the gentrifying Carroll Gardens neighborhood. Its spa - located at 252 Smith Street - offers a wide-variety of services, like facials, massages and body treatments. Yoga classes are held in the third floor of 252 Smith Street, a charming Brooklyn walk-up. The lilac-colored walls, drapes and the candle-lit altar at the front of the room give a soothing ambience. The classes themselves are quite challenging. The basic class that I took was more difficult than many open classes I have taken at other studios. One word of advice - be on time for class. Once the class starts, the doorbell is turned off and you are out of luck.

### BIKRAM YOGA OF BROOKLYN HEIGHTS
*106 Montague Street between Henry and Hicks Street, 2nd floor*
*718-797-2100*
*www.bikramyogabrooklyn.com*
*Drop in class: $18*
*Closest subway: N/R to Court Street;*
*4/5 to Borough Hall; 2/3 to Clark Street*
While all Bikram studios practice the same 26 poses in 100+ degree heat, not all studios are the same. Elizabeth Issacs, who opened her Bikram studio in 2001, has created one of the most unique Bikram

**YOGA** | ESOTERIC GROUPS | WITCHCRAFT | OCCULT UNDERGROUND | BOOKS | UFOS | BOTANICAS | TANTRA | ASTROLOGERS & PSYCHICS |

studios in the country. She designed the studio as
"a holistic environment using the concepts of green
architecture and feng shui." The problem with many
Bikram studios is that the heat and humidity can
create a moldy smell and feel. Issacs, however, uses
a state-of-the art heating system that controls the
amount of humidity and circulates the air. Hi-tech
filters remove bacteria and mold spores, making it
a fresh-smelling environment. She insulated the studio with recycled blue jeans and used "fruit-based"
paints on the walls. Issacs was trained by Bikram
Choudhury at his Beverly Hills studio and has assisted Bikram at his seminars in Kripalu Yoga in Lenox.

## ENERGY CENTER
*53 Wykoff Street off Court Street*
*718-243-1285*
*www.theenergycenter.com*
*Drop in class: $15*
*Closest subway stop: 4/5, 2/3 M, N/R to Jay*
*Street/Borough Hall; F, G to Bergen Street*
The Energy Center has been Brooklyn Height's holistic health center since the mid-1980s. The center is
located in a house on tree-lined Wykoff Street and
shares the space with the Providence Day Spa.
Joyce Cossett, the center director, is a certified
Kripalu yoga teacher and an Integrative Yoga therapist. The center offers a full-schedule of Vinyasa
and hatha yoga classes, along with a number of
courses like Yoga and Pregnancy, and The Alexander
Technique and Yoga. The intermediate class that I
took was taught by Stephanie Artz, an Iyengar and
Jivamukti trained yogi. She put the primarily female
class though its paces with a diverse mix of down-
ward and upward dogs, chatarangas and lunges.
The studio itself is airy and light-filled.

## GO YOGA
*218 Bedford Avenue between North 4th and*
*North 5th Streets*
*718- 486-5602*
*www.goyoga.ws*
*Drop in class: $15*
*Closest subway: L to Bedford Avenue*
Lilia Mead opened Go Yoga in 2000 to offer
Vinyasa-style yoga to her Williamsburg neighborhood. Mead - who grew up in Greenwich Village -
says that the studio is geared to the local community. Classes are "Vinyasa-based, while combining
Ashtanga, Iyengar and Jivakukti styles." The yoga
space itself is located in a sun-drenched store-front

ESOTERIC GUIDE TO NEW YORK                    **47**

**YOGA** | ESOTERIC GROUPS | WITCHCRAFT | OCCULT UNDERGROUND | BOOKS | UFOS | BOTANICAS | TANTRA | ASTROLOGERS & PSYCHICS |

at the Girdle Factory Mall. Mead herself trained at Jivamukti with David Life and Sharon Gannon, as well as with Sri Pattabhi Jois in Mysore, India. In addition to Vinyasa, Go also offers Prenatal and Restorative Yoga and meditation classes.

### GREENHOUSE HOLISTIC
*88 Roebling Street between North 7th and North 6th Streets*
*718-599-3113*
*www.greenhouseholistic.com*
*Drop in class: $12*
*Closest subway: L to Bedford Avenue*
David Greenhouse sees yoga and holistic health as an extension of the punk rock movement that he was once part of. "Our philosophy here is DIY - do it yourself," says Greenhouse, who once was a member of the band Colored Greens. "If you need soap, learn to make it yourself. We are offering an alternative to consumerism." Greenhouse - a licensed massage therapist and ta'i chi instructor - opened the holistic health center that bears his name in the summer of 2001. "I opened the studio as a healing center for myself, as well as for the community," says Greenhouse. The holistic center has the feel of a community center; it offers free tea, water and has a lounge with a library for students to socialize after class. Yoga classes are taught primarily by teachers from the Williambsburg neighborhood. "We like to think that this is more than a yoga center, but rather is someplace to go, hang out and heal yourself," says Greenhouse. In addition to yoga, the center offers a full-range of services like massage, acupuncture and steam treatment.

### HIPJOINT YOGA STUDIO
*281 North 7th Street between Havemeyer and Meeker Streets*
*718-349-1066*
*Closest subway stop: L to Bedford Avenue*
Hipjoint Yoga offers Iyengar-style yoga "in a beautiful practice space." The studio offers about six classes a week. Call for schedule.

### HOT YOGA PEOPLE
*659 Fulton Street between Ashland Place and Rockwell Place*
*718-237-2300*
*www.yoga-people.com*
*Drop in class: $16*
*Closest subway: G to Fulton; C to Lafayette;*

*D/M/Q/N/R/W to DeKalb and Flatbush*
The Yoga People studio has expanded to open a
"Hot Yoga" studio in the Fort Greene neighborhood.
The majority of classes are a series of postures in
100+ degree heat to enhance flexibility. The studio
also offers non-heated Vinyasa classes. The program is directed by Anita Ruderman, who has been
practicing yoga since 1988 and was certified as
a teacher by Yoga Spectrum in 1992.

### JAYA YOGA AND WELLNESS CENTER
*1626 8th Avenue between Windsor Place and
Prospect Avenue*
*718-788-8788*
*www.jayayogacenter.com*
*Drop in class: $14*
*Closest subway: F to Prospect Park/Windsor Place*
Jaya means "victory and success" in Sanskrit, and
this Prospect Park studio lives up to its name. The
studio offers at least five classes a day, ranging
from beginner to open and a "heat-producing"
Vinyasa class. Director Maryann Donnelly has gath-
ered together a talented and varied group of teachers who bring a variety of styles to their classes.
Donnelly is a certified Kripalu teacher, who studied
with Prem Shakti. "Our studio is very friendly and
inviting," says Donnelly. "It is a real part of the community. Most people who come to class live within
a walking distance."

### KUNDALINI YOGA IN PARK SLOPE
*473 13th Street between Prospect Park West
and 8th Avenue*
*718-832-1559*
*Drop in class: $15*
*Closest subway: F to Prospect Park/Windsor Place*
Siri Sevak Khalsa runs her Kundalini Yoga studio out
of a beautiful brownstone. Classes are held in the
big room on the parlor floor. Classes are based upon
the teachings of Yogi Bhajan and the 3HO organization. Once a month, Khalsa offers "chanting, as well
as a vegetarian dinner." Classes are held five times a
week, with classes on Wednesdays at 7 p.m. and
Saturdays at 6 p.m.

### MIND-BODY BALANCE YOGA AND
### HEALING CENTER
*759 President Street between 6th and 7th Streets*
*718-636-3950*
For Phyllis Kanti Berg, yoga is a constantly evolving
art form. "I'm a perpetual student, I always try to

break the mold," says Berg, who has been practicing yoga since 1974. Berg has created her own, unique style of yoga that incorporates her various esoteric interests. Her Integrative Yoga Therapy classes include hatha poses, sound, visualization, breath-work and "toning." She has also developed Kabbalistic Yoga, which combines Kabbalistic chanting with yoga poses. Students say that Berg's approach is "etheric," and that she is "more angel than human." Berg says that ever since she met her first teacher, "Baba" Muktananda, she has felt she has been on a spiritual mission. "I left my body when I met Baba," she says. "It was a powerful experience." Berg's role is more of a spiritual teacher to her students. She teaches nearly all the classes herself and does not advertise or have a web site, so it is best to call her first to find out when the most appropriate class is held. Berg, whom some have described as a "sixth dimensional angelic being," also conducts healing session with vibration and sound. "Our classes here deal with the whole person," says Berg. "I don't consider myself only a yoga teacher; I am more a teacher of life."

### PARK SLOPE YOGA CENTER
*792 Union Street between 6th and 7th Avenues*
*718-789-2288*
*www.lifeinmotion.com/ParkSlope.htm*
*Drop in class: $14*
*Closest subway: 2/3 to Grand Army Plaza*
Park Slope Yoga is one of the "most community-oriented yoga studios" in Brooklyn. It offers 66 classes a week and also runs a community center across the street from the studio. The studio owner, "Vee," is a long-time yogi with extensive experience in Vinyasa yoga and teaching. The studio features hatha, Vinyasa, Jivamukti and Prenatal classes.

### SANTOSA YOGA AND BIRTH
*359 4th Street between 5th and 6th Avenues,*
*first floor*
*646-234-6222*
*www.santosayoga.com*
*Drop in class: $10*
*Closest subway: F to 7th Avenue; N/R/M to Union Street/Ninth Street*
Santosa Yoga and Birth is a "haven" for pregnant women in the Park Slope area who want to enhance the birth experience. "We are a very local, grass-roots organization," says director Kristin Sasser. "We have a very casual atmosphere where expec-

tant mothers can come for a communal experience."
Sasser says that the studio offers yoga classes,
as well as educational classes in pre-natal nutrition,
birthing classes and emotional support. In addition
to having a yoga teaching certificate from Kripalu,
Sasser is also a certified Labor Support Doula.
Classes are held in the studio nicknamed the Womb
Room, located in a stately Victorian brownstone,
decorated with photographs of children from
around the world and luxurious silk wall hangings.
"We are not a yoga factory," says Sasser. "We are
more of a support network for new moms and
provide fitness to a like-minded community."

## SATTVA YOGA CENTER
*126 13th Street at corner of Third Avenue*
*718-965-1245*
*www.sattvacenter.com*
*Drop in class: $12*
*Closest subway: F/N/R/M to 4th Avenue*
Sattva Yoga Center is based upon the principles
of Integral Yoga, founded by the late Swami
Satchidananda. Owner Sandy Phillips teaches
many of the hatha classes, while she has several
other teachers trained in Jivamukti and Vinyasa-
style yoga. The yoga space is located in a building
filled with artist studios, giving it an edgy, yet
peaceful feel. The studio is a bit small, lending
itself to an intimate class, with plenty of assistance from the teacher. "We give all of our
students personalized attention," says Phillips.
"We don't let our class get bigger than ten students.
That way we can tailor the class to the needs of
the students."

## SHAMBHALA YOGA AND DANCE CENTER
*348 St. Marks Avenue between Washington and*
*Underhill Avenues*
*718-622-9956*
*www.shambhalayogadance.com*
*Drop in class: $12*
*Closest subway: 2/3 to Eastern Parkway/Brooklyn*
*Museum*
The Shambhala Yoga Center offers 25 classes a
week. The Park Slope studio bills itself as a "non-
competitive community and family-oriented yoga
center." Cathy Calderon, an award-winning filmmak-
er and theater director, opened the studio to create
a "warm and nurturing community space where
people of all backgrounds could come together."
Calderon studied with Todd Norian and teaches

Anusara style yoga. The studio also teaches African Dance, Belly Dancing and Salsa classes.

## SOLAR YOGA CENTER
*373 Ninth Street at Sixth Avenue*
*718-499-3669*
*www.solaryogacenter.org*
*Drop in Class: $12*
*Closest subway: N/R, F to 4th Avenue/9th Street*
Solar Yoga is one of the most intriguing classes I have taken in New York. It is the opposite of the Bikram "hot yoga" craze - because it features a "cold shower" in the middle of the yoga session. The mysterious French yogi Dr. Serge Raynaud de la Ferriere "Mahatma Chandra Bala Guruji" founded the Solar Yoga movement in the 1948. The unique yoga system took off in South America, but never really made it big in the United States. Every Solar Yoga class begins with a half-hour or so of psycho-physical exercise, that mixes yogic breathing with active exercises like arm swings, leg lifts and abdominal rolls. The teacher then announces that it is "shower time" and students march to the four showers in the back of the class and take a frigid, cold shower. Then it is back to the mats for a 45-minute asana practice, relaxation, and then a 10-minute period of Gnani Yoga "sharing and questions". The shower itself is shockingly cold, but afterward you feel as though your body is glowing with energy. Marian, who taught the class I took, said that the shower forces all of the blood to the surface of the skin and pushes the pranic energy into the body. The two-hour classes are taught by volunteers in the three-story, cultural building, and run by Solar Yoga's non-governmental organization known as the Universal Great Brotherhood.

## SPOKE THE HUB
*748 Union Street between 6th and 7th Streets*
*718-857-5158*
*www.spokethehub.org*
*Closest subway: 2/3 to Bergen Street;*
*D/Q to 7th Avenue*
Spoke the Hub is a "multi-purpose, multi-faceted community arts organization" that offers, among other things, several yoga classes each week. The center is focused on creative arts and fitness classes for toddlers through adult professionals. Other classes include Sambaerobics, Mindfulness, Meditation and Stress Reduction, and Men's Energizer, plus a whole range of classes for children

and teenagers. The "Spoke the Hub Re-creation center" was founded in 1995, and grew out of a group of "cultural pioneers" who have been involved in more than 100 performance presentations. The center offers primarily Kripalu and Integral styles of yoga.

## THE STABLE - DANCE AND YOGA IN WILLIAMSBURG

*281 North Seventh Street between Meeker and Havemeyer*
*718-387-3962*
*Drop in class: $14*
*www.stabledanceyoga.com*
*Closest subway stop: L to Bedford; G to Metropolitan/Grand Street*
What happens when you mix the art of boxing with Kundalini yoga "as taught by Yogi Bhajan"? The result is a hybrid called Boku, an exercise which "pumps you up and gives and experience of deep relaxation at the same time." And where else would you practice this discipline than The Stable, one of the more innovative yoga centers in the city. This beautiful and sunny Williamsburg studio offers yoga, theater arts, dance and music. Philippa Woolley "Ram Rang Kaur", a certified Kundalini yoga teacher, founded the Stable as a community center offering an eclectic mix of spiritually-based exercises. The Stable also runs a children's summer camp, geared toward the creative arts and drama.

## YOGA CENTER OF BROOKLYN

*519 Court Street at West 9th Street*
*718-858-4554; 718-858-7394*
*www.brooklynyoga.com*
*Drop in class: $13*
*Closest subway: F/G to Smith and Ninth Streets*
Brooklyn native Jonathan Gordon opened the Yoga Center of Brooklyn as a "yoga/wellness" center in the heart of the Red Hook/Carroll Gardens neighborhood. Gordon is both a certified yoga teacher as well as a reiki master; he is also trained as a hospice counselor. Gordon teaches many of the classes, which are primarily Vinyasa-style. The studio has a "community feel" to it and Gordon recently started a non-profit organization with some of his teachers called the Heart of Brooklyn, which provides free yoga classes to nursing homes, corrections centers or other organizations which may be in need. "I have watched yoga help so many people in so many ways," says Gordon, who sees his studio as a "base of operation" to reach out to the community. The

philosophy of the studio is to use yoga as tool to bring "a sense of bliss and inner peace."

## YOGA PEOPLE
*157 Remsen Street between Court and*
*Clinton Streets*
*718-522-9642*
*www.yoga-people.com*
*Drop-in class: $16*
*Closest subway stop: 2/3/4/5 to Borough Hall*
Yoga People offers a solid yoga program in a nice, clean space. Yogi Wendy Chanelis founded the Brooklyn Heights studio to provide a center where "all people can practice in a joyful, playful environment." She has been a student of yoga for 15 years and has hired a diverse and talented group of yoga teachers. The class I took was taught by a teacher who trained at Om Yoga in Manhattan. The class was a well-paced Vinyasa flow. The studio includes two practice spaces and a massage room.

## QUEENS
### ANANDA MARGA
*97-38 42nd Avenue between 98th and 99th Streets*
*718-898-1603*
*www.yoginnewyork.com*
*Drop in class: $10*
*Closest subway: 7 to Junction Boulevard*
Yoga classes at the Ananda Marga ashram are gentle and geared toward preparing the body for meditation. They include non-vigorous movements combined with the breath, usually done in repetitions of eight. The teachings are based upon the work of the late Shri Shri Anandamurti, a former Indian railway official who began the Ananda Marga organization to spread the teachings of "self-realization and service to humanity." Anandamurti's focus included ecology, environment, science, music, art and literature. In addition, the center teaches tantric meditation, which students claim was first systematized by Shiva more than 7,000 years ago and "reintroduced" to the world by Anandamurti. The tantric teachings have very little to do with sex "a perversion of the system according to Anandamurti", but rather mantra and philosophy. The meditation classes are taught by Dada Rainjitananda, who was a direct disciple of Anandamurti.

## DEVANAND YOGA CENTER
*95-06 Roosevelt Avenue between Warren and*

*94th Streets*
*718-426-4643*
*www.devanandyoga.org*
*Drop in class: donation of $10 or $50 for the year*
*Closest subway: 7 to Junction Boulevard*
The Devanand ashram offers yoga as a community
service in this primarily Hispanic neighborhood.
Hatha yoga and Mantra Yoga Meditation classes are
held daily. The ashram was founded on the teachings
of the late Swami Guru Devanand Saraswati Ji
Maharaj, a spiritual teacher of the ascetic order of
Shankara. He called mantra yoga meditation the
"ultimate mystical key to contact the inner self."
"We are not a commercial yoga studio," says teacher
Sarah Aponte. "The center is completely run by volunteers. We are here to serve the community."
Classes are generally held every weekday evening
at 6 pm, but call to reserve a space. The center also
holds twice daily meditations.

### EGYPTIAN YOGA

*Camille Charles*
*718-793-6047*
Camille Charles teaches a unique style of yoga
based upon the teachings of Dr. Muata Ashby,
the author of the Egyptian Yoga series of books.
Charles went to Ashby's Florida ashram and learned
a style of yoga that is "spiritual and mystically-
based" upon the teachings of the ancient Egyptians.
Charles teaches private, one-on-one classes for $45
an hour, which includes a "free 15-minute reiki session." Charles offers classes in her Kew Garden
home and also will travel to clients. She describes
the classes as gentle hatha, with some Vinyasa
movements. Charles advocates a "raw food" diet
to "revitalize the body" and offers nutritional counseling. "Many people study the ancient Egyptians
and how they lived," says Charles. "But the Egyptian
yoga system actually follows the spiritual path of
the Egyptians - it is a living system."

### QUEENS YOGA INSTITUTE

*102-19 Jamaica Avenue between 108th Street*
*and Woodhaven Boulevard*
*718-850-YOGA*
*www.queensyoga.com*
*Drop in class: $12*
*Closest subway: J to 111th Street*
The Queens Yoga Institute is centrally located in
Queens, conveniently serving Forest Hills, Kew
Gardens, Richmond Hill, Woodhaven and Howard

Beach. It offers hatha, Ashtanga, hot yoga, senior yoga and pre-natal yoga. The center has two ambient studios, plus a hot room, massage room and offers ayurvedic body-wellness. Director Kris Ingram Lanzaro says that yoga, for him, is much more than a physical exercise. "I started doing yoga strictly as a physical practice. I was very depressed at the time," says Lanzaro. "However, the more I did yoga, the more my life became transformed." Lanzaro has studied a number of different styles, including Ashtanga, Bikram, Vinyasa and Iyengar styles. He ended up traveling to India where he earned certificates in Ayurvedic bodywork and Panca Karma therapy, along with various yoga styles. As a singer and songwriter, Lanzaro says that he sees yoga as an extension of his music. "Both are very meditative and can get you into that zone," Lanzaro says. "Like music, yoga can connect you to spirit. This is how the healing takes place in yoga."

### TREE OF LIFE YOGA CENTER

*102-19 Metropolitan Avenue between 71st and 72nd Avenues*
*718-544-5997*
*www.genesissociety.org*
*Drop in class: $15*
*Closest subway: E/F to Continental/Forest Hills (need to walk from station or take 223 bus)*
Rene David Alkalay is well-known in the yoga community for his spiritual approach to the ancient discipline. Alkalay has an eclectic and "interfaith" approach to yoga. He trained under Swami Rama of the Himalaya Institute and also has certificates in the Kundalini, tantra and Kriya yoga traditions. Of late, Alkalay - a survivor of the Holocaust - has been concentrating on Kaballah studies and has been working to develop Ophanim, a yoga based upon the Kaballah, which combines asana with visualization on the Kabbalistic sephirot. Alkalay, along with his wife Rachelle, also runs the Genesis Health Center, offering nutritional and wellness counseling. Classes range from Gentle Yoga to Kaballah and Kundalini classes.

### YOGA ROOM

*32-32 Steinway Street between Broadway and 34th Avenue*
*718-274-0255*
*www.the-yoga-room.com*
*Drop in class: $17*
*Closest subway: R/V to Steinway Street*

YOGA | ESOTERIC GROUPS | WITCHCRAFT | OCCULT UNDERGROUND | BOOKS | UFOS | BOTANICAS | TANTRA | ASTROLOGERS & PSYCHICS |

Astoria resident Zhana Galiasevic wanted to practice yoga in her Astoria neighborhood, so she opened her own studio. The Croatian-native began studying yoga after enduring a chronic leg injury from running. She says that when she began studying Bikram yoga, the numbness and pain "completely disappeared." She eventually went on to get her teacher-training certification from Bikram's Yoga College of India in California. Galiasevic says that her studio uses a gentler "radiant heat," as opposed to the heat blowers that most hot yoga studios use. The 700 square-foot mirrored hot yoga studio is bathed in natural sunlight. Classes are 90 minutes long and consist of a set of 26 poses, each done twice. The studio also offers tradition Vinyasa style classes.

## YOGA-LIFE-PERFECTION OF NEW YORK
*148-59 87th Avenue 718-523-1430*
*www.lifeperfection.com*
*Drop in class: $13*
*Closest subway stop: F to Parsons Blvd.*
Located in the heart of the Sri Chinmoy community in Queens, Yoga Life Perfections offers daily "classical yoga in a relaxing, quiet atmosphere." Sarama - a long-time Chinmoy disciple - has been teaching yoga out of her home since 1974. She originally trained with the legendary yogi Swami Vishnu Devananda. Sarama says that her focus is on breathing and gentle asanas. The classes are two-hours long and end with a meditation.

## YOGASHAKTI YOGA CENTER
*114-41 Lefferts Blvd. between Linden and Rockaway*
*718-529-2153*
*www.teachyoga.org*
*Drop in class: $14*
*Closest subway: A to Lefferts Blvd.*
The Yogashakti Yoga Center is part of the Yoga Shakti Mission, a religious organization based upon the energy and teachings of the yogic monk "Ma Yoga Shakti." Disciple Ma Makshapriya Shakti runs the Queens Yoga center. Mokshapriya has been teaching yoga and meditation since 1970 and still teaches many of the hatha yoga classes at the center. The classes are traditional, with an emphasis on pranayama breathing and philosophy. The center also has a highly respected teacher-training program as well; Mokshapriya co-founded the Yoga Teachers Training Institute, which "prepares and teaches the curriculum for

yoga teachers in the New York area."

## YOGI GUPTA ASHRAM
*90-16 51 Avenue in Queens*
*718-592-3217*
*Walk-in class: $11*
*Closest subway: G to Grand Avenue*
The Yogi Gupta Ashram is located in house identical to my grandmother's home in Revere, Mass. Located on a residential street in Queens, the vinyl-sided ashram has been US headquarters for Yogi Gupta "Swami Kailashananda" since the late 1960s. Yogi Gupta, however, was nowhere to be seen and his disciples did not seem to know where he was physically, or at least they wouldn't say. One disciple answered that: "He is here. You can feel him in the quiet peace of the ashram." The ashram yoga program has apparently seen better days; I was the only one who showed up for the 7 p.m. hatha class and no one showed up for the 8 p.m. meditation. The class was a bit slow moving, as we went through a routine that included "topsy-turvy pose" (half-plough) and "transverse pressure pose" (dancer pose). Manhattan yoga teacher Sri Dharma Mittra studied under Yogi Gupta. According to printed material, Yogi Gupta came to the United States in 1954 upon the advice of his disembodied guru, to spread "true yogic teachings" to the West. He began teaching yoga and meditation New York City in 1959 and now apparently spends much of the year, at least on the physical plane, in India.

## *STATEN ISLAND*
### RELAX ON CLOUD 9 SPA
*694 Clove Road at Raleigh Avenue*
*718-448-3412*
*www.relaxoncloud9.com*
*Drop in class: $14 ($6 for first class)*
The Relax on Cloud 9 Spa offers yoga classes four days a week at its Clove Lake facility, which is located across from the Staten Island Zoo. The spa offers an eclectic style of yoga, which mixes Vinyasa and traditional hatha. After class you can treat yourself to a massage, facial, hydrotherapy, or one of the many other healing modalities offered at the elegant estate.

## SHAKTI YOGA CENTER
*3 Victory Boulevard at Bay Street Landing*
*Residential Complex*

*718-442-9400*
*www.shaktiyoga.com*
*Drop-in class: $13*
*Closest subway: SIRT (Staten Island Rapid Transit)*
*to Tompkinsville*
This beautiful little studio is within walking distance
from the Staten Island Ferry, and is located right
off the promenade, overlooking the water. Alice
Waldman and Pam Flynn opened the studio in 1995
to offer a full-time yoga studio to Staten Island res-
didents. Waldman studied at Kripalu and Flynn did
her training with Dharma Mittra and Jivamukti. The
style at the studio is Vinyasa flow, though they do
offer several "gentle" yoga classes each week. "Yoga
is a great stress reliever," says Waldman. "It brings
the body and mind into balance and equanimity."

# Got a Guru? Esoteric Groups, Learning Centers and Teachers in New York

Nearly every major spiritual teacher on the planet has either lived in New York City, or at least visited the Big Apple at one time or another during the past century. If Jesus and Mohammed were alive today, no doubt they would try to try to hold at least a weekend workshop in Manhattan.

New York has a plethora of spiritual and esoteric groups for every taste. They say there are thousands of paths to the truth, and New York has nearly as many groups and centers. The groups listed mirror the varied and diverse paths available to the general public in the city.

The goal of each group is transformation of the self and elevation of the individual's consciousness through esoteric means. New York has the accepting and multi-cultural environment necessary for many of these groups to thrive. To get involved, all you have to do is pick up the phone.

### A BETTER WORLD
*Mitchell Rabin*
*212-420-0800*
*www.abetterworld.net*
Many people, when they first meet Mitchell Rabin say, "haven't I met you before?" This is because Rabin is everywhere in the esoteric community; as host of A Better World TV, Mitchell has interviewed diverse spiritual teachers, from Terrence McKenna to Bhagavan Das. Rabin, a holistic psychotherapist and acupuncturist, has been giving workshops on healing and spirituality since the early 1980s.

Rabin operates out of his office/home near 14th Street, a book-filled space that doubles as his television studio. Rabin was one of the first to introduce flotation tanks in New York City, with his Center for Creative Well-Being in the 1970s. He has also been practicing t'ai-chi chuan since 1976, and deeply involved with Gurdjieff work. He is a certified Healing Tao instructor and teaches the Micro-cosmic Orbit, Healing Sounds, Chi-Kung, and the Tao of Love, privately and in groups. "Taoist meditations are very self-empowering and help you to cultivate your own chi body, health, well-being and ultimately, immortality," says Rabin.

Rabin's passion, however, is in using the media to help transform society. He began A Better World ten years ago to bring the "great minds and sages of our time" to the general public. His guest list is eclectic and esoteric. Recent guests have included J.J. Hurtak, author of the Keys of Enoch, and Derek O'Neil, an Irishman who also happens to be one of Satya Sai Baba's top disciples (and some say an ascended master). Rabin interviews each guest with sense of humor and an ability to ground their message. The show can be seen locally on Manhattan Neighborhood Network every Wednesday evening at 8 p.m.

"The goal of the program is to create a better world," says Rabin. "We are going through difficult times and need to get a spiritually uplifting message out in the media. We need to speak about human potential that translates ideals into action."

### ADIDAM NEW YORK
*P.O.Box 270*
*New York, NY 10025*
*212-726-2820*
*www.adidam.org/new york*
Queens native Franklin Jones transformed himself from a working-class guy to world-class guru who now lives "somewhere in the Fiji Islands" with his nine wives. Jones periodically changes his name, presumably to reflect his "inner state." When I first came across him, he was calling himself Da Free John, and had the charisma of a rock star, giving shaktipat transmission of energy to his ecstatic followers. He now goes by the name Adi Da Samraj, the promised "God-man."

When Jones was a student at Columbia University in the early 1970s, he began studied with American teacher Swami Rudrananda (Rudi), who had an ashram in Greenwich Village. Jones then went on to study with Rudi's own teacher, Swami Muktananda and, according to published reports, claims to even studied the "archetype of the Virgin Mary." Jones claims that he achieved "yogic liberation" while studying with Muktananda, transcending the need for a teacher. His followers consider him to be an "avatar," a direct representation of God on earth.

While Jones no longer makes public appearances, he has active groups throughout the world, particularly in his hometown of New York. The New York center holds regular meditations and classes on his teachings in both Brooklyn and Manhattan, to share "the bright, profound relationship our spiritual teacher offers."

### AGNI YOGA SOCIETY
*at the Nicholas Roerich Museum*
*319 West 107th Street between Broadway and*

*West End Avenue*
*212-864-7752*
*www.agniyoga.org*
*Closest subway: 1/9 to 110th Street*
Russian mystic and artist Nicholas Roerich is probably best-known as the spiritual guru of former vice president Henry A. Wallace, the politician responsible for putting the pyramid and "all-seeing eye" on our dollar bill. Roerich and his wife Helena founded the Agni Yoga Society in 1920, teaching a synthesis of Eastern and Western thought. Roerich had traveled through India, Tibet and Nepal and his students believe that he came into contact with the "ascended masters," most notably Mahatma Morya, the spiritual inspiration behind the Theosophical Society. Although there is no formal study course or classes at the Agni Yoga Center, the center does have an extensive selection of books by Roerich and his wife. The center also is rumored to have unpublished private writings from Roerich, which have not yet been released to the public. The Agni Yoga Society holds an informal "discussion group" every Thursday evening at 7pm.

## ALL-FAITHS SEMINARY INTERNATIONAL

*7 West 96th Street between Central Park West
and Columbus, suite 19B*
*212-866-3795*
*www.allfaithseminary.org*
Chances are, if you meet an ordained minister in New York City, they got their start with Rabbi Joseph Gelberman (see feature). Gelberman founded both the New Seminary, along with his latest project, the All-Faiths Seminary International. Students receive a solid grounding in the mystical traditions of the major world religions. The seminary offers both a two-year program and an accelerated one-year program. The seminary is modeled after the "ancient schools of wisdom, where in-depth training and experience were imparted through personal association." The seminary says it produces clergy who are spiritual practitioners rather than functionaries.

Graduates of the seminary can perform marriages, give sermons, conduct baby namings, give workshops and provide spiritual education. Several graduates have gone on to found their own seminaries. The seminary also offers a Physician of the Soul correspondence program that teaches Kabbalistic healing techniques, along with other holistic modalities like rebirthing, shamanic healing, creative visualization and hypnotherapy.

## *Rabbi Gelberman: An Interfaith Vision for a Peaceful World*

Rabbi Joseph Gelberman was trained as an orthodox Rabbi when he lived in Hungary. But when he moved to New York City, Gelberman definitely became "unorthodox."

"I became a hippy during the 1970s - I was the Rabbi to all of the hippies in Greenwich Village," Says Gelberman, the founder of the New Seminary and All Faiths Seminary International. Gelberman came to the United States in the 1940s, after fleeing Nazi Germany. Tragically, members of his family - including his wife at the time - were killed during the Holocaust. When he arrived in America, Gelberman joined the Army as a chaplain, "to give back to this great country." "I loved America then, and I love it now," says Gelberman. "In this country, you are immediately accepted. In Europe, as Jews, we were completely separated - we couldn"t even play with the other children."

Gelberman eventually rented space in Greenwich Village for his synagogue, directly over the yga studio of Swami Vishnu Devanand. "We became very good friends," says Gelberman. "One day he said to me 'you need to do yoga.' And I have been doing it every day since then." Gelberman eventually excelled at the discipline, and was often called upon in class by Devanand to demonstrate the "headstand" pose.

Gelberman has recently combined his love of yoga with his passion for the Kabbalah, the mystical body of Jewish esoteric knowledge. Gelberman has created *Kabbalah in Motion*, a yoga practice that combines yoga-style physical movements with 12 Kabbalistic mantras, focusing on the "energy centers of the Kabbalistic Tree of Life as found within one's body."

However, Gelberman's life mission has been a bridge, bringing religions together by showing their common roots. Deeply affected by the horrors of religious-based violence, Gelberman vowed to work for unity and affirming the "truth in all faiths and religious paths."

Gelberman says that the idea for an interfaith seminary came to him while he was walking in Greenwich Village and came across a group of teenagers, from all different ethnic backgrounds, walking hand-in-hand.

"I had a vision at that moment. I didn't see the people, instead I saw Jesus, Mohammed, Buddha, Moses and Krishna walking together," says Gelberman.

In 1971, Gelberman turned this vision into a reality and, with the aid of clergy of various faiths, he founded the New Seminary, the first interfaith seminary in the country. Since then, Gelberman has trained hundreds of interfaith ministers to "serve the needs of the world community." Many have gone on to create their own seminaries and learning centers.

Gelberman retired from the New Seminary in 1988, but he continued his divinely inspired work by starting the All Faith Seminary, which offers an accelerated modern interfaith minister program, as well as a correspondence course for those who live outside the New York area.

Though in his late 80s, Rabbi Gelberman still actively promotes peace through understanding, that God is one, and there are many paths to the truth.

"The seminary is like an ancient mystery school. We study all major spiritual paths," says Gelberman. "Our motto is: never instead of, always in addition. We can learn something from every religion."

"These programs are designed to meet the needs specifically of working professionals in all walks of life," says Rabbi Gelberman. "The seminary fosters respect of all paths leading toward a deepening of one's relationship with one's own conception of God."

### AMERICAN SOCIETY OF DOWSERS
*Norman Leighton Chapter of Manhattan Dowsers*
*Meets last Tuesday monthly (except July, August and December) at 7:30 pm in the Community Room, ground floor, 303 West 66 Street*
*Contact Judy Olsen 212-736-0711*

Dowsing isn't just used for finding water. "In dowsing, you become a channel for a higher power," says Gerry Adler, New York Dowser's in-house dowsing instructor. "The pendulum is simply a tool that you use to connect to the divine." Adler teaches the monthly dowsing class that precedes the regular monthly meeting of the group. The group attracts a large and loyal following, many of which are healers,

YOGA | ESOTERIC GROUPS | WITCHCRAFT | OCCULT UNDERGROUND | BOOKS | UFOS | BOTANICAS | TANTRA | ASTROLOGERS & PSYCHICS |

psychics and occultists. Some of the best exorcists got their start in Manhattan dowsers, since dowsing gives them an ability to "sense" negative entities.

Dowsers use either a pendulum, or a set of "L-rods," a pair of metal rods that look like bent coat-hangers. Dowsers generally use dowsing charts to ask a question. The chart can indicate a simple yes or no, or the chart could be more intricate, indicating, say, parts of the body which need healing. Each month the club features a different speaker, usually on health or spirituality.

The focal point of every meeting, however, is Adler's dowsing class, which begins at 7p.m. Students form a circle around Adler and hold their pendulums up as Adler gives them tips on how to "clear" themselves and become a channel for divine guidance. "Dowsing can be used for mundane purposes like finding water, or even trying to decide what shirt to buy at the store," says Adler. "But I like to use dowsing as a tool for healing and self-transformation."

## AMERICAN SOCIETY FOR PSYCHICAL RESEARCH
*5 West 73rd Street between Central Park West
and Columbus Avenue
212-799-5050
www.aspr.com
Hours: M-Th: 11am-6pm
Closest subway: 1/2/3/9 to 72nd Street*
The American Society for Psychical Research is the oldest "psychic research" organization in the United States. Philosopher William James was one of the original founders who began the center to explore "the realms of human consciousness" in 1885.

Today the center operates more like a "clearing house" for "unexplained phenomena including telepathy, clairvoyance, precognition, psychokinesis, out-of-body experiences and poltergeists. Members receive the quarterly Journal of the ASPR as well as use of the library and assistance from the ASPR staff.

The ASPR is canvassing the public for precognitive "dreams" about the 9-11 terrorist attack. The center says that a large number of New Yorkers dreamed about the World Trade Center attack before it happened.

## ANOMALOUS PHENOMENA RESEARCH CENTER
*Alexander Imich, Ph.D.
305 West End Avenue between 73rd and
74th Streets, Suite 1401
212-874-6433*

*aimich@juno.com*
Alexander Imich dreams of a day when the general public will believe in the paranormal.

Imich - who recently celebrated his 100th birth-day - has spent the better part of his life investigating psychics and paranormal events, publishing hundreds of his reports in various journals, including a book Incredible Tales of the Paranormal. "My specialty is psychic phenomena with physical manifestation," he says. That would be people who can levitate, bend spoons and make objects appear and disappear.

There is a spiritual component to Imich's interest in the paranormal. "I always wanted to be a yogi," says Imich. A picture of Indian guru Satya Sai Baba sits on his mantel. "I wrote Sai Baba several letters, but he never responded to me," says Imich, a bit ruefully. Imich was also a student of Queens guru Sri Chinmoy for several years, but left because he says: "I just didn't feel anything. I've visited with nearly every guru who came to New York City," says Imich. "I meditate every day, but I guess I'm a bit too grounded. I don't have any of the paranormal abilities that I study."

Many of Imich's psychics do seem to have "yoga siddhi" power. Like Sai Baba, they apparently can manifest physical objects. For instance, Imich is currently studying an Egyptian psychic who recently visited New York. Imich claims that the middle-age man was able to produce wads of money, moss from Sweden and make candles light by themselves.

Imich pulls out an old, plastic container from his kitchen to demonstrate. "I held this in my hand. It was empty," says Imich, holding up the container. "When the Egyptian told me to open it, it had 50 one hundred dollar bills in it and a personal check from Cairo."

The Egyptian told Imich that the money came from someone's personal account and his spirit guide - "Abu Afiya" - ordered him to return it. When Imich closed the box and opened it again, the money was gone. Imich says that the Egyptian "does not want any publicity" for safety purposes. Imich claims that the Egyptian was forced "at gun-point" to produced $3 million dollars for a Shaykh in Cairo. "He produced the money, but it belonged to someone else, so the money disappeared when the Shaykh got home," he says.

Similarly, Imich is studying a disabled man who lives in rural Pennsylvania and can bend objects with his mind, similar to the famed Uri Geller. "I see this with my own eyes and I wonder why science can't see this as well," says Imich.

Imich has not always made his living as a parapsychologist. He once wanted to be a zoologist, but the anti-semitic climate in pre-World War II Poland prevented him from following his dream. During the war, he and his wife escaped the Nazis, but ended up spending the war in a Russian labor camp. He and his wife moved to New York City in 1951, where he worked as a chemist and his wife worked as a psychotherapist.

He founded the Anomalous Phenomena Research Center (APRC) in 1999, as a non-profit organization to raise awareness about parapsychology. Some of the board members include John Keel of the Mothman Prophecy fame, Patricia Corbett and Michael Mannion from the Mindshift Project, and noted author Ingo Swann. Imich's priority now is raising money for his public psychic demonstration, in which he will gather the top psychics in the world to perform paranormal feats in front of a group of scientists.

"I would like to see a day when instead of just studying about clairvoyants and psychics, that we study to become just like them. Do you understand what kind of revolution this would be for the human race?" Imich asks. "If everyone became like yogis, we wouldn't need scientists or researchers any more to find the cure for diseases. People could live without food and perform amazing feats. Yes, this is the future of the human race."

## ANTHROPOSOPHY NYC
*138 West 15th Street between 6th and 7th Avenues*
*212-245-8945*
*www.nyanthroposophy.org*
*Closest subway: 1/9/2/3 to 14th Street*
Rudolph Steiner was a mystic and Theosophist who eventually broke away from the group to pursue his more "Christ-centered" philosophy. Theosophy teaches that Jesus Christ was merely one of many esoteric teachers, while Steiner believed that Christianity had replaced the older, Eastern religions. Steiner promoted the idea the mankind has always existed on the earth, but at one time was a being of spirit, who became material and now has forgotten his spiritual roots.

Steiner eventually formed his own group called the Anthroposophical Society, which had its headquarters in Switzerland. The society encompasses all facets of life - spiritual study, art, agriculture and music. He became best known for the development of the "Waldorf Schools," which allow students to explore their creative sides.

| YOGA | **ESOTERIC GROUPS** | WITCHCRAFT | OCCULT UNDERGROUND | BOOKS | UFOS | BOTANICAS | TANTRA | ASTROLOGERS & PSYCHICS |

Steiner - an initiate of the Rosicrucians - claimed to have "occult vision" and could directly perceive the "inner worlds." He claimed that he could read the "akashic record," which is the "cosmic memory" of the planet. Through this clairvoyance, Steiner "witnessed" such events at the crucifixion of Jesus on Golgotha, which he called the "pivotal point of time in the entire history of creation."

Steiner was considered by many to be a "Grail initiate" who uncovered the "Satanic" energy behind the Thule Group, active in pre-World War II Germany (members claimed that he watched the Thule meetings from the astral plane). Steiner was marked for death by Adolph Hitler and narrowly missed being assassinated by the occult group in 1922. Although Steiner died in 1925, his work lives on, particularly in New York City.

Steiner wrote several books and gave thousands of lectures on mysticism and occultism. This grand body of work can be found at the New York Anthoposophical bookstore and center near Union Square. Members meet the first Friday of the month at 7 p.m. and several study groups meet during the week to discuss Steiner's work and occult philosophy. The goal of the New York center is to "spread Anthroposophic knowledge and apply these ideas to the various areas of life: art, architecture, education, youth culture, economics and others."

## AQUARIAN FOUNDATION
*235 East 4th Street between Avenue B and Avenue A*
*212-460-5820*
*Closest subway: 5/6 to Astor Place; N/R to*
*8th Street*
Members of the Aquarian Foundation believe that founder Rev. Keith Milton Rhinehart - also known as Master Kumara - is the avatar of the Aquarian Age. Rhinehart founded the Aquarian Foundation in 1955, ushering in the Age of Aquarius, his followers say. According to New York Aquarian Foundation Director Rev. Jeff Earnshaw, the Aquarian Foundation is a "mystery school" that incorporates all religions and beliefs.

Walking into the East Village church is a mind-blowing spiritual experience. A stunning crystal covered altar shares space with a statue of liberty wearing a necklace. Pictures of diverse spiritual masters, such as St. Germaine, Jesus, Parhamansa Yogananda and Master Koot Humi, hang next to drawings of extraterrestrials. Two life-sized space aliens sit in glass cabinets in the back of the church. An entire wall is devoted to Rev. Rhinehart's public miracles that followers say he performed during an eight-day span in the 1970s. One photo appears to show the white, gauzy "ectoplasmic" appearance of the Angel Gabriel, streaming from Rhinehart's mouth. Others show Rhinehart undergoing the "stigmata," when he "channels Jesus Christ." Several photos show "trumpet phenomena," in which a megaphone-like instrument is seemingly suspended in mid-air as the "disembodied voice" of various "ascended masters" comes through the floating instrument.

"Keith Rhinehart was the most tested medium in history," says Earnshaw, who runs the Lower East Side church with his wife. "He produced hundreds of pounds of clear white crystal stones under the supervision of a group of scientists. There is simply no other explanation." In a glass case, Earnshaw points out several of the crystals that he says "came out of Rhinehart's eyes."

Earnshaw says that the Aquarian foundation is a mystery school, known as the Order of Melchizadek. The teachings are based upon the channeled information from Rhinehart, whom Earnshaw says channeled such diverse teachers as Babaji, St. Germaine, Martin Luther King and several "extraterrestrial beings." All of the channeling sessions were taped and the Aquarian lessons are based upon these transcripts.

"We get the information directly from the source," says Earnshaw. "The ascended masters speak directly to us through Reverend Rhinehart. Where else can you study directly with ascended masters from Ancient Egypt and Atlantis, not to mention from other planets?"

In addition to the lessons, church members can take classes and learn such techniques as spiritual healing and spiritual psychic readings. During the Wednesday healing service I attended, church members conducted a "hands-on healing," in which church healers came around and placed their hands on parishioners, transmitting "healing energy."

Earnshaw claims that some of the Aquarian Foundation's more famous early members include Mark Prophet, who went on to found The Church Universal and Triumphant. "We are essentially a teaching order," says Earnshaw. "Our teachings embody the promises of the New Age."

The Foundation holds Sunday services at 11 a.m. and Wednesday healing services at 7:30 p.m. The Foundation also teaches various courses to members, based upon the voluminous taped lectures.

## ARCHANGEL HEALING LIGHT CENTER

*Sondra Shaye*
*718-398-7560*
*www.archangelhealinglightcenter.com*

Sondra Shaye was a lawyer at a prestigious corporate law firm in Manhattan when she had a series of powerful "spiritual awakenings" that led her on a spiritual quest. Her quest led her to the Rocky Mountain Mystery School in Utah, one of "seven mystery schools" currently active on the planet, where she was initiated as an adept and healer. "I felt like I had a calling," says Shaye, a New Jersey native. "I felt like a spiritual door opened for me."

Shaye calls herself a "lightworker" and says that she is in contact with the "hierarchy of light," which oversees the planet. After abruptly quitting her Manhattan law job, she moved to Park Slope, Brooklyn and opened the Archangel Healing Light Center. "It was really a leap of faith," she says. "I gave up a good salary. But the healing center is working out very well. The universe takes care of those who make the first step."

In the few years that she has had the center, Shaye has created a growing network of "lightworkers" who she has trained. Shaye conducts regular "adept initiations," a weekend-long series of rituals and lectures that promises "ten times more spiritual power," "four new spiritual guides," and clearer communication with "God, the archangels and masters of light." It is the lightworkers who are "keeping things together," and working with the hierarchy "to prevent disasters" in the world.

Shaye also offers a unique spiritual service called 22-Strand DNA activation, which she says "activates" all 22 strands of DNA (most people only have 2-3 strands activated, she teaches). Shaye says that the 22-Strand activation helps people adjust to the "influx of new planetary energy" that began shifting on "July 7, 1997."

"We are going through a time of ascension," says Shaye. "This gradual shift in our spiritual consciousness is bringing us more joy, peace and harmony. But it is also creating emotional upheaval and physical stress in some people. These techniques help us to make the transition into a higher consciousness gracefully."

## ASSOCIATION FOR RESEARCH AND ENLIGHTENMENT OF NEW YORK

*Center for the work of Edgar Cayce*
*150 West 28 Street between 6th and 7th Avenues,*

## *Eugenia Macer-Story:*
## *Sorcery and the UFO Experience*

If you are an evil polter-geist or alien entity, Eugenia Macer-Story is one person you don't want to mess with.

Macer-Story runs the "Magick Mirror," located at 315 West 39th Street, and she is considered one of New York City's top "ghost busters" and UFO experts.

"People come to me with certain problems when conventional means don't work," says Macer-Story. "Whether it be a missing person, polter-geist or possession by an evil entity, I use my own powers to resolve the problem."

Macer-Story recently released her latest book, *Doing Business in the Aidirondacks: True Tales of the Bizarre and Supernatural*, which recounts UFO sightings and Macer-Story's battles with "evil Thantatos sorcerers" in the New York area. The book also ties in the terrorist attack on the World Trade Center. She claims that Islamic fundamentalists use black magic to achieve their goals.

"Many people don't realize that the Blind Shaykh (Abdul Rahman) is also a psychic," says Macer-Story. "Shortly before the first World Trade Center attack, I coincidently was helping a young woman who was also consulting with Rahman. He was interpreting her dreams and dong the same type of psychic work I was doing."

Macer-Story is a familiar and somewhat controversial figure at UFO conferences. She regularly attends the New York meet-ings of Budd Hopkins "Intruders Foundation," however disagrees with the idea that all UFO encounters are "extraterrestrial." "Many so-called UFO encounters can be explained much better through knowledge of the history of spirit contact and the powers of conjuration," she says. For instance, in a recent article, she pro-posed that many negative "alien encounters" aren't extraterres-trial at all ñ but rather "inter-dimensional," from the astral plane. The "grey" aliens of modern-day accounts are actually supernat-ural entities known as the "Kelippah," which are described in Kabbalistic literature. Modern-day UFO abductions are really attempts by the Kelippah to create "hybrid" race so that they can incarnate onto the Earth plane.

Macer-Story is also a poet and much of her writing veers between art and supernatural exploration. Her 1997 book *Dark Frontier* is a brilliant and poetic look at the "multi-dimensional reality" of New York City, as she weaves together a story of synchronicities, vampires, UFOs and sorcery.

Macer-Story says that she was born with psychic powers. Her grandfather was a Mason and involved in the esoteric; she says that her psychic sensitivity comes from her Irish roots, on her mother's side of the family.

She originally came to New York City in the late 1960s as a theater student at Columbia University. She then moved to the Boston area with her husband, and lived in Ipswich, Mass. She began attending spiritual activities there and had a paranormal experience with a UFO at an Ipswich train station, in which she witnessed a spacecraft hovering near her as she waited on the platform. This experience led her to write her first book, *Congratulations to the UFO Reality*. Macer-Story opened her first incarnation of "Magick Mirror" in Salem, Mass., in 1976.

Macer-Story moved to Manhattan in the early 1980s, when one of her plays was produced. She has made her home in Manhattan ever since. She says that her paranormal talents are very much in demand in New York City, the site of a great deal of supernatural occurrences. Macer-Story is able to see auras, and offers "astral drawings" for clients, that show the astral body.

She uses a number of occult means to get rid of evil entities, including spells. But the most important aspect of helping someone get rid of possession is convincing the victim to stop cooperating with the problematic spirit.

"A poltergeist will not bother a person unless there is a conscious - or unconscious - agreement made," says Macer-Story. "In a way, it is like being in an abusive relationship. You have to convince the victim of abuse to cut contact with the abuser."

Macer-Story's involvement in the occult has led her to the discovery of an esoteric energy form she has termed "fluidice." Macer-Story discovered this energy while meditating on a candle. She noticed that, by her concentration, she could make the candle flame grow, leading her to explore where this energy came from. She has attracted a great deal of attention in the scientific community because of her discovery and has given several presentations at physics conventions.

"The energy has to have come from somewhere," she says. "If we can tap into this energy, we could solve a lot of our energy problems."

Macer-Story is truly a renaissance woman - playwright, artist, writer and occultist. Her store is open by appointment only and features her *Yankee Oracle* journal, books and her art.

*Magick-Mirror is located at 315 West 39th Street, suite 710, located between 8th and 9th Avenues. Macer-Story can be reached at 212-727-0002 and through her website, www.magickmirror.com.*

*suite 1001*
*212-691-7690*
*www.mindspring.com/~areofnyc*
*Closest subway: 1/9 to 28th Street*
Edgar Cayce was known as the "sleeping prophet,"
who would go into a "trance state" to diagnose illness and received spiritual information on subjects
like Atlantis, the future of America and the past
lives of famous people. His work lives on at the
Association for Research and Enlightenment (A.R.E.)
in Chelsea. This relatively new and active chapter of
A.R.E. offers a robust calendar of classes and lectures, based on Cayce's work. Cayce healed thousands of people, based upon the diagnoses he gave
while in his trance state. Cayce also provided
numerous predictions of future events, many of
which have come true. Regular classes include
Psychic and Intuitive Development with Coni Buro,
Spiritual Healing with Sam Daniels and Rose and the
Scorpion with Tom Eisle, an exploration of the
Kabbalah, astrology and tarot. The center sponsors
ongoing group work, such as a healing prayer group
on Thursday nights (7:30-9:30 pm), dream study
group on Sundays (2-4 p.m.) and a Revelations Class
on Saturdays (6:15-8:30pm), which looks at the
Book of Revelations as interpreted by Cayce. A.R.E.
New York is run by a group of dedicated volunteers,
including Lynn and Peter Miceli, Ken Klein, Michael
Lopez, Teresa Soru, Leonard Cassara and Helen Lee.
The A.R.E. bookstore stocks Cayce books, as well as
his health products.

## BUILDERS OF THE ADYTUM

*www.bota.org*
Builders of the Adytum (BOTA) was founded by Paul
Foster Case in New York City during the Vernal
Equinox in 1922. Case, a Golden Dawn member and
Mason, received permission to open this mystery
school by the "Secret Chiefs of the Inner School,"
after the Golden Dawn had become "corrupted" by
"dangerous alien elements in the rituals and knowledge lectures" (most likely referring to Aleister
Crowley's influence in the organization.) Many
believe that BOTA is the "reincarnation" of the true
Golden Dawn teachings. Adytum means the "inner
shrine" of a temple and BOTA members see their
work as "perfecting the human being" and bringing
about a "true brotherhood of man."
    BOTA now has its headquarters in Los Angeles
and operates a wonderful correspondence course
on the Holy Qabalah and Sacred Tarot. It takes more

than ten years to finish the entire BOTA course curriculum. Study includes intensive work on tarot symbolism (including coloring your own tarot cards), development of "supersensory powers," and visualization and occult meditation techniques.

The New York chapter of BOTA meets on the 4th Saturday of the month at the Masonic Building, 71 West 23rd Street, 12th floor Chapter Room.

## CHILDREN OF LIGHT
*Center for Personal Healing*
*2672 Broadway between 101st and 102nd Streets*
*212-932-9433*
*www.childrenoflight.com*
*Subway: 1/9 to 103rd Street*
Did you ever want to study directly with the Archangel Gabriel? Now you can. For the past 13 years, Robert Baker claims to have regularly channeled Gabriel, the archangel that allegedly dictated the Koran to Mohammed. Baker directs the Children of Light Center, along with his partner, Ron Baker (no relation), and channels Gabriel every Sunday at 7 p.m. The Sunday program begins at 5 p.m. with a Tibetan Open Eye meditation, in which the Bakers stare into the eyes of their students to "transmit energy."

During the channeling portion of the evening, Baker sits in a chair, grimaces and contorts his face as "Gabriel" takes over his body. The somewhat high-strung Baker is suddenly transformed into a serene, paternal, Mr. Rogers-type individual who refers to his students as "my dear ones." On the evening I went, the channeled "Gabriel" gave out visualization and meditation techniques to "open the crown chakra" and warned the upcoming summer months would be "very trying times indeed." During the question and answer portion of the evening, most of the 15 or so students asked for a "weather report," essentially an evaluation of their spiritual progress. Each session is taped and then sold as a set of ten or so classes, since Gabriel seems to favor giving out information in a series of related classes.

Following the channeling, Baker told me that he was formerly a make-up artist with the New York City Opera Company when a several coincidences led him to attend a mediation class with a noted medium in New York. During one meditation, Baker says that he "lost consciousness" and when he awoke 45 minutes later, he was told that he had "brought them the Angel Gabriel." He eventually learned to channel Gabriel "at will." Robert left the theater world and earned his degree in psychotherapy; he and Ron have since traveled the world spreading Gabriel's message and teaching people "spiritual ascension." Baker says that we are about to enter into the Aquarian Age, and that the human race is about to take a quantum leap ahead in its spiritual evolution. "But we have some tough times ahead of us. It is not going to be easy," says Baker. "Gabriel is really concerned about what is happening on the planet right now. And he's really pissed about what George Bush and the Republicans are up to."

## CHURCH UNIVERSAL AND TRIUMPHANT

*1133 Broadway between 26th and 25th Streets, suite 204*
*212-645-2680*
*www.tsl.org*
*Closest subway: 1/9/R to 28th Street*

I could smell the cleansing smell of Frankincense incense the moment I got off the elevator on my way to the 11 a.m. Sunday morning service at the Church Universal and Triumphant, the New Age church founded by Mark and Elizabeth Clare Prophet. Mark Prophet established the church in Washington, DC in 1958, to disseminate the messages of the "ascended masters," disembodied enlightened beings who assist the spiritual evolution of mankind. Mark Prophet passed away in 1973 ("ascended" his followers say), but his wife Elizabeth, known as the "Mother," has continued his work. The New York Church occupies a small suite that includes a bookstore and chapel. Wallace, one of the church elders, said that church is the primary vehicle that the ascended masters use to communicate with the human race now.

The primary spiritual exercise of the church is a form of vocal affirmation known as "decreeing," in which church members shout out chants, such as: "I am a being of violet fire! I am the purity God desires!" Members decree during the first hour of the three-hour service. Then, the service moves into singing, more decreeing, a short sermon from a lay minister, and then a videotape of a "dictation," in which Elizabeth Clare Prophet channels an ascended master.

On the Sunday I attended, Prophet dictated a message from "Jesus Christ," who admonished church members to get with the Aquarian consciousness and stop thinking in a Piscean modality. Overall, the message was positive and uplifting. The service ended with "communion" of a holy wafer and a sip of grape juice. The ascended master Saint Germain features prominently in the church, since Saint Germain is considered the avatar of the Aquarian Age - as well as the patron saint of the United States. The church tends to be very patriotic, since it considers the United States of America to be a divinely inspired country founded by enlightened masters. The service attracted a small but eclectic group of followers. First-time attendees are encouraged to attend the Thursday night beginner's class at 7 p.m. to become familiar with the spiritual practices and philosophy of the group.

## ECKANKAR
*853 Broadway between 13th and 14th Streets, suite 712*
*212-475-2061*
*www.eckankar.com*
*Closest subway: 5/6/N/R to Union Square*
The spiritual path of Eckankar was founded in 1968 by American Paul Twitchell, who claimed that he was the 971st "Eck Master," the latest in a long lineage of spiritual guides. Originally, Eckankar practiced a very Eastern-oriented spirituality, which included "soul travel," and meditation on the "inner sound and light." The church became more Western-oriented when the present Eck Master, Sri Harold Klemp took the organization over in 1981. Klemp, the author of The Art of Spiritual Dreaming, has stressed "conscious dreaming" as a way to contact one's spiritual guide and gain wisdom. The pantheon of Eck spiritual guides that practitioner say guide them from the "inner plane" includes an Egyptian named Gopal Das, an Arab named Shamus-i-Tabriz and a Tibetan named Rebazar Tarz. Eck members received monthly discourses by Klemp that provide spiritual exercises. The Eck Service I attended on a Friday night was full of a diverse group of people - African, Anglo, Latino, Christian and even Muslim.

The Eck minister began the service with a reading from Klemp's Autobiography of a Modern Prophet. The group then chanted the mantra Hu (rhymes with phew) for five minutes (practitioners say that this is the ancient name for God). The chanting was surprisingly uplifting; my mind filled with geometrical images. After a short, but inspiring musical performance by an Eckist who sounded a lot like Norah Jones, we broke up into "discussion groups." The topic of the evening was: "How did you first become aware of spiritual guides in your life?"

The students seemed passionate about their Eck experiences and nearly all had a supernatural contact with an Eck master in their dreams before joining the group. One member, a Nigerian Muslim, described how he had a dream that his fellow Muslims threw him off a ship, forcing him to swim to an island after nearly drowning. Waiting for him on the shore was an old Asian man with a flowing white beard, who greeted him and hugged him. The man later recognized the Asian man as Eck Master Lai Tsi. As a result of this vision, he left his Islamic community to study with an Eckankar group in India, before immigrating to the United States. The tightly knit group seemed as much social as it was spiritual, and after the service many stayed for fellowship. The group welcomes the public to its services, held at 6 p.m. on Wednesdays and 7 p.m. on Fridays.

## FIRST CHURCH OF RELIGIOUS SCIENCE
*14 East 48th Street between Madison and*
*5th Avenues*
*212-688-0600*
*www.fcrsny.org*
*Closest subway: 6/E/F to 51st Street*
The First Church of Religious Science is one of the most prominent "new thought" organizations in country. Based on the writings of Ernest Holmes, the church has the attitude: "If you can conceive it, you can achieve it." The midtown center has a bookstore with titles by positive thinking authors like Emmet Fox and Vernon Walters. Every day at noon, the center holds a service in which people can submit requests for "spiritual treatments," sort of like prayer requests, except the congregation uses "affirmations" to actualize the request. During the noon service I attended, most of the requests were for more money and better jobs, including one actor who wanted "to be able to act in principled films and yet still make an excellent salary." The Rev. Joyce Jackson read each treatment aloud and then gave a series of affirmations.

Every Sunday, the pastor Rev. Wade Adkisson holds the famous 11 am service at Alice Tully Hall in Lincoln Center. The service includes spiritual treatments, as well as a lecture. The parishioners of the church include many creative types. Every Thursday, the center holds the popular Artist and Actors Workshop, which teaches people how to use the power of positive thinking to land that dream role. The center also has a number of trained, licensed practitioners who can provide one-on-one spiritual treatments for those who need more focused help with their creative visualizations.

## GURDJIEFF FOUNDATION
*123 East 63rd Street between 2nd and 3rd Avenues*
*212-838-7727*
*www.gurdjieff.org/foundation*
Since 1953, the Gurdjieff Foundation of New York
has kept the work of the mystic Georges Ivanovitch
Gurdjieff (1871-1949) alive. Gurdjieff - known as the
"Master" - promoted the idea that most humans "were
asleep." His "sacred dance" exercises, based upon esoteric Sufi movements, are aimed at "breaking habits"
and creating an "awakened" person. Gurdjieff once
said that "200 fully conscious people could change
the whole world." Foundation members consider
themselves "purists" when it comes to Gurdjieff's
work. The foundation says it is "dedicated to preserv-
ing the essence, specificity and integrity" of the
Gurdjieff teachings. Members say that the New York
foundation is extremely "selective" and only interested in sincere, genuine seekers. In order to participate
in the weekly lectures and sacred dance lessons, you
need to call the office number for an initial contact. It
may take several personal interviews to be accepted
as a full-fledged member. One former foundation student said that it took him a year of personal meetings
before he would participate in a "poly-rhythmic" session at the East Side headquarters. In the 1960s, a
group of students, led by Willem Nyland, broke away
to establish the "Institute for Religious Development,"
the other main Gurdjieff group in the area.

## HOLISTIC STUDIES INSTITUTE OF NEW YORK
*208 West 30th Street between 7th and 8th*
*Avenues, suite 201*
*212-337-3017*
*www.holisticstudies.com*
According to Stephen Robinson, anyone can be a
psychic like "John Edwards" and "James Van Praagh."
"Being psychic is like breathing," says Robinson,
director of the Holistic Studies Institute of New
York. "Everyone is psychic; they just need to
become aware of it."
     Robinson is an ordained spiritualist minister,
who began the school in Albany in 1977. He opened
the Manhattan branch two years ago. The school's
most popular course is the four-level Psychic
Development Course that Robinson teaches with his
assistant Charlene Robbins. "Being a psychic can literally save your life," says Robinson, who has trained
more than 10,000 people. He gives several examples where his students have used their psychic
abilities to avoid disaster, including one case where

his student got a "psychic impression" and did not board a commuter plane that later crashed.

Robinson is also a certified psychic-medium and hosts séances every Tuesday evening at the Institute. The séances are open to the public and Robinson will channel information from the spirits who have accompanied individuals to the event. "Spirits make much better psychics that people do," says Robinson. "They have a much better vantage point to see the future." Robinson also teaches mediumship skills during the 40-week psychic development course.

While many of Robinson's students go on to become professional psychics, many enroll in the course simply to expand their own awareness. "This is an important life tool," says Robinson. "In this program, we take a skill that is unconscious and make it conscious. We teach people to recognize it, validate it and express it."

## HEAVEN IN HELL'S KITCHEN
*Rebecca Scott*
*212-315-4075*

Hell's Kitchen seems like an unusual place to find a spiritual sanctuary. However, Rebecca Scott has created a cutting-edge center offering classes in astral travel, channeling and sacred divine geometry, along with healing modalities like 22 Strand DNA Activation, and Emotional Cord Cutting. Scott spent many years as a massage therapist before discovering the Rocky Mountain Mystery School (RMMS), where she was initiated into the "hierarchy of light."

"You can benefit a great deal from the New Age movement, but not everything is grounded in solid metaphysics," says Scott. "This school has thousands of years of lineage behind it, a lineage that can be traced back directly to King Solomon." The RMMS is one of seven mystery schools on the planet, and the only public mystery school, she says. "For instance, if you went to Tibet and you knew the general location of the mystery school there, you would not find it unless they wanted you to," she says. Scott also channels the "masters of the planets," as well as "tarot archetypes," during public meditations. She channeled the "master of Mars" when Mars was extremely close to the Earth in August 2003. "Many people received powerful messages during this channeling, particularly on how to exercise and develop physical strength, which is an attribute of Mars," says Scott. "Every session and class we do is designed to provide people with lasting empowerment."

## I AM SANCTUARIES OF NYC
*159 East 35th Street between 3rd and
Lexington Avenues*
*212-686-9088*
*www.saintgermainfoundation.com*

In 1930, a mining engineer named Guy W. Ballard was hiking on Mount Shasta in California, when he claims that he came into contact with the "ascended master Saint Germain," one of the "great beings from the spiritual hierarchy who govern this system of worlds." The result of this meeting was the formation of the "I AM" organization, which has inspired countless other groups which also claim to be in touch with the ascended masters, "living, tangible beings who raised their bodies into ascension, as did Jesus the Christ." Ballard produced more than eleven textbooks and countless transcripts of the teachings that Germain allegedly gave him.

The real Saint Germain was a mysterious diplomat and occultist who lived in 18th century France, and claimed to be several centuries old. Many believe that Saint Germain played a crucial - yet behind-the-scenes - role during the formation of the United States of America (some say he was the nameless man whose stirring speech urged the Founding Fathers to sign the Declaration of Independence).

The I AM Sanctuary of NYC holds nightly services at its midtown center; however none of the services are open to the public. The center does not seek publicity and does not proselytize. In order to become a member, you must read Ballard's first three books, The Unveiled Mysteries, The Magic Presence and the Discourses. Then you need to take the I AM fundamental lessons course. After a meeting with New York Temple director Tammy Tanaka, then you are eligible to attend the nightly services. This weeds out the "agitators" who would disrupt the public I AM meetings during the intolerant 1950s. Each service includes a reading, "violet flame" meditation/visualization, and ends with a series of "decrees," or affirmations.

When I contacted the center, Tanaka said that my "mental body" was most likely in touch with the ascended masters, since I was expressing a interest in organization. "We don't choose the masters, it is the masters who choose us," says Tanaka, who invited me to come by the temple and pick up Ballard's first book.

The temple itself is stunning and has the feeling of exclusivity. Well-dressed and bright-eyed men and women filed in for the 6pm service. As the door

YOGA | ESOTERIC GROUPS | WITCHCRAFT | OCCULT UNDERGROUND | BOOKS | UFOS | BOTANICAS | TANTRA | ASTROLOGERS & PSYCHICS |

opened, I could here the chanting of the "decrees" and see purple drapes, candles and flowers on the altar (Saint Germain is said to be the master of the "Purple Ray" and the color purple is prevalent, from the decor to the clothing that members wear).

Tanaka says that she came into contact with the I AM teachings more than 40 years ago, while a journalism student at Columbia University. Tanaka says that Saint Germain will often take on a physical body to come to the Earth and "check out what is happening." She says that Saint Germain has done this more frequently as of late, given the tense political situation and the "time of purification" that we are going through.

"You probably have seen Saint Germain walking the streets of New York yourself," she says. "He is the best dressed person on the street, the most stylish. He walks among people every day and most don't even notice."

## INSTITUTE FOR RELIGIOUS DEVELOPMENT
*New York City Nyland group*
*845-258-4655*
*www.nyland.org*
Willem A. Nyland was a direct student of mystic George Ivanovitch Gurdjieff and helped found the Gurdjieff Foundation in New York. In the early 1960s, Nyland and several students broke away from the foundation to start their own Gurdjieff group. While the foundation is focused more on theory, Nyland took a more "hands-on" approach. Many of Nyland's students moved out to his rural farm in Warwick, NY to work with their hands and put the Gurdjieff teachings "into action." The Nyland group teaches Work-on-oneself, based upon the original teachings of Gurdjieff. Contact Elaine Knight at the website above for the information on the New York City group.

## INTERNATIONAL SOCIETY FOR KRISHNA CONSCIOUSNESS (ISKCON)
*26 Second Avenue between First and*
*Second Streets*
*212-420-8803*
*www.krishnanyc.com*
*Closest subway: F to 2nd Avenue*
If you have ever spent any time in the lower East Village, you no doubt have been treated to an impromptu parade of Hare Krishnas chanting and dancing down Second Avenue. The ISKCON center in the East Village is the oldest Hare Krishna center in

America. His Divine Grace A.C. Bhaktivedanta Swami Prabhupada - who brought the Hare Krishna movement to the United States - lived right around the corner in the Bowery when he first came to this country. His followers say that he was "subjected to the bitter New York winter, theft of his meager belongings, as well as abuse from his drug-crazed roommate, yet he was determined to bring about a spiritual revolution."

Swami Prabhupada and two disciples opened the storefront at 26 Second Avenue in 1966, establishing ISKCON, which grew into the international organization that he envisioned. The Hare Krishna organization soon outgrew the Second Avenue location, however Krishna followers renovated the historic Temple and re-opened it in 1991, making it the "beacon" of the Krishna movement in Manhattan.

The Second Avenue temple holds regular Tuesday and Friday evening events starting at 6:45 pm, which includes a lecture, devotional chanting and a vegetarian feast. The temple also sponsors a Saturday Sanskit class, taught by Dayananda Das.

The primary spiritual practice of ISKON is chanting the holy names of Lord Krishna and devotional. Followers are vegetarian and do not drink alcohol. "Through yogic chanting, devotees purify their consciousness and develop their relationship with Krishna, the Supreme Lord," says the organization.

### JAIN MEDITATION INTERNATIONAL CENTER
*212-362-6483*
*www.jainmeditation.org*
When Gurudev Shree Chitrabanhu first came to the United States in 1971, the Jain religion was barely known. Yet Chitrabanhu had a powerful vision of the Jain principle of ahimsa (non-violence) becoming ingrained into the consciousness of the Americans.

"The Western world has a great material capacity, enough to reach the moon," says Chitrabanhu, who lives on the Upper East Side. "But many in the West are also fighting and creating violence. If they don't have a reverence for life, they will use guns to kill their own people."

Chitrabanhu's vision has come true; there are now 80,000 members of JAINA, the organization the he founded. The Jain religion is one of the oldest in the world, based on the teachings of non-violence. Although he is in his 80s, Chritrabanhu still teaches meditation every Wednesday evening in Manhattan during the summer months.

Jain meditation is a very powerful technique

# Ralph White: Creating an Open Center for the Esoteric Community

For the past 20 years, the New York Open Center in Soho has been New York's premier holistic learning center, teaching classes in healing, metaphysics and indigenous spirituality.

Much of the success of the center is due to the vision of John White, an Englishman who now calls New York City his home. White founded the center, along with Walter Beebe, in 1984. "New York City is the most influential vortex of humanity on the planet earth," says White. "To create a center devoted entirely to holistic values in an environment like New York was a formidable achievement - it did not come easy."

White came to the United States in 1970, as a Fulbright Scholar in American studies. However, the voice of the counter culture beckoned him and, rather than finish his degree, White took to the road and fulfilled a boyhood dream, to "drive Route 66 from Chicago to California."

It was during this trip that White had a profound spiritual experience that would alter his life direction forever. With his female traveling companion - who was an astrologer - White had an "opening of the heart" experience while in the Arizona desert. "For me, it was the spiritual turning point of my life," says White. "It was an inner, mystical experience, and nothing in the academic approach spoke to this."

White embarked on a "vision quest" that took him to California, the mystical mountains of *Machu Pichu* and finally to the Scottish spiritual community of Findhorn, where he lived for three years.

Using the knowledge he gained during his nearly ten years of journey and spiritual quest, White returned to the New York City area and became the program director for the Omega Center in Rhinebeck, NY. His goal was to recreate the "open-hearted, inclusive spiritual practices" of Findhorn.

At about the same time, White met Walter Beebe, a Wall Street lawyer with a strong vision of social justice and holistic living. Beebe felt that New York City needed a spiritual center for holistic education like Omega.

"It was a crazy idea," says White. "But Walter is a genius at fundraising. It turned out that Walter's idea was right."

Since opening, the non-profit center has offered cutting-edge classes and certificate programs. Unlike many other holistic centers, the Open Center has a very strong emphasis on the Western esoteric tradition, as well as courses on the indigenous spirituality of the African and Latin American diaspora.

White's new project involves opening similar holistic centers in the former Soviet Union countries. Particularly since the 9-11 attacks, White says that it is crucial that the holistic philosophy be spread throughout the world.

"What many around the world don't realize is that America is not just about trade and economy - we are about an inclusive culture and a haven for people on the spiritual path, for cultural creatives," says White. "Human freedom resides in the civil society and culture sphere. The long-term solution is for us to create a more just, caring and sustainable world - these are the American values that the world should be seeing."

that combines breathing with mantra. Adherents breathe in, bringing energy in through the third-eye chakra, down the spine, to the chakra at the base of the spine. During the out-breath, adherents chant the mantra Ha-reem, bringing the energy back up the spine to the third-eye chakra.

Before coming to the United States, Chitrabanhu lived in India as a Jain monk for 28 years; he spent the first five years of his monk hood in complete silence and meditation, achieving a state of enlightenment.

The New York Jain meditation group meets every Wednesday at 7:15 p.m. in Manhattan at TRS, 44 East 32nd Street, 11th floor.

"There is no greater power than meditation," says Chitrabanhu. "It keeps you alive, fresh, unsoiled and ever-flowing. In meditation, what becomes magnified in our awareness helps us to have a flow of energy and oneness with life around us."

## KABBALAH CENTER
*155 East 48th Street between Second and Third Avenues*
*212-644-0025*

*www.kabbalah.com*
*Closest subway: 6/E/F to 51st Street*
Love them or dislike them, the Kabbalah Center
has done more to spread the esoteric wisdom of
Judaism than any other group in the world. Kabbalah
purists claim that the center has "commercialized"
this spiritual wisdom, while its supporters say
that the center has exposed the Kabbalah to those
who otherwise would not have access. Traditionally,
the high Kabbalah was only taught to married
males over the age of 40, as an oral tradition. The
Kabbalah Center, on the other hand, has opened
these once secret teachings to all who can pay the
course fee. The Center offers courses like Kabbalah
101, From Chaos to Connection, Zohar Class and
Kabbalistic Astrology.

The Kabbalah Center claims that it was founded
in 1922 in Jerusalem by Rabbi Yehuda Ashlag. It
went international when Rabbi Phillip Berg opened
the first center in the United States in 1969. Since
then, 40 Kabbalah Centers have been opened
throughout the world. The Los Angeles Center has
attracted movie and music stars as students, such
as Madonna and Roseanne Barr.

The New York center has a chic ambience, with a
bookstore on the ground floor and classrooms on
the upper floors. Attractive young women - most
from Israel - staff the bookstore with the zeal of
missionaries. The day I went in, the clerk nearly had
me convinced into buying the 23-volume Zohar, the
mystical text that the center uses for its "scripture."
The woman told me that just by "meditating on the
Hebrew letters" every day, amazing shifts in consciousness would occur in my life. At $415 for the
set, it was a bit much for me. However, many students swear by the book, and the center. "Before I
learned the Kabbalah, I had no direction in my life,"
says one student I met there. "But now I understand
the purpose in my life. Everything makes sense in
light of the Kaballah - even world events."

### DR. JOY LEO
*396 Broadway between Canal and White Streets,*
*suite 302*
*212-966-7577*
*www.joy-light.net*
*Closest subway: 6/N/R/A/C/E to Canal Street*
Joy Leo spent years as a Buddhist monk and scholar. She says that the "ascended masters" guided her
to move to New York City, just before the 9-11
World Trade Center attacks. "When I first set foot

YOGA | **ESOTERIC GROUPS** | WITCHCRAFT | OCCULT UNDERGROUND | BOOKS | UFOS | BOTANICAS | TANTRA | ASTROLOGERS & PSYCHICS |

on Manhattan, I knew I was on sacred ground, I knew that I was on Atlantis," says Leo, an attractive, former Hong Kong television personality. Leo says that her decision to move to New York was part of a "soul agreement," she made to help uplift the energy of Manhattan. Leo saw the 9-11 attacks as a "planetary initiation." "The attacks ripped apart the fabric of everything that felt secure," say Leo. "The feeling of vulnerability rips at the heart and consciousness opens."

Leo is also a one of three Sekhem masters living in the United States. Leo says that she channels healing energy from a "very high place." Sekhem was originally taught to healing priests in ancient Egypt. Since arriving in New York, Leo has attracted a growing body of spiritual students. Her mix of Buddhism and western mysticism is powerful and she has a charismatic, caring presence. She holds a meditation at her Chinatown office every Tuesday evening. Leo is a spiritual teacher who combines both Eastern and Western wisdom, for profound healing and transformation.

Leo and her meditation group say they are working behind the scenes to integrate the "Atlantis-Lemurian energy still present in New York," thus creating a new type of spiritual awareness. She says that Manhattan was actually part of Atlantis, the fabled and spiritually advanced continent that sank. "New York is the New Jerusalem," says Leo. "Manhattan is on the cutting edge of the new paradigm as the planet ascends to a higher consciousness. Mankind is collectively elevating itself. The 9-11 attacks were destructive, but also transformative. It is like the myth of Phoenix, from the flames of the WTC, a new culture and consciousness will rise. The dark forces that control the planet are weakening."

### LUCIS TRUST
*120 Wall Street between Water and South Streets, 24th floor*
*212-292-0707*
*www.lucistrust.org*
In 1919, a Theosophist named Alice Bailey was contacted telepathically by "The Tibetan," known as Djwal Khul, who asked her to write and published certain books of his in the West. For 30 years, Bailey - who was living in Manhattan - wrote and published 24 books, including Initiation, Human and Solar, and A Treatise on the Seven Rays. Bailey founded the Lucis Trust in New York City in 1922. Its first office was in an office building at 11 West 42nd Street.

Lucis Trust has become primarily a teaching organization and its focus is at the United Nations. Bailey started the "Arcane School" in 1923, as "training school in meditation techniques and the development of spiritual potential." The Lucis Trust runs the Arcane School now as a correspondence course.

Members of the Lucis Trust consider themselves as "lightworkers" who work with the "ascended masters" to create a peaceful, more evolved world. The vision of the Lucis Trust is one of universality, of individuals rising above their ethnic and religious differences to engage in "world cooperation." The Trust promotes both a one-world government administered through the United Nations and a "New World Religion." They believe that only when individuals come together as a "New Group of World Servers" will there be true peace on earth.

Lucis Trust holds public full Moon meditations once a month at the Marriott East Side Hotel, 525 Lexington Avenue to send "spiritual light" to the world, particularly world leaders. The group's primary full Moon meditation is the "Wesak Festival," which occurs when the full Moon is in Taurus. During this day, also known as the "Festival of the Buddha," members say that a "door into Heaven" opens so that contact can be made with the "spiritual hierarchy of light." "The light in Lucis Trust reveals the unity of all human beings, of all planetary beings," says Lucis President Sarah McKechnie.

### MAMA DONNA'S TEA GARDEN AND HEALING CENTER

*718-857-2247*
*www.donnahenes.net*
For the past 28 years, Donna Henes, also known as Mama Donna, has created a "community of spirit" in Brooklyn, offering public ceremonies, drumming circles and personal rituals. Henes, a sculptor by training, began her spiritual journey after experiencing a vision. "At the time, all of my sculpture work involved making huge spider webs," says Henes. "One day I had a vision that everything in the universe was interconnected. From that day, I realized that my work was to always to connect people together through ritual, and to build community." Henes went on a series of spiritual journeys, primarily to Latin America and Mexico, and was initiated as a shaman. Her spiritual quest culminated with a nine-day "Vision Quest" at the top of a mountain. In addition to her new and full Moon drumming circles, she also offers ongoing "spirit support group sessions," as well as private "rit-

ual consultancy," that includes tarot readings, spiritual counseling and soul path coaching.

Mama Donna's has both a ceremonial ritual space, as well as a "Spirit Shop," which offers unique spiritual tools from around the world. Mama Donna gained fame as the "Urban Shaman" after she began doing public ceremonies in the 1970s, including the yearly Spring Equinox Eggs on End: Standing on Ceremony, which was held at the World Trade Center, in which participants would stand eggs on their ends (the gravitational pull of the equinox creates a phenomena that allows the eggs to stand). Although her training is in Latin American shamanism, she says that her outlook is universal. "Our circles represent the multi-culture of New York City; we have every race, sex and religion," says Henes. "We are urban shaman. We aren't constrained by any one culture - we accept them all."

## MASONIC LODGE
*71 West 23rd Street between 6th and 7th Avenues*
*1-800-3MASON4*
*www.nymasons.org*
*Closest subway: 1/9 to 23rd Street*
The 12-story Masonic Lodge building on West 23rd Street is one of the "hidden secrets" of the city. Since 1908, the stunning building has been home to nearly 75 individual Masonic lodges, as well as related groups like the Scottish Rite, Knights Templar, and even non-Masonic groups like the Golden Dawn, Builders of the Adytum and Ordo Templi Orientis (OTO) (who rent space in the building).

"There is a strong esoteric tradition within Masonry and some would say that Masonry is the source of many esoteric traditions," says Tom Savini, director of the Masonic Library and Museum. "However the vast majority of current members know little about the esoteric side of Masonry and that is not what originally drew them to organization." Savini says that Masonry was originally designed "as a system of ethics and lessons to build character." The purpose of the Masonic ritual is to instill these ethics through the memorization of ritualistic dialogue. "That way it really stays with an individual," says Savini. "Masonry is also an intensely symbolic system, and symbols are also a language."

Masons trace their lineage back nearly 300 years, when the first Grand Lodge was established in England in 1717. Since then, Masonry has spread throughout the free world, dedicated to the "Brotherhood of man under the Fatherhood of God."

Masonry played a big role in the formation of the United States. Many of the Founding Fathers were Masons; their Masonic ideals of "individual liberty, fraternity and equality" were completely consistent with the ideals of the Revolution. The Boston Tea Party was conducted by members of the St. Andrews Lodge; Paul Revere, Thomas Paine, Thomas Jefferson and Benjamin Franklin were all active Masons.

While Masonry has become much more of a "fraternal organization," esoteric knowledge can still be found within the ritual and symbols. There are some Masons who claim that the lineage of Masonry goes back directly to Solomon's Temple - and even further to the mystery schools of Atlantis.

Mason and Golden Dawn initiate Michael Lewis sums it up this way: "What you get out of Masonry depends on what you put in. Masonry is the original spiritual tradition of the West, the heir to all other lineages of wisdom, the custodian of the mysteries. But like the Stone of the Wise, it is everywhere apparent, but not esteemed by the many. For a few, Masonry is an ongoing revelation of the Secret of Secrets."

According to Savini, it is quite easy to apply to become Masons. "Many people are under the impression that you have to be invited to be member," says Savini. "All you really have to do is come to the Masonic building and ask for an application form." Applicants must be "of good moral character" and must undergo a home visit before the particular lodge they are applying will accept their application.

Tours of the Masonic building are given daily during the week between 11 a.m. and 2:30 p.m. Marble craftsmen from Italy were flown over several years ago to renovate the historic building. The centerpiece is the grand ballroom on the third and fourth floors, which has Tiffany skylights and is reportedly identical to the ballroom of the fated ship the Titanic. The TV show Law and Order regularly films there and the New York Philharmonic Orchestra practices there because of the excellent acoustics.

"Freemasonry relies on an individual to be active in their own spiritual path," says Savini. "At the same time, Freemasonry opens the initiate's mind up to other paths and promotes the idea of tolerance and responsibility. It encourages us to think, study and learn more."

**MINDSHIFT INSTITUTE**
*3 West 87th Street, suite 1D*
*212-721-6785*
*www.mindshiftinstitute.org*

For Trish Corbett and Michael Mannion, public accep-
tance of extraterrestrials and paranormal experiences is crucial for world peace, as well as our continued existence on the Earth. "Only then will we see ourselves as human beings, members of one big family,"
says Mannion. "The differences of nationalism, eth-
nicity, religion and ideology will all become irrelevant."

Mannion and Corbett founded the Mindshift
Institute in 1999, as a non-profit organization dedicated to "opening people's minds" and challenging
the dominant world view. The institute organizes
regular conferences and interactive workshops it
calls "conversational evenings." "Most people are
asleep," says Corbett. "We are about awakening people to a new reality and making them more aware of
what is happening around them."

Mannion and Corbett met while volunteering at
the Friends of the Noetic Sciences in New York.
Mannion is the author of a number of health and
parapsychology titles, including Project Mindshift, a
book that deals with "UFOs and the alien presence"
in the world. Corbett is a healer and a graduate of
the IM School of Healing Arts.

Mannion says that it was an interest in the work
of the late Dr. Wilhelm Reich that led him into the
field of parapsychology and "new thought." Mannion
even constructed a Reichian Orgone Accumulator,
which he and Corbett use on a daily basis in their
Upper West Side apartment. Like Dr. Reich, Mannion
says that he "follows the energy" to get at the truth.
Reich claimed that he discovered a "universal cosmic energy" that he called orgone, which can promote vitality and heal diseases such as cancer.

Much like Reich, Mannion and Corbett accept
the existence of UFOS and the paranormal, but have
come to no conclusions about these phenomena.
"Most groups focus on parapsychology, psychic phenomena, or UFOs," says Mannion. "We accept these,
but we are more interested in the underlying unity
of this phenomenon. We want to open people's
minds. We don't force people to believe as we do, we
are only asking that people use their awareness to
decide for themselves."

And what would a society look like that is full of
esoteric "believers?" Mannion and Corbett say that
many sincere people work on projects to clean the
environment or end world conflict. But with the
"shift in thinking," these problems would not exist in
the first place. "Rather than dealing with the symp-
tom, we are dealing with the primary cause," says
Corbett. "With a change in world view, we wouldn't

YOGA | **ESOTERIC GROUPS** | WITCHCRAFT | OCCULT UNDERGROUND | BOOKS | UFOS | BOTANICAS | TANTRA | ASTROLOGERS & PSYCHICS |

even think of polluting our rivers. We would see everything as being interconnected and sacred."

## NEW YORK KRIYA YOGA
*917-453-7752*
*http://users.aol.com/nyckriya*
When people think of Kriya Yoga, they immediately associate the spiritual practice with Paramahansa Yogananda, the author of Autobiography of a Yogi. However, the late Paramahansa Hariharananda formed one of the other main, though lesser-known, Kriya lineages. Kriya Yoga is a set of mystical exercises which circulate pranic energy in the energy centers of the body.

The New York Kriya Yoga center teaches Kriya Yoga according to the teachings of Hariharananda, who entered mahasamadhi in 2002. His students say that Hariharananda achieved a state of samadhi (enlightenment) when he was in his 20s and maintained a high state of consciousness throughout his life.

"Hariharananda had an amazing presence," says Don "Baba" Abrams, the head of the New York center. "Although he passed into mahasamadhi, we can still feel this presence."

Abrams says that Hariharananda was the only Kriya master to publicly teach all six Kriya techniques. Even Yogananda's school, Self Realization Fellowship, only teaches the two primary Kriya exercises. Abrams says that Hariharananda learned the higher Kriya techniques from disciples of Sriyukteshwar, who originally initiated him into Kriya Yoga.

"Yogananda never publicly taught the higher Kriyas," says Abrams. "Hariharananda believed that the West was ready for these advanced techniques."

Abrams was given the authority to initiate students into Kriya Yoga; the six Kriya techniques are given to students over a period of years, as they master each one.

Hariharananda's successor, Paramahansa Prajnananda, visits the New York center several times a year to give in initiations and provide guidance. "Kriya Yoga will give you amazing benefits, both physical and spiritual," says Abrams. "It will make you a more peaceful person, but the ultimate goal of Kriya is to give you a direct experience of God, to contact the spark of the divine within you."

The Kriya meditation group meets Wednesdays and Thursdays from 7- 8:30 p.m. at the Sri Radha Govinda Temple, 93 St. Marks Place, second floor.

They also meet Sundays at Sufi Books, 227 West Broadway at 9 a.m. (first Kriya) and 9:30 a.m. (second Kriya). Suggested donation is $10.

## NEW YORK OPEN CENTER
*83 Spring Street between Broadway and Lafayette Street*
*212-219-2527*
*www.opencenter.org*
*Closest subway: 6 to Prince; R to Spring Street*
Since the early 1980s, the New York Open Center has been the largest holistic learning center in the United States. The center is a hotbed of cutting-edge spiritual and healing disciplines. The center has one of the best Polarity Therapy programs in the country, along with certificate programs in herbology, foot reflexology, Thai Yoga and feng shui. Some of the world's most creative minds in the esoteric world have lectured at the center. Each semester the center features classes on Kabbalah, the Western mystery tradition, Native American spirituality, Latin American spirituality and a myriad of other disciplines.

The center was originally founded by Ralph White (see feature) and Walter Beebe and is staffed by volunteers who get to take free classes in exchange for their time. The center was founded to help create a "paradigm shift" into a more holistic world view.

## NEW YORK THEOSOPHICAL SOCIETY
*253 East 53rd Street between 2nd and 3rd Avenues*
*212-753-3835*
*www.theosophy-ny.org*
*Closest subway: 6/E/F to 51st Street*
Madame Petrovna Blavatsky (or HPB as she is known to TS members) arguably created the New Age movement in the West with the publication of the Secret Doctrine in 1888. Blavatsky claimed to have been in contact with the masters and mahatmas, members of the "Great White Brotherhood," a group of highly evolved individuals who assist the spiritual growth of mankind. Many don't realize that Blavatsky penned this influential book right in Manhattan, at 46 Irving Place, where the Russian-born mystic made her home for many years.

The Theosophical Society grew out of the spiritualist movement. This movement began in Hydesville, NY on March 31, 1848 when teenagers Margaret and Kate Fox began a series of communication with spiritual entities through "rapping and knocks" that they heard in the home. The Fox sisters went on to have a celebrated 30-year career as America's most celebrated "public rapping mediums" (no, not that kind of rapping).

The sisters began a phenomenal growth of mediums and séances, accompanied by supernatural appearances, prophecies, levitations and communication with the dead. By the 1870s, there were an estimated 10 million Americans who described themselves as "spiritualists," the majority of whom were from the New York City area. During a two-week stay at a spiritualist center in Chittenden, Vermont in 1874, Blavatsky made a fated meeting with New York City lawyer Colonel Henry Steel Olcott. Olcott was a lawyer and a journalist who was also interested in the spiritualist movement. Olcott convinced Blavatsky to live in New York City.

Blavatsky, along with Olcott, founded the TS in 1875, to "investigate the nature of the universe and humanity's place in it, to promote an understanding of other cultures, and to be a nucleus of universal brotherhood among all human beings." The society promoted such groundbreaking ideas (in those days) of reincarnation, karma, the existence of worlds beyond the physical, the duty of altruism and the ultimate perfection of human nature, society and life.

Today, the New York TS is ably guided by President Don Conte, a long-time TS member and also Lucis Trust member. The society holds regular members-only meetings on Tuesdays, along with a robust selection of public lectures and workshops. Some recent offerings include The Enneagram and Spiritual Evolution, Creating Personal Prosperity in This Lifetime, and Mars and Pisces Need not be a Crisis.

### THE NORTH AMERICAN TEMPLATE
*Formerly Emin Foundation*
*161 West 22nd Street between 6th and*
*7th Avenues*
*212-929-3381*
*www.natemplate.org*
*Closest subway: F/1/9/R to 23rd Street*
The charismatic guru "Leo" (Raymond John Armin) died in 2002, however his occult group, the Emin Foundation, continues to live on as the "North American Template." NAT New York meets several times a week, with regular public lectures at its new space in Chelsea. Center director Tuval Ariel has come up with an intriguing schedule of workshops. For instance, he recently taught a three-part

YOGA | ESOTERIC GROUPS | WITCHCRAFT | OCCULT UNDERGROUND | BOOKS | UFOS | BOTANICAS | TANTRA | ASTROLOGERS & PSYCHICS |

Wednesday evening series on The Human Aura, which gave students techniques for sensing the aura, "making the aura shine," telepathy, clairvoyance and creating "mental projections" with the aura. "We need this type of knowledge more than ever," says Ariel, a native of Israel. "The energy of the planet is changing and the level of stress is increasing. We need to strengthen our aura to protect ourselves."

The NAT remains true to the teaching of the enigmatic Leo, who promoted the idea that the human skull was "melting" as the brain expands in the evolution of the human species, that everything in the world can be categorized into a 16 "templates," and that there are "seven layers of astral light" that humans are constantly connecting to. The key is to connect with the "high astral light and beings" and to continually "cleanse" the lower astral entities from your aura. "High astral beings can only be invited, they can't be commanded to appear," said Leo, in his heyday in London.

The Emin Foundation, at its height, was quite a scene in late 1970s London. Each night hundreds of people would sit with Leo as he held court in the "Putney Center," the Emin headquarters that had a vaulted ceiling with wire mesh where the "invited high astral spirits" would gather. Leo taught elaborate space clearing rituals, using clapping, a special incense and bell ringing (space clearing guru Karen Kingston got her start with Emin) to get rid of lower astral entities. He called the high energy that would gather the "fizz." "Do you understand what our religion is about?" he would say, when the high astral entities would fill the center. "It is called the human story!"

In Leo's cosmology, the gods did exist, and were to be respected for running the universe, but should not be worshiped. "When I meet God, I will meet Him face-to-face, standing, not kneeling in front of Him," he was fond of saying. He had no use for organized religion, which he called a "diseased mentality." He likewise, had little regard from other occult organizations which attempted contact with the astral energy of "ancient and outmoded" gods.

The Emin Foundation began with humble roots. Leo was an encyclopedia salesman who went bankrupt and decided to devote his life to esoteric learning. He developed a love of Eastern philosophy from a stint as a pilot with the RAF in India. He developed an elegant, yet intricate belief system, based partly on the wisdom of ancient Egypt. Everything in the material world has some type of spiritual significance - it is up to each student to discern the meaning. Leo wrote hundreds of books and pamphlets, which are available only from the NAT.

The NAT was formed by Emin students David and Joanna Francis and Aviv Shahar in March 2001 in Canada and now has centers in five US cities. One can become a NAT member after attending a few meetings and getting to know the group.

### PARAPSYCHOLOGY FOUNDATION

*"Psychic Explorer's Club"*
*228 East 71st Street between Second and Third*
*Avenues*
*212-628-1550*
*www.parapsychology.org*

The staff at the Parapsychology Foundation cringes whenever any reference is made to the movie Ghostbusters. "That was the Hollywood version of what we do and it has been difficult to shake," says Simon Pettet, a Brit who is in charge of the film archive. "What most people don't realize is that parapsychology is a science and an academic discipline."

The foundation has worked hard to bring credibility to this arcane science. It even publishes a list of universities which sponsor a "parapsychology" major. It also has one of the best parapsychology libraries in the world, with the latest books and videos on all types of paranormal phenomena - from Marion apparitions to UFO sightings, to plain, old occultism.

The foundation was founded more than 50 years ago by Eileen J. Garrett, a prominent medium and spiritualist. The foundation used scientific methods to test Garrett's paranormal abilities. The foundation is now run by Garrett's granddaughter, Lisette Coly.

Eventually, the foundation became a "clearing house" for scientific research on psychic and paranormal phenomena, like remote viewing, extra-sensory perception, out-of-body experiences and psycho kinesis. Unlike its Hollywood counterpart, the foundation steers away from studies on haunted houses.

"From a scientific viewpoint, it is much harder to examine ghosts or hauntings in a laboratory setting," says Pettet. "It is difficult to predict when a ghost will appear, so it is nearly impossible to use scientific principles to examine this phenomena."

For the layperson who wants to get involved, the foundation recently started up the Psychic Explorer's Club. Members can attend the foundation's lectures and seminars and can participate in a "members only" forum on the foundations website.

## ROSICRUCIAN ORDER, AMORC

*32 Irving Place between 14th and 15th Streets*
*212-982-6520*
*www.amorc.org*
*Closest subway: 4/5/6/L to 14th Street*
Many people think that they have to travel to Egypt in order to see a genuine Egyptian temple. But many New Yorkers don't need to go further than Union Square, where the AMORC New York Lodge holds its regular rituals. The New York center has a working Egyptian temple inside. There's only one catch - you have to be an initiated member to see it.

New York native H. Spencer Lewis founded the Ancient and Mystical Order Rosae Crucis (AMORC) in Manhattan in 1915, after "making contact" with the "secret chiefs" of the Rosicrucian Order. Lewis, a member of the Golden Dawn, claimed that AMORC was the latest incarnation of an order that traces its lineage back to the mystery schools of ancient Egypt. Rosicrucians claim that the original founder of their order was Egyptian Pharaoh Thutmose III (1500-1477 B.C.)

AMORC disseminates its information through mail-order lessons, though after studying for one year, students are eligible to join a "lodge" such as the New York Lodge. AMORC functions as an initiatory organization, using elaborate rituals to alter the consciousness and instruct the candidate. The first-degree initiation into AMORC is held several times a year in New York and occurs over a two-day period. While students are required to take an oath of silence regarding the ritual work, it can be said that the rituals are recreations of ancient Egyptian rituals, complete with Egyptian costumes, incense and symbols. Like Masonic initiations, AMORC requires students to remember passwords and rituals can be quite dramatic.

Over a period of years, AMORC students learn telepathy, astral travel, visualizations techniques, healing techniques, and development of psychic powers. Also affiliated with the AMORC lodge is the "Traditional Martinist Order," an esoteric, initiatory order based upon the Kabbalah.

The New York Lodge has a definite family feel to it; many of the lodge members also happen to be from Caribbean countries. There are lodge "convocations" nearly every evening for members, along with special classes on Kabbalah and psychic development. What sets AMORC apart from other spiritual groups is it powerful egregore, a group of spiritual masters on the "inner plane" who guide

YOGA | ESOTERIC GROUPS | WITCHCRAFT | OCCULT UNDERGROUND | BOOKS | UFOS | BOTANICAS | TANTRA | ASTROLOGERS & PSYCHICS |

members of the organization. AMORC's goal is the spiritual development of both the individual, and society as a whole. As one member put it: "When you become initiated into AMORC, you have no idea how powerful this is. You are connected to with a very strong set of teachings. It will transform you."

## SACRED LIGHT FELLOWSHIP
*208 West 30th Street between 7th and*
*8th Avenues, suite 201*
*212-877-6937*
*www.sacredlightfellowship.org*
Spiritualism and mediumship lives on in New York City. The Sacred Light Fellowship grew out of Rev. Clifford Bias' First Universal Spiritualist Church, the home of New York's best mediums (like Frank Andrews and Alexander Murray). After Bias passed away, and his Church eventually dissolved, three members of that church - Rev. George Brooks, Rev. Daniel Neusom and Rev. Lyn Skreczko Van Riper - decided to form their own spiritualist church in 2000.

"We wanted to have a place for healing and metaphysical teaching in New York," says Rev. Skreczko. "We are essentially continuing the work of Clifford Bias." The church rents space from the Source of Life and meets faithfully on Sunday mornings and Monday, Wednesday and Friday evenings.

The church teaches psychic development and mediumship. The Sunday service also provides "psychic messages" for each parishioner from the ministers. The ministers also regularly "channel" guest teachers, who give workshops. Some of the channeled "guest teachers" have included Edgar Cayce, Paramansa Yogananda, Swami Satchidananda and an American Indian shaman. Part of the ministry includes hands-on healing and there is a "healing prayer group" held every Monday evening. Skreczko says that the church has created a close community of like-minded people, who come to the classes for fellowship, as well as learning.

"This is ultimately about shifting energy to live more true to our soul mission," says Rev. Skreczko. "From sacred light and sacred love, we can create and live a sacred life."

## SACRED MERKABA TECHNIQUES
*212-289-3831*
*www.nymerkaba.com*
The word merkaba in Hebrew means chariot, the "throne of light" that the Prophet Elijah ascended up into heaven on. But for those in the New Age

community, the merkaba is the "rotating energy field" that surrounds every living human being.

In most humans, the merkaba is dormant and not moving very well. But adepts say that the merkaba can consciously be activated through visualization and mediation.

Practitioners of the Sacred Merkaba meditation proclaim this as that ultimate mediation for the New Age. The Sacred Merkaba technique was developed by Gary Smith. Although it is similar to the technique of Drunvalo Melchizadek, who in turn received it from an entity named "Thoth," practitioners of Smith's technique claim that it is a bit different and is not affiliated with Melchizadek. Teacher Thomas Victor says that he has tried "numerous spiritual paths," and that the merkaba activation technique created a quantum leap in his spiritual development. He says the technique creates a "wall of light" around a person, protecting them from negative influences. The merkaba also connects the practitioner to higher, spiritual intelligences. The system is used both for spiritual ascension and healing and takes about ten minutes every day. The New York Sacred Merkaba group offers regular two-day basic workshop, for about $200 a weekend, which teaches the basic technique. The group also offers more advanced training with Gary Smith, for those who want to become adepts and teach the meditation themselves.

## SAHAJA YOGA
*212-269-9642*
*www.yoganewyork.org*
Sahaja Yoga bills itself as the "true meditation" that will raise the "kundalini" (cosmic energy) in a student's spine for enlightenment and health. The meditation technique was "revealed" to the West by Shri Mataji Nirmala Devi, a mother and grandmother, who was born with self-realization, according to her students. Mataji, as she is called, was involved in the Indian Independence movement as a young woman and lived on Mahatma Gandhi's ashram. "Most enlightened masters live in caves in the Himalayas and don't come down anymore," says Jerry, a volunteer at the New York Sahaja Yoga Center. "But Mataji decided that humanity needed this meditation."

The Manhattan Sahaja yoga group gets together once a week for a meditation and then a short video-talk by Mataji. The meditation consists of affirmations on the chakras and a "Kundalini raising"

| YOGA | **ESOTERIC GROUPS** | WITCHCRAFT | OCCULT UNDERGROUND | BOOKS | UFOS | BOTANICAS | TANTRA | ASTROLOGERS & PSYCHICS |

exercise in which students place their left hand in front of the abdomen, then raise the hand, while rotating the right hand around the left hand in a clockwise direction.

Following the formal meditation, Sahaja yogis - wearing photos of Mataji around their necks - "work on" the newcomers to awaken the "dormant" Kundalini at the base of the spine. A young, Indian yogini named Anita volunteered to be my guide. She stood behind me and put her right-hand on the top of my head, while using her left hand to "raise the energy" in my spine.

"When someone has their Kundalini raised, they are like a candle," she says, gently rubbing the sahasrara chakra on the top of my skull. "Once your candle is lit, you can share the fire. "

I could feel my Kundalini rising already. The New York center meets in Manhattan every Monday at 7 p.m. at the American Indian Community House, 404 Lafayette Street, 8th Floor.

## SCHOOL OF IMAGES
*73 5th Avenue between 15th and 16th Streets, suite 8B*
*212-627-2345*
*www.schoolofimages.com*
*Closest subway: 4/5/6/L to 14th Street*
The School of Images is a western esoteric "wisdom school," based upon Sephardic Kaballistic principles. School director Catherine Shainberg founded the school 22 years ago, after spending a number of years in Jerusalem, studying with the famed Kabbalist Madame Colette Aboulker-Muscat. "The work we do is the Kaballah of light," says Shainberg. "We plunge inside ourselves to find the inner place where vision can occur. We use the imagination for both insight and transformation."

Images are at the heart of Shainberg's Kaballistic system. Students learn visualization techniques, as well as "cleansing and clearing of old patterns." By visualizing something, you can make it become reality. Students generally take four years to finish the school's core curriculum, but Shainberg says she has many students who still are with the school after 20 years. "It becomes a spiritual practice and a community," says Shainberg.

Shainberg's school is extremely popular among bodyworkers, artists and psychotherapists because "it teaches you how the imagination functions." Students learn imagery, group dreaming and prayer. One of the most popular classes is Morphology, the esoteric study of the human shape. "We can read people simply by looking at their body type and observing the way they walk into a room," says Shainberg. "It is extremely useful for healers and bodyworkers."

Unlike other Kabbalistic schools, the School of Images does not deal with archetypes or the "formulaic" use of Hebrew letters. "All of the early Kabbalah masters used images," says Shainberg. "The images and dreams are all of a personal nature. The images must be powerful and shocking in order to create the necessary change. When you tap into your imagined mind, it is like a barometer. It tells you where you are and, if it is clear, it will respond to your wishes."

## SCIENCE OF SPIRITUALITY
*at the Community Church of New York*
*40 East 35th Street between Park and*
*Madison Avenues*
*516-483-3898*
*www.sos.org*
*Closest subway: 6 to 33rd Street*
The Science of Spirituality advertises itself as the "path of inner light and sound," also known as Sant Mat and Surat Shabd Yoga. The current spiritual guru of the organization is Sant Rahinder Singh, who visits New York City once a year.

Students of the meditation system say that the system was once a secretive teaching, based upon the teachings of Hazur Baba Sawan Singh Ji Maharaj. The meditation itself is quite simple. Students close their eyes, concentrate on the third eye chakra, repeat a mantra, and look into the darkness until they see "flashes of light." The light will eventually take form into a star, then a Moon and finally the Sun, and all of the "internal planets."

The second part of the meditation is concentration of the "inner sound." Students plug their ears with their fingers and "listen with the inner ear" to the cosmic sounds of the astral and causal planes. Members report hearing the Om mantra, celestial music and the "voice of the saints." Singh recommends that his students meditate at least ten percent of their day - which means a two and a half hour session each morning.

The Manhattan group meets every Saturday morning at the Community Church on East 35th Street. A one-hour meditation is held at 10:30 am. Then the weekly satsang talk is held, when the group leader picks a topic and then conducts read-

| YOGA | **ESOTERIC GROUPS** | WITCHCRAFT | OCCULT UNDERGROUND | BOOKS | UFOS | BOTANICAS | TANTRA | ASTROLOGERS & PSYCHICS |

ings and videotaped messages from Singh on a
particular topic

Singh initiates students into Sant Mat during
his yearly visits, in which he gives a secret mantra
that should be silently chanted during the light meditation. Members say that the Sant Mat meditation
is safe and effective, because it does not try to control bodily functions, but allows a person to become
aware of their spiritual nature.

"We are souls living in a physical body, and the
key is to experience the spiritual self," says Maurice,
a member of the New York group who has been
practicing for more than 20 years. "With this meditation, we ride the light and sound right back to the
seat of God."

### SELF REALIZATION FELLOWSHIP
*217 East 28th Street between 2nd and 3rd Avenues*
*212-689-3622*
*www.yogananda-srf.org*
*Closest subway: 6 to 28th Street*
In 1920, Autobiography of a Yogi author
Paramahansa Yogananda came to the United States
at the request of his guru to spread the ancient
science of Kriya Yoga. He founded Self Realization
Fellowship (SRF) as the official teaching and initiatory body for Kriya Yoga.

Following Yogananda's mahasamadhi, in 1952,
SRF has continued as the world's largest Kriya orga-
nization. Students interested in learning the Kriya
Yoga technique generally enroll in the SRF corre-
spondence course lessons, in which they learn the
Energization Exercise, Hong-Sau Technique, and the
Aum Technique." After a little more than a year, and
after passing a written test, students are then eligi-
ble to become initiated and receive the secretive
Kriya Yoga technique, a profound breathing exercise.

SRF claims that the Kriya Yoga meditation was
practiced in the "golden age" of human history,
including by the Hindu deity Krishna. In modern
times, it was "reintroduced" by the mysterious yogi
"Babaji," in 1861 to Lahiri Mahasaya, known as the
"father of Kriya Yoga." Mahasaya then taught Sri
Yukteshwarji, who was Yoganananda's teacher. The
techniques are only taught through initiation, so
they won't become corrupted or commercialized,
SRF officials say.

The New York Center meets on Thursdays,
Fridays and Sundays for meditation and prayer
services, which are open to the public.

| YOGA | ESOTERIC GROUPS | WITCHCRAFT | OCCULT UNDERGROUND | BOOKS | UFOS | BOTANICAS | TANTRA | ASTROLOGERS & PSYCHICS |

## JODI SEROTA

*212-961-9131*
*www.jodiserota.com*

For years, Jodi Serota dreamed of crystal skulls. Her dreams would include green skulls, clear quartz skulls, sometimes accompanied by intricate geometrical shapes.

"At the time, I really didn't know the significance of the dreams, it only became clear after time," says Serota, who has since become a channel for "otherworldly celestial beings." By day, Serota is an attractive and hip artist. But by night, Serota is one of Manhattan's most eclectic metaphysical teachers and channels. She now teaches her techniques to others with her Tuesday evening metaphysical classes held in her Upper West Side apartment.

Serota has become most known for her work with the "crystal skulls," the enigmatic crystal objects found throughout the world. Legend says that there are 13 "authentic" skulls, placed around the globe by ancient and advanced civilizations - possibly Atlantis or possibly extraterrestrial.

"The skulls are like time capsules and contain a great deal of information," says Serota. "They are being discovered now because the information in the crystal needs to be released. When the human race is ready, all 13 skulls will be found." Serota says that the skulls are "activated" through sound, color and light and are waiting for "light workers" such as her to release the stored information.

Serota works with her own green jadite crystal skull that she found in Mexico, as well as the famed crystal skull, "Max." Joann Parks, of Texas, brings Max to New York City twice a year. Serota channels information from both skulls. She also does individual divination sessions and vibrational healing using the energy from the crystal objects. Max was tested by the British Museum and is considered by many to be one of the 13 authentic skulls.

Serota says that the first time she heard someone channel information from the Max skull, she intuitively knew the language. "I have worked with crystal skulls before in another lifetime," Serota says. "When I channel, I create a vortex, balancing out energy from the star systems. I am very connected to the Sirius star system."

Serota says that she has had a number of profound visions revolving around the crystal skulls. "I had vision of light beings from another dimension that once inhabited the Earth plane," says Serota. "In my vision, I saw the light beings placing crystals all over the Earth. In the vision, I was one of those light beings, and I had originally placed spiritual information in those skulls. I feel that it is my mission to bring this information back to the human race."

When Max is brought to Manhattan, Serota usually conducts a public ritual, channeling the ancient language from the skull. The channeled material sounds like a cross between a mantra and celestial singing.

"Like any of us, the skulls want to be touched; they activate you by just being in the same room as them," says Serota. "When you are with the skull, you need to breathe and connect with its energy. Ask it to give you what you need."

## SHARE INTERNATIONAL
*718-797-9520; 212-459-4022 (rec message)*
*www.share-international.org/newyork/*
World teacher or Antichrist? In May 1982, British artist Benjamin Creme announced at a press conference that the "world teacher, Maitreya, the Christ, was alive and well and living in the Pakistani-slums of London. Maitreya "appointed" Creme as his "messenger," and Creme sees himself as the heir to the esoteric spiritual revelations begun by Theosophy founder Helena Petrovna Blavatsky and Lucis Trust founder Alice Bailey. Maitreya has allegedly appeared to 60,000 villagers in Nairobi in 1988, who "saw him as Jesus Christ." Creme says that Maitreya "works behind the scenes in world politics," meeting with high-level government and media officials. Creme's "Share International" organization even has representation at the United Nations, allegedly preparing the world for the "one world government," headed, of course, by Maitreya.

This has gotten certain Christian groups quite upset (not to mention some Theosophists and members of Lucis Trust). Psychic Sean David Morton calls Creme the "dark prophet" and Catholic writer Katherine Keating has repeatedly written about the "Antichrist at the UN." However, Share International has developed a substantial following and some positive press (from the New York Times, of course).

During a recent talk in New York at the Pennsylvania Hotel, Creme - an 80-year-old with a mop of curly white hair - began the evening by meditating on each member of the audience, "overshadowed," he says, by Maitreya. He then went on a diatribe against the United States, which he called "a land without justice." He called the 9-11 terrorist attacks "karmic retribution" for "the injustice that fills the world" and he urged the United Nations to gather every country together and "stand against" the United States and Israel.

Creme said that Maitreya would appear publicly "after the collapse of the American and European economies," an event that Creme and Maitreya are apparently waiting in glee for.  Maitreya will appear on "every TV worldwide" and will "form a telepathic rapport with the whole of humanity." Only then will the world's (i.e. America's) wealth "be redistributed" to the poor people in third world countries, leading to a "golden age of peace that the world has never seen."

If Creme sounds like a communist, well, he is. He stated in previous press interviews that he has been a "card-carrying member" since the 1950s. Only difference between him and other "fellow travelers" is that he in "telepathic" communication with a mysterious entity that he believes is the second-coming of Christ - and a load of well-meaning people believe him.

Share International practices a discipline called "transmission meditation," originally given to Alice Bailey by "The Tibetan." During the sessions, students receive "energy" from the ascended masters and then "channel" this energy to the earth for the "benefit of humanity."

"If what I say is true, then this is most important event in the whole history of the world," says Creme. "Some people say I am mad. But it is for you to decide. I, for one, believe that Maitreya is coming."

## SILVA MIND CONTROL
*Tony Mitchell*
*212-698-0123*
*www.silvamethod.com*
Tony Mitchell was a struggling actor when he discovered the Silva Mind Control program back in the 1970s. He was skeptical at first; however after doing the Silva exercises, he began getting lucrative acting jobs. Now, every time he wants an acting gig, he simply goes into the "alpha" state and pictures it in his "mind's eye."

"In the Silva method, you consciously create your success," says Mitchell. "We use the mirror of the mind to visualize and achieve our goals. We are constantly programming our future; why not consciously program the future we want?"

Mitchell became so enthusiastic about the program, that he eventually became a full-time Silva instructor and now owns one of the top Silva franchises in the city. He still occasionally takes acting jobs, but the Silva Method is his true passion. He regularly gives weekend Silva workshops at the

Source of Life Center on 34th Street, teaching both
basic and advanced Silva techniques. The basic
course teaches relaxation, visualization, sleep control, weight loss, dream control and clairvoyance.
The graduate course teaches remote viewing,
"acquiring guidance from higher intelligence," "programming" water for healing and advanced mind
success programming techniques.

Founder Jose Silva founded the program in
1966, after studying self-help techniques for more
than 20 years. Silva's method combines the best of
all the "new thought" practices, his students say.

"If you can conceive of something in your mind,
you can achieve it," says Mitchell. "Everyone has
within them the power to be successful, but most
people don't tap into it. The Silva Method gives you
a number of proven tools to do this."

## SPIRIT NEW YORK
*530 West 27th Street between 10th and*
*11th Streets*
*212-268-9477*
*www.spiritnewyork.com*
*Closest subway: 1/9 to 28th Street*
Spirit New York wants to bring back the "rave" to its
spiritual roots. Founder and Dublin native Robbie
Wootton says he had a "religious experience" a few
years back in Los Angeles, while backstage at a U2
concert. He saw visions of himself opening "mind,
body and soul" centers throughout the world. He
started by opening "Spirit Dublin" last year, "Spirit
New York" this year, and plans other centers in Cape
Town, Sydney, Shanghai, Rio de Janeiro and Athens.

"The rave was always meant to be a spiritual
event and was, until drugs hijacked the scene," says
Wootton. "The rave is the closest thing we have to
indigenous tribal music.

Spirit New York is much more than a Saturday
night rave. During the week, its Mind center offers
holistic energy healing and its Soul restaurant
offers organic and "live" food. The Body is a
Saturday evening show that changes with the
solstices and equinoxes.

"It's an interactive creation myth, and attending
a show is a cross between De La Guarda and Cirque
de Soleil," says Wootton. "The entertainment is
directly connected to the rhythm of the Earth."

In addition to dancing, patrons will also be able
to sneak down to the "sensual yet mystical" holistic
health center and - until 4 a.m. - get a Swedish massage, Thai massage, "body painting," tarot card read-

ing, palmistry, or simply lie down in a bed, amid the incense and "chillout soundz from our musical gurus."

Wootton says that this is not a business for him, but rather a "spiritual path." He says that after his mystical experience, he began reading a lot of spiritual literature and was most influenced by Conversations with God, by Neal Donald Walsh.

"I woke up and realized that life is a river and I was standing on the shore," Wootton says. "I finally got the courage to jump into the water."

## SRI CHINMOY CENTER

*86-24 Parsons Boulevard in Jamaica, Queens*
*718-297-6456*
*www.srichinmoy.org*
*Closest subway: F to Parsons Blvd.*

Sri Chinmoy has become the unofficial "guru" of the United Nations; he gives twice-a-week meditations there and considers his mission to "bring peace to all nations." His followers are legion in the UN area and have been encouraged to get jobs there to "spread the light." If you see a starry-eyed Anglo woman near the UN wearing a sari, no doubt she is a Chinmoy disciple. Chinmoy and his disciples gained notoriety a few years back for their often-bizarre physical feats, many of which landed them in the Guinness Book of World records - like riding a pogo stick underwater and running backwards.

The process of becoming a Chinmoy student usually begins with a free meditation class given by disciple. Interested students are encouraged to provide a photograph to Chinmoy, who meditates on it and decides whether to accept them as a student. The path of a Chinmoy disciple is pretty tough; it's the "Opus Dei" of the esoteric Hindu world. Disciples are encouraged to give up their outside friends and activities and move near the "mother ashram" in Queens. The primary spiritual discipline is meditating on a photograph of Chinmoy, which shows him reportedly in the state of samadhi.

Chinmoy certainly seems to have "mojo." During meditations, many report feeling "white heat, white light" while staring into his eyes. But like any drug, it has its side effects. Chinmoy, who originally moved to New York as a "clerk" with the Indian Consulate in the 1960s, has been criticized for being over-controlling in the lives of his students. A small but vocal group of ex-disciples have gone public with their complaints.

Chinmoy gives regular "Friday night" meditations at a large open tennis court near his Queens

| YOGA | **ESOTERIC GROUPS** | WITCHCRAFT | OCCULT UNDERGROUND | BOOKS | UFOS | BOTANICAS | TANTRA | ASTROLOGERS & PSYCHICS |

home. His disciples believe that he is a "God-realized" spiritual teacher, who became enlightened after spending 20 years of spiritual practice in the Sri Aurobindo ashram in India. Chinmoy also regularly gives music concerts in which he "plays" 20 or so different instruments on the stage.

"This is a rare opportunity to be able to actually meditate with a God-realized guru," says one disciple "In the past, disciples would have to travel miles and make an arduous journey to spend time with an enlightened master. Here, all you have to do is take the F train to Queens."

### ALEX STARK
*Shaman,* feng shui *master, teacher*
*718-840-2820*
*www.alexstark.com*
Back in the day, it was tough work to become a shaman. First of all, you had to be born deformed, or at least struck by lightning to be marked as "gifted." Then, to be accepted as a student by another shaman - fuggedaboutit. Many times you had to sleep on the doorstep of a prospective teacher for a year just to get an interview.

Alex Stark, a genuine shaman from Peru, has streamlined the process with his five-year shamanic apprenticeship program called the Path of Love and Power. "We are in a time in human evolution when this information needs to get out to people," says Stark, who originally came to New York as an architect with the United Nations. "Many people don't know how lucky they are. In Peru, it is very difficult to become an apprentice to a shaman." Stark does not look fit the image of a traditional shaman. He dresses stylishly, favoring dress slacks and wears a neatly-trimmed goatee. His path to shamanism was quit arduous, however. He was marked as having "the gift" after being struck by lightning - twice in one evening. He spent years in Peru studying with his master, learning ritual, magic, divination and healing. He used much of his shamanic knowledge in his feng shui work, offering ground-breaking ceremonies, house blessings, space clearing and altar building, along with the traditional Chinese elements of the art.

The Path of Love and Power meets twice a year for a weekend workshop and includes spiritual exercises and hands-on homework. Students learn traditional shamanic arts such as building altars, "communing with the gods," space clearing, astral travel and healing. It is an intensive program designed to "transform the individual," so the individual can transform society.

Stark is the real deal; he begins each workshop module by "cleansing the negative entities" off each student by spraying Florida Water on each participant with his mouth and blowing the smoke of a special herbal substance to "see the entity." He then "cuts the entity off" the person with a huge eagle feather (in New York City, apparently all sorts of things can latch onto you).

Many of Stark's students are also feng shui consultants, since Stark is most well-known for his feng shui consultations. He lectures internationally on feng shui, as well as shamanism.

## SUBUD NEW YORK
*230 West 29th Street between 7th and 8th Avenues*
*212-563-1196*
*www.subudnewyork.org*
*Closest subway: 1/9 to 28th Street*
I'm sitting in the greeting area of Subud New York with Mahmoud (formerly James) and Michael (formerly William), both long-time members of the mystical group Subud. Both look far younger than their real ages and both extol the virtues of the spiritual path developed by Indonesian mystic "Bapak" Mohammad Subuh Sumohadiwidjojo.

In order to join a Subud group, you need to meet with a Subud "helper" for at least 12 times, every Monday evening at about 8 p.m. On each successive meeting, the helper reveals a bit more about the path. "In general, you need to show your sincerity," says Michael. "You need to know what we are about and we need to find out a bit about you."

"Bapak" discovered Subud in the 1920s, when he was walking home from a Koran-study class in Indonesia. He reported that a "white light" descend over him and then felt his entire body energized. Over a period of years, the energy settled and resulted in Bapak's enlightenment, his students say.

Bapak discovered that he could replicate this experience with other people, with a technique called latihan, loosely translated as the "exercise." The latihan occurs when the "divine energy" descends on a practitioner. A typical service begins with the group coming together and sitting in silence. When the atmosphere is still, the leader will simply say: "begin." The latihan will then descend, and each practitioner will experience the energy in a different way. Some will stay quiet, some will "speak in tongues," and others may actually cry, sing or fall on the floor. The latihan is described as a powerful vibration that one feels inside, "which connects directly to God."

Once a seeker proves his/her sincerity, the seeker will then be invited to a latihan session to experience "the opening," one's first Subud experience. "After a person has their first opening, the latihan will then descend on them during the regular latihan sessions," says Michael, who changed his name upon the recommendation of Bapak. "It is a mystical thing," explains Michael, on the name change. "Sometimes you are given a name that may not be appropriate for your spirit. Health problems can go away when you change your name."

New York Subud holds several latihans each week for the men's group and women's group. "Subud practice is very simple, but very profound," says Michael. "You can't really explain it. The latihan is something that you just have to experience for yourself."

## SUFI ZIKRULLAH: CIRCLE OF DIVINE REMEMBRANCE MASJID AL-FARAH

*245 West Broadway between White and Franklin Streets*
*www.ashkijerrahi.com*
*Closest subway: 1/9 to Franklin Street*
Traditionally, Sufis were the "hidden" mystics of Islam; if someone told you they were Sufi, they probably weren't. However, Sufism has become much more accessible in the modern, particularly for Westerners. One of the most open Sufi paths is the Nur Ahki Jerrahi Sufi Order, based out of the Al-Farah mosque in Tribeca. Every Thursday at 7:30 p.m., the group comes together for chanting, a talk and Sufi ritualistic dancing.

Unlike many other Sufi orders (particularly in the Arab world), men and women pray and dance together at the Tribeca mosque. The group is also headed by a female dervish, Shaykha Fariha al-Jerrahi, an American convert to Islam. Anyone can attend the free zhikr - and you don't have to be Muslim.

The group says that it traces its spiritual lineage directly back to the Prophet Mohammed. In modern times, the New York group was started by the late Lex Hixon (Nur al-Anwar al-Jerrahi), a spiritual master in several different disciplines, who was "crowned" by the Turkish head of the Al-Jerrahi Sufi order, Shaykh Muzaffer Ozak al-Jerrahi. After Hixon's death, Shaykha Fariha took over the group.

The evening I attended the zhikr, the group

included a Jewish holy man, a Buddhist Sensei and several Christian ministers (including an Episcopalian Bishop) taking a course in comparative religion. Most of the Sufis were American converts to Islam. The evening began with chanting and then a talk. The Sufi "dancing" did not kick in until around 10:30 pm, but the wait was worth it. The group holds hands and dances around in a circle, chanting Islamic mantras and moving their heads and bodies in a specific rhythm, as directed by the Shaykha (who stands in the middle of the circle).

"You lose yourself in the zikhr," says one dervish, who is originally from Sudan. "Zhikr means to remember. When we dance in the circle, we forget ourselves and remember God."

## SUKYO MAHIKARI
*72 Madison Avenue between 27th and 28th Streets*
*212-447-5811*
*Hours: M-F:9am-8pm; Sat/Sun:9am-6pm*
*www.mahikari.org*
*Closest subway: 6 to 28th Street*
At around 5:30 pm every weekday, the "dojo" at the New York Sukyo Mahikari Center begins to look like an emergency room triage center; there are bodies lying on the ground, being attended to. But instead of IVs, these "lightworkers" use their hands to infuse the patient's bodies with "divine energy."

"The dojo really gets busy after work," says Ravi, one of the 12 or so volunteer Sukyo Mahikari healers on hand. Ravi is a computer programmer who is "between jobs." So, he has been spending his days at the Mahikari center, giving free light treatments to whoever walks through the door. "Mahikari is light from a very high source, the divine," says Ravi, as he places his hands on my back.

Anyone can become a channel for divine energy, says the Sukyo Mahikari literature. Mahikari began in 1957, after Lt. Col. Yoshikazu Okada, a Japanese Imperial Guard, claimed to have received "revelations from God." Mahikari claims to be "supra religion," that is, the resurrection of the "original religion" from which all others have come from. Mahikari does have some controversial beliefs. Its beliefs are quite Japanese-centric; some members claim that the Japanese are the "true Jews, who are God's chosen people." Some members also claim that both Jehovah and Allah are Japanese deities, and that the true "Mecca" is actually somewhere near Tokyo, and not in Saudi Arabia.

Most Americans who join Mahikari are more

YOGA | **ESOTERIC GROUPS** | WITCHCRAFT | OCCULT UNDERGROUND | BOOKS | UFOS | BOTANICAS | TANTRA | ASTROLOGERS & PSYCHICS |

interested in learning the Art of Divine Light, which members say purifies the body from toxins and evil spirits. For those "who want to save others and change this world," the New York Center offers a regular three-day basic Mahikari Seminar, in which students are taught to radiate divine light from their hands. After the training they receive a special holy pendant, which is "connected to the higher dimensional world."

### THE TAROT SCHOOL
*at the Source of Life Center*
*22 West 34th Street*
*1-800-804-2184*
*www.tarotschool.com*
Wald Amberstone picked up his first tarot deck in 1959, starting a lifetime of fascination with the divinatory art. Amberstone opened the Tarot School in 1995, to share his more than 35 years of professional reading experience. The school, which Amberstone runs with his wife, Ruth Ann, meets every Monday from 6-9 p.m. at the Source of Life Center. The classes are "open ended" and eventually lead to a degree, provided that the student attend at least a year's worth of classes, as well as several one-day intensives on Kaballah, journeywork and meditation. "Many people study with us for years, since we cover a different tarot card every week," says Amberstone. "Others stay with us only for the professional program and go on to become full-time readers."

The Tarot School has one of the most respected tarot programs in the country and recently began offering a tarot correspondence course for those who live outside the New York City area. Amberstone stresses that the correspondence course is not a duplication of the Monday evening classes and, in a way, he says that it is much more demanding than the live sessions. In the correspondence course, students cover 12 lessons in about 16 months and get coaching session with Ambestone each lesson. Students are expected to submit at least 40 pages of homework each month and end up "writing their own book" on tarot. "They become experts," says Amberstone. "How many tarot readers write a book on the subject?"

Amberstone says that once someone learns to become a reader, they can "read anything, from sidewalk cracks to smoke" in order to tell the future. "But tarot is a matter of knowledge," says Amberstone. "During the course, many students go through a great deal of introspection. Tarot lets us look at everything under the Sun under a really, high-powered color microscope. In the course, you learn to become a professional reader, but the real pleasure is that you learn more about yourself in the process."

## TESLA SOCIETY OF NEW YORK
*P.O. Box 863837*
*Ridgewood, NY 11386*
*718-417-5102*
*www.teslasociety.com*

Famed scientist Nikola Tesla resides in the nether-world where spirituality meets science meets conspiracy theory. In the exoteric world, Tesla is credited with 40 patents, including alternating polyphase electricity, wireless transmission of electrical energy, the Tesla coil, fluorescent light and the use of the ionosphere for communication.

But in the esoteric world, Tesla remains an enigma, a "man out of time," whose research is so advanced, that scientists are still trying to figure out his theories. Tesla's more secretive side includes his intercepted communications with extraterrestrials, whom he claims "were secretly controlling mankind," preparing the Earth for a complete extraterrestrial take-over. Some even go as far to suggest that Tesla himself was an alien, a walk-in who came from an advanced extraterrestrial race.

Tesla spent his most productive years living in New York City, first at the Waldorf-Astoria, and later at the Hotel New Yorker (room 337). When he died in 1943, many of his papers and research went missing. Some say it was the FBI, and others claim the papers were taken by Nazi secret agents, who ransacked his room shortly after his death, looking for plans of his rumored "death ray."

The Tesla Society of New York has been working to keep the memory of Tesla alive. Society President Ljubo Vujovic has been working with the United Nations to have July 10 named the international "Tesla Day," and create a worldwide "Tesla movement."

"Nikola Telsa was one of the greatest discovers of all time, he was a mystic man," says Vujovic. "There is even a religious sect in California that believes Tesla was not a human being at all, but a being who came from the planet Vanera. They say he spent several years of his life on Earth then went back to Vanera on the spaceship, which he designed. The spirit of Nikola Tesla is living with us today."

## THE UNITED LODGE OF THEOSOPHISTS

*347 East 72 Street between 1st and*
*2nd Streets*
*212-535-2230*
*www.ult.org*
*Closest subway:6 to 72nd Street*
Members of the United Lodge of Theosophists
consider themselves "purists" when it comes to
Theosophical teachings. The lodge promotes the
works of Theosophical Society founder Helena
Petrovna Blavatsky, such as her book The Secret
Doctrine. The group does not promote the work of
the Theosophists who came after her, such as Annie
Besant, C.W. Leadbeater and Lucis Trust founder
Alice Bailey. The works of HPB contemporary
William Q. Judge are included in the pantheon of
ULT teachings.

Rather than teach courses, the ULT gets together for Sunday evening discussions on topics like
Reincarnation of Men and Nations, and Seven
Categories of Dreams. The group also holds Monday
and Wednesday evening discussions on various esoteric topics.

## UNITED NATIONS SOCIETY FOR ENLIGHTENMENT AND TRANSFORMATION

*United Nations Clubroom, GA-37*
*Lina Arellano, president*
*212-963-0889*
*arellanol@un.org*
Come rub shoulders with diplomats and UN staff
members at the monthly meetings of The UN Society
for Enlightenment and Transformation (SEAT). One
Friday a month SEAT hosts a metaphysical speaker
who has a "global vision." During the past few years,
speakers have included Keys of Enoch author J.J.
Hurtak, Buddhist teacher Joy Leo, spiritual teacher
Eckhart Tolle, metaphysical writer Ted Andrews and
international psychic Martin Zoller. The UN-related
Lucis Trust also has a once-a-year public meeting
with SEAT.

SEAT grew out of the UN "Parapsychology" club,
originally founded by UN employee Mansour Faridi.
The organization is now under in the capable hands
of long-time member Lina Arellano, who is also
active in the UN Feng Shui Club.

The UN itself has quite a metaphysical background; one needs only to take a visit to the meditation room, with its "black cube" altar (made from a
meteorite). Several Secretary Generals have been
deeply interested in the esoteric and one - Javier

Perez de Cuellar - reportedly witnessed the famous "Brooklyn Bridge UFO Abduction."

## WORLD MATE, INC.
*150 East 57th Street between Lexington and*
*3rd Avenues, apt. 9D*
*www.worldmate.info*
*646-414-1366; 917-362-5414*
*Closest subway: 4/5/6/N/R to 59th Street*
I went to World Mate for a "spiritual consultation." The mystical Japanese non-profit is located in a swanky Upper East Side apartment building, complete with a meditation area and an altar where the TV should be.

Maiko, the young, lithe, Japanese spiritual adept, had my case down in a few minutes. "You have angry ghosts bothering you," she says, matter-of-factly. "This affects the way you think and feel." The cure? An exorcism for a donation of $100. Visions of Linda Blair's head-turning and vomiting green ectoplasm went through my mind. "No, no," Maiko says. "We do prayer and spiritual purification. We ask the angry ghosts to leave and they usually comply. You just have to sit and the monk does the rest."

According to Maiko, the actions of our ancestors affect us today. If an ancestor killed or wronged someone, the "vengeful spirit" of that person may attack you. Thoughts of my grandfather getting into barroom brawls in Boston began to make me feel a bit nervous. "Yes, it could be the vengeful spirits from these types of fights," she says.

World Mate was founded by Aiko Uematsu, known as the "Japanese Mother Mary," who received a "revelation from God to guide young people to follow the true path of virtue." The Shinto organization is now headed by Toshu Fukami, a prolific author who has propelled World Mate onto the international stage as a philanthropic organization.

The New York branch opened about five years ago and now has 35 members - many of them non-Japanese - who participate in monthly Shinto rituals, palm reading sessions, Japanese horoscope readings and drawing of the omikuji (sacred oracle).

I never did end up getting the World Mate exorcism. As my grandfather once said: "Beware of the demons that you cast out - you may be getting rid of the best part of yourself!"

YOGA | **ESOTERIC GROUPS** | WITCHCRAFT | OCCULT UNDERGROUND | BOOKS | UFOS | BOTANICAS | TANTRA | ASTROLOGERS & PSYCHICS |

# Witchcraft and Pagan Groups in the Big Apple

New York City has one of the largest numbers of pagan groups and witchcraft covens in the world. Witchcraft in New York City has a unique style, reflecting the multi-cultural, multi-religious atmosphere of the city. Only in New York can you walk into a Wicca store and find Santeria supplies, side-by-side with pentagrams, ritual daggers and swords. The beauty of New York is its multi-ethnic make up; people share and learn from each other. And spiritual groups are no different. From diversity comes beauty and power.

Witches worship the "old ways," that is pre-monotheistic, nature-based practices focused on the goddess. Witch covens generally meet once or twice a month and, of course, during the eight Sabbats, the times on the calendar when "magic and power" on the Earth are most intense - like Winter *Solstice*, *Beltane*, *Spring Equinox* and *Samhain* "Halloween".

Pagans, on the other hand, are harder to define. Witches are pagans, but not all pagans would consider themselves witches. Like witches, pagans follow a cyclical world view, living according to the changing seasons. Pagans can worship any number of pre-monotheistic pantheons of deities, from the Norse Gods (*Asatru*) to the African *Orisha* deities (Santeria).

No introduction to witchcraft in New York City would be complete without mentioning the late Herman Slater and Edmund Buczynski, the innovative "fathers" of the modern Wicca movement in New York City. Nearly every coven in the city today owes its existence somehow to Slater and

>>>

## CIRCLE OF ARA

*212-663-5642*
*www.phylliscurott.com*
*aradia@mindspring.com*

Phyllis Curott brought "Wicca to the masses" after her first book, The Book of Shadows, became an international bestseller. Curott, a lawyer by profession, has created her own style of witchcraft called Circle of Ara, a coven that she says is "liberated from outdated and inappropriate ideas." The focus of the Circle of Ara is a Wiccan practice without any "cultural baggage." "We concentrate primarily on practice, casting a circle, calling of the four directions and the basics of Wicca," says Curott. "People are encouraged to explore whatever pantheon of deities that speaks to them, but we don't force any one pantheon on anyone."

Curott was originally initiated into the Minoan

<<<

Buczynski, who operated the Warlock Shop in Brooklyn Heights, and later, the famous Magickal Childe, on West 19th Street in Manhattan.

Slater and Buczynski went on to initiate hundreds of witches who, in turn, have branched out and formed their own traditions. Most notable is Lady Rhea (see feature article), who went on to found Enchantments with Carol Bulzone in 1982, and then opened her own store, Magickal Realms, in the Bronx. Rhea has established the *Edwardian* tradition of Wicca, in honor of Buczynski.

Paganism is said to be the fastest growing religion in the United States and it is diverse enough to fulfill the needs of nearly every spiritual seeker. The average modern American is alienated and disconnected from the natural world; the cycle of the seasons is not measured by the movement of the Moon and Sun anymore, but rather from television reruns and football games. Paganism and witchcraft speak to this modern disconnection by offering an acknowledgement of the sacred rhythm of the Earth and a community that values both wisdom and fellowship.

There are plenty of covens in the New York area and two of the best ways to find an appropriate coven is through *www.witchvox.com* or *www.waningmoon.com*. Some of the more established covens do not accept new members and are very difficult to find. This is especially true of the more traditional *Gardnerian* covens, groups which trace their lineage to the British witch Gerald Gardner, whom many believe founded modern witchcraft in the 1950s. The following is a listing of some of the more eclectic and open covens and organizations in the city that I have come across.

Sisterhood by Lady Rhea and Carol Bulzone in the early 1980s. Although Curott comes from the same-sex Minoan tradition, her coven is coed and the worship of deity is up to each individual member. Curott also runs a teaching coven every year, from June 4 - Oct. 31, in Central Park, where elders of Ara tradition teach her unique vision of the Craft. The goal of the Circle of Ara teachings is to connect members with the divine, putting them in rhythm with the natural world.

Although Wicca is based upon ancient teachings, Curott notes that its practitioners constantly update its practices and the religion is evolving. Curott uses her talents as a lawyer to fight for the rights of witches and other religious minorities in the United States. "Wicca is the fastest growing religion in the United States," says Curott. "Although it has an ancient lineage, we are really creating a new religion each day." The Circle of Ara coven meets every other Wednesday in Manhattan and its teaching grove is open to sincere seekers. "Wicca is becoming so popular because people want to live in harmony with the natural world," says Curott. "We, as witches, seek to live in a sacred manner because we live in a sacred world."

## COVEN WILLOWSTAR

*www.willowstar.org*
Coven Willowstar is a traditional Wiccan coven founded during Samhain, 1988. The coven offers an "initiatory path," that combines such traditions as the New Reformed Orthodox Order of the Golden Dawn (N.R.O.O.G.D), Gardnerian Wicca, Blue Star, Nordic myth, along with Thelemic and Masonic ritual. It has been described as more of a "clan" than a teaching/training group. Originally, the coven was a group of solitary practitioners before finding each other. Led by the High Priestess Balachandra, the coven holds regular rituals in Manhattan. The coven "rarely advertises for new members," and those who "truly belong" show up at the right time. Contact the coven through its website.

## ENCHANTMENTS PAGAN WAY GROVE

*341 East 9th Street between 1st and 2nd Avenues*
*212-543-0334*
*www.joeandjezibell.com;*
*www.enchantmentsincnyc.com*
Since 1983, the Enchantments Pagan Way Grove has been New York City's preeminent learning center for paganism and witchcraft. Originally founded by Enchantments owner Carol Bulzone, the grove is now run by Joe and Jezibell (see feature article). All Sabbats and classes at the Grove are free, with a one-time fee of $30. You can't get a better deal than this in New York City. The Grove meets every Saturday, from 2-5 pm, beginning with the Spring Equinox in March and ending with Samhain in October. Joe and Jezibell teach with humor and wisdom, based upon their years of occult study and involvement in the Wicca movement. Joe and Jezibell have created a wonderful community; the Saturday Grove Beltane ceremony that I attended included about 50 participants from all ages and experience levels. If you decide to attend the Grove, expect the real deal and getting a solid basis in Wicca practice. Many Grove graduates choose to continue their studies in the sponsoring coven Kyklos ton Asterion (Circle of Stars). The Grove

YOGA | ESOTERIC GROUPS | **WITCHCRAFT** | OCCULT UNDERGROUND | BOOKS | UFOS | BOTANICAS | TANTRA | ASTROLOGERS & PSYCHICS |

## *Joe and Jezibel: A Fresh Vision for the Wicca community*

For Joe and Jezibell, Wicca is an evolving, open-ended religion.

"We are pagans in 21st Century New York City," says Joe, the High Priest of the Kyklos von Asterion coven and employee at Enchantments in the East Village. "We arenít living in the mythical land of our ancestors. The path of Wicca spirituality is one of self-examination and self-transformation."

Joe and his partner Jezibell have been running Enchantment's Pagan Grove from the back of the East Village store since 1997. The grove was originally established in 1983 by Enchantments owner Carol Bulzone, as a training ground for those interested in Wicca.

Since then, the Enchantments Pagan Grove has become one of the premier Wiccan training groups in the country. Thousands of spiritual adepts have gone through the demanding, eight-month program, which begins on the *Spring Equinox* and ends on *Samhain* in October every year.

Since taking the teaching duties over, Joe and Jezibell have put their stamp on the Grove teachings, creating a unique pagan philosophy they have termed "Thelemic Wicca, which mixes the magical philosophy of Aleister Crowley with pagan ritual.

"We have found that many Wiccans tend to be sloppy in their research and tend to mix mythology with history," says Jezibell, who has been active in the New York pagan community since moving to New York City in the early 1990s. "In the Grove, we are sticklers about being factual and true to our sources."

Raised in Georgia, Jezibell originally came to New York to pursue a career as an actress, belly dancer, writer, singer and drummer. She has written and directed several pagan-themed musical productions, including Inanna, A Journey of Darkness and Light.

Joe seems a perfect match for her fiery intensity. Nicknamed the "Bear" by students of the Grove, Joe projects an earthy power. He was initiated into his first coven in 1976 and became the youngest member of the coven to become High Priest, in 1979. Joe has spent the past thirty or so years exploring various magical and mystical paths.

Joe says that his entire outlook on paganism changed, however, after he attended at Gnostic Mass celebrated by the Ordo Templi Orientis (OTO) Tahuti Lodge, the mystical organization which was heavily influenced by Aleister Crowley.

"When I first saw the Mass, I realized that this was the source from which modern Wicca draws its rituals from," says Joe. "We embrace the philosophy of Aleister Crowley. Our intention here in the Grove is to help each person strengthen and reinforce their will. Every person is a self-creating individual."

Joe and Jezibell seek to take the superstition out of witchcraft. They say they are "skeptics" who don't put much credibility into the more fanciful concepts, such as Atlantis, channeling or other beliefs which can't be proved.

One of the required books for the Pagan Grove is Jared Diamond's Guns, Germs and Steel: The Fates of Human Societies. Joe says that it gives a very accurate view of history.

"People in spiritual movements tend to idealize the indigenous people of the past, like the Native American Indians, and blame all of the world's problems on the modern white European," says Joe. "The truth is that all civilizations and cultures have had their problems."

At the Enchantment's Grove, Joe has taken his years of experience and teaches the philosophy and techniques that he believes work.

"Magic is nothing more than psychology with props," says Joe. "And religion and spirituality and deities were created by man, to serve man. We should never forget this."

Unfortunately, Joe and Jezibell have announced that they are taking a sabbatical from running the Pagan Way Grove in 2004, in order to work on writing projects. Although Sabbats will be held, the classes will be suspended for a year. While Sabbat ceremonies will still be celebrated, the teachings will not be held during the year.

"The Grove will continue in one form or another," says Joe. "We have been teaching for a number of years and feel that it is time to focus on some of our personal projects. It's all part of the path."

practices a unique form of paganism created by Joe and Jezibell called Thelemic Wicca, which incorporates pagan ritual with the Thelemic philosophy of Aleister Crowley. The Thelemic Wiccan path is one of "liberation, growth and self-knowledge," with recognition that we are all "self-creating individuals."

## THE GROVE ARGENTUM
*c/o Rev.Carol Linda Gonzales*
*340 West 28th Street, Apt. 2G, New York, NY*
*www.webnik.com/dana*
The Grove Argentum practices Druidic form of paganism in the lineage of the Druid Clan of Dana. The group follows a Celtic spirituality and "honors both the feminine and the masculine in divinity through the study of the sacred in all cultures." Rev. Carole Linda Gonzales and Richard Spendio founded the Grove in 2002. Members include initiated Wiccans and pagans from other traditions. The Grove traces its lineage to Rev. Lawrence Durdin-Robertson, of Ireland, whose own spiritual legacy "connects the group to names like W.B. Yeats and Robert Graves." Lady Olivia Robertson continued the lineage when she founded the "Society of the Fellowship of Isis" in 1976 at Clonegal Castle in Ireland, and initiated Gonzales into the Fellowship in 1997. The group is always looking for new members who share their outlook and beliefs.

## MAGICKAL REALMS GROVE
*2937 Wilkinson Avenue between Westchester and*
*Hobart Avenues in Bronx*
*718-892-5350*
*www.magickalrealms.com/EventsClasses.html*
*Closest subway: 6 to Pelham Bay Park (last stop)*
Lady Rhea (see feature article) has continued to share her wisdom through her store, Magickal Realms. Rhea and her partner, Lady Zoradia run the Magickal Realms Pagan Way Grove, which meets every Tuesday evening from 7:30-9p.m. and on Sundays from 2-4p.m. For those interested in becoming an initiated witch, the Magickal Realms Grove is one of best places to learn the Craft. The curriculum also reflects Lady Rhea's eclectic spiritual interests. According to Rhea, a pagan is one who "worships the original gods and refuses to be stamped out." In addition to Wicca, the Grove covers Hinduism, Native American religion, Santeria, Voudon, Buddhism, Minoan tradition, Strega, Celtic, Welsh, Egyptian and Norse paths. You'll walk away from the Grove with knowledge about spells, charms,

magic, astrology, feng shui, trance and meditation. Full Moon and New Moon circles are also held every month. The donation for each class is only $3. Some of the guest teachers include Lord Tammuz, Mercurius (Matthew Sawicki) and Lord Julian (Paul J. DeLuca).

## MINOAN BROTHERHOOD

*c/o Matthew Sawicki*
*MDS1877NYC@earthlink.net*
After being dormant for many years, the Minoan Brotherhood coven in New York City is being brought back to life by initiated High Priest Matthew Sawicki, who intends to restore the coven to what it once was - a teaching and initiatory path for gay witches.

"Ever since coming to New York City, it was my quest to become initiated into the Minoan system," says Sawicki. However, it took Sawicki more than five years and trip to Canada to find a Minoan priest who was still initiating witches into the tradition.

"The AIDs epidemic wiped out 75 percent of the Minoan priests in the late 1980s," says Sawicki. "There are a few active covens around the country, but none in New York City, the birthplace of the tradition."

In ancient civilizations, it was the homosexual who was revered as the high priest or priestess, since the gay priest was able to channel both god and goddess energy. Yet in the modern resurgence of witchcraft, particularly the Gardnerian lineage, there was a bias against gay priests, since, in their opinion, the high priest and high priestess must lead all ceremonies. The late Edmund Buczynski, who was the "father" of the New York tradition of Wicca in the early 1970s, rediscovered the important role of gay priests in witchcraft, after he founded the Minoan Brotherhood coven in 1975. The Minoan Brotherhood - and later the Minoan Sisterhood founded by Lady Rhea and Carol Bulzone - became a place for primarily gay witches to gather, train and participate in single-gender rituals. Buczynski wrote a Book of Shadows for the coven, using a pantheon of deities from the Minoan period of civilization in Crete "the main deities are Rhea the "mother goddess" and her male counterpart Asterion, the "brother of the stars".

The Minoan Brotherhood is an initiatory order and the names of the other Minoan deities are given as the initiate progresses through the ranks. Given the fact that the Minoans thrived in 2500 B.C. and the proximity to Egypt, there is an "Egyptian flavor" to many of the deities.

## *The Magic of Lady Rhea*

Lady Rhea is considered the godmother of the modern Wicca movement in New York City. She, along with the late Edmund Buczynski, created the Minoan Tradition of Wicca - and inspired a generation of pagans and witches in the process. Lady Rhea has also started the "Edwardian" style of Wicca, based upon the teachings and philosophy of Buczynski.

"Eddie was magic," says Lady Rhea, from her store Magickal Realms in the Bronx. "He founded so many magical systems and influenced so many people."

Lady Rhea became interested in spirituality as a young child growing up in the Bronx, fascinated by the practice of Santeria. However, it was when she walked into "The Warlock Shop" in Brooklyn Heights that her magical education really began. The store was owned by Buczynski and the Herman Slater, who eventually went on to open the world-famous "Magickal Childe." Lady Rhea ended up working for both stores, learning the Craft and making a network of friends at the same time.

It was at Magickal Childe, in the late 1970s, that Lady Rhea first created the "Enchanted Candle," a candle that is "dressed" with specific oils, magical sigils and glitter to achieve a specific magical goal, like finding a job or new romance. Her style of candle carving has inspired other books and has become a uniquely New York magical practice. Due to the popularity, Lady Rhea published the book, *The Enchanted Candle*, in 1986. Although the book is currently out-of-print, Lady Rhea says that it soon will be re-published by a major publishing company.

Lady Rhea came up with the concept of the Enchanted Candle by accident. She ordered 26 cases of "pull-out" candles by mistake, rather than the more popular filled candles.

"Herman (Slater) was a hard boss, and when he saw the pull-out candles, he began screaming that no one would purchase them," says Lady Rhea. "I came up with the idea of carving and dressing the candles. The first one, I carved a pyramid and money sign, then rolled it in glitter and put oil on it. Herman became convinced after his business that day doubled. Candle carving is an art form and a powerful form of magic."

Lady Rhea and Buczynski became very active in the Minoan tradition, which they formed in 1972. The Minoan tradition broke away from the idea that every coven must have a high priest and high priestess to conduct a magical working. The Minoan tradition allowed same-sex magical partners to lead rituals, opening up coven work to gay and lesbian witches.

Lady Rhea initiated Carol Bulzone into the Minoan Tradition in 1975. The two eventually decided to open their own witchcraft shop, Enchantments, which is still in the East Village. Lady Rhea spent five years as co-owner of Enchantments. In 1987, she sold her half of the store to Bulzone, to pursue motherhood full-time. Around this time, Lady Rhea's love for Santeria took hold again and she began working part-time doing readings at Original Products in the Bronx, one of the top *botanicas* in the country. Lady Rhea can still be found at Original Products every Friday. Lady Rhea says that the pagan community and Santeria community have learned a great deal from the other and, in a typical New York fashion, you will find Santeria supplies in many of the witchcraft stores

"New York is a melting pot, with many magical traditions," says Lady Rhea. "How could traditions not cross?"

Lady Rhea, herself, is a Buddhist, a witch and highly knowledgeable about Santeria. She remains one of the most respected Wicca elders in the community, a compassionate and wise teacher. She says that the ideals of witchcraft that first got her interested are still valid today, particularly concern for the environment.

"The Earth is our mother and the witch is her voice," says Lady Rhea. "The Wicca community in New York City has certainly changed, and we have all had our differences. But at the end of the day we all agree on one main principle - the love of the God and the Goddess. That is our collective purpose."

The Minoan Brotherhood, however, was cut down in its prime by the AIDS crisis; Buczynski himself succumbed to the disease in 1991.

Sawicki says that he is determined to continue the legacy of Buczynski. He is re-forming the coven and anyone interested in being initiated into this system, should contact Sawicki through his e-mail.

"This system works. The gods do respond," says Sawicki. "This system is for someone who has a strong passion for life, confidence in themselves and an interest in learning more about the nature of divinity in themselves as a gay man."

### NEW MOON NEW YORK (NMNY)
*212-388-8288*
*www.newmoonny.faithweb.com*
Founded in 1991, New Moon New York is the city's oldest pagan networking organization. All "life-affirming" goddess-worshiping pagan paths are welcome to participate. Its website contains pagan

YOGA | ESOTERIC GROUPS | **WITCHCRAFT** | OCCULT UNDERGROUND | BOOKS | UFOS | BOTANICAS | TANTRA | ASTROLOGERS & PSYCHICS |

links, as well as business links. New Moon New York is most known, however, for its wonderful annual Beltane celebration held in Central Park. New Moon also organizes eight seasonal festivals which are open to the public.

## NEW YORK METRO ASATRU SOCIETY

*www.nycpagan.com*
Members of the NYMAS are "heathens" and proud of it. Heathen is actually the Germanic word for "pagan." The NYMAS was founded in 2000 and is dedicated to the Germanic and Norse pantheon of deities - that is, Odin, Friya and the most muscular of Gods, Thor. NYMAS events are usually held in public places around the metro New York City area. Asatru events have traditionally involved consumption of home-made "mead," and many members specialize in Runic divination. Contact nycheathen@aol.com for information on current events.

## POLYHYMNIA COVEN

*c/o Richard Wandel*
*Box 726*
*Jackson Heights, NY 11372*
*rwandel@pipeline.com*
Polyhymnia Coven is one of the more prominent traditional Gardnerian Covens in New York City that is devoted to promoting the vision of witchcraft according to the "father" of the modern Wicca movement, Gerald Gardner. Richard Wandel and his magical partner Lady Ryonan formed the Queens coven in 1993, after "hiving" off from the Kathexis Coven. Kathexis eventually moved to Long Island and is now known as Our Lady of the Seashore.

"We are primarily a teaching coven," says Wandel. "Our main focus is training new clergy in the Gardnerian tradition." Wandel, who once lived in a Catholic monastery, says that he first became involved in witchcraft more than 20 years ago. "After leaving the monastery, I did a lot of spiritual searching and I found what I was looking for in the Craft," says Wandel. The training to become a high priest or priestess in Polyhymnia takes, at the very least, three years and three days and encompasses three degrees.

Those who would like to join Polyhymnia need to first write a letter or e-mail explaining their background and why they are interested in becoming a witch. Then Wandel and Lady Ryonan will arrange a one-on-one meeting "usually in a diner" that is close to the Queens location of the coven "so people get an idea of how far they have to come." Students at Polyhymnia are taught a traditional style of Gardnerian witchcraft - having the goddess and the god in equal partnership, casting the circle and having all magical workings male to female. "We appreciate the idea of having an ongoing tradition, as opposed to making the tradition up," says Wandel. "We like the idea that we can magically trace our roots back directly to Gerald Gardner."

### THE SHADOWFOLK TRADITION TEACHING COLLECTIVE
*www.shadowfolk.org*
*grove@shadowfolk.org*
The Shadowfolk Tradition Teaching Collective meets on the Upper West Side every Saturday, from 2-5 p.m., from March until October. The seven month course, First Steps on the Spiral: The Wiccan Way, focuses on "magickal communication with the elemental forces" and introduces students to ritual work and comparative mythology. The classes include art and crafts, including the making of masks, incense and mandalas. The course is run by the Temple of the Spiral Path, a family of covens which practice the Shadowfolk Tradition of witchcraft. Although the Shadowfolk follow a Celtic tradition, they are also eclectic and open to other traditions.

### TRIPLE STAR
*www.paganpath.com/welsh.htm*
*Avagddu@aol.com*
This is a coven in the Welsh/Celtic tradition, the Welsh Rite Gwyddonaid, which worships a Welsh pantheon of gods and goddesses. The Triple Star - located in Greenwich Village - is led by Lord Gwion and Lady Gwyndra. It is an initiatory order, in which the prospective members must spend an introductory period in the "outer court," before becoming initiated. The Gwyddonaid "requires a strong follower with a sincere heart ... in order to understand the ways of the wise." Lord Gwion has blended the New York Welsh Traditionalist Wicca (NYWTW), founded by Edmund Buczynski, with its original sources, creating a "cohesive, fully functional tradition." Triple Star is still accepting applicants for its outer court.

### TEMPLE OF THE ETERNAL LIGHT
*www.totelny.com*
The Temple of the Eternal Light (TOTEL) bills itself

as a Kaballistic Wiccan Temple. The coven is still active in Brooklyn, though now has its administrative offices in California after two of its founding members, Karen DePolito and Jerome Peartree, drove their motor home across the country and settled "somewhere in Lake County." DePolito joined the coven in 1987 introducing a neo-pagan element to the coven, which had previously concentrated on Kaballah and ceremonial magic. Those who live outside the New York area and still want to study with TOTEL can order the home-study program Yiddush Yoga: Thirteen Tools Toward Enlightenment. TOTEL promises that the eleven lessons will "reveal the Kabbalistic secrets from the Bible Code."

### UNCOVEN OF THE SOLITARIES
*www.uncoven.com;*
*www.angelfire.com/ny3/tucots/index.html*
*TheEntwife@yahoo.com*
The Uncoven of the Solitaries describes itself as a "floating pagan party," a group of socially-compatible pagans and pagan-friendly folk who get together periodically for rituals and fun. "First of all, we are not a coven," says Uncoven founder Persephone Yavanna. "There are no initiations, degrees, lineages or inner court vs. outer court distinctions." Yavanna formed the "uncoven" in 1990, after she began hosting an eclectic weekly group ritual in her Manhattan apartment. The group tends to identify itself more with paganism than Wicca. "Our tradition is folkloric, we tend to engage in practices that are as similar as possible to those of other living polytheistic/animist traditions such as Taoist, Shinto, Hindu, Native American and Voudou/Ifa," says Yavanna. The pagans who join Uncoven are usually solitary practitioners. Uncoven is willing to accept new members; however they can be quite selective in making sure "there is a good fit" with the rest of the group. Yavanna made it clear that Uncoven does not teach paganism or witchcraft. "We are a social group. If you join, be prepared to socialize," she says. "And just because you are a solitary practitioner does not mean that you can't be social."

### WICCAN CIRCLE OF QUEENS
*www.webnik.com/circleofqueens*
*mriggiola@nyc.rr.com*
The Wiccan Circle of Queens began as a small teaching circle in a store-front in Flushing, Queens. Riannon-Lia and her ex-daughter-in-law Anuskaadi began to practice the Craft together and started a

small business, making spell-kits, along with decorated brooms and wreaths. The "circle" began to grow, and pretty soon it became a "close-knit family." The group meets regularly to celebrate the eight Sabbats, as well as full Moon rituals.

"What makes our group unique is that there is absolutely no hierarchy and everyone participates as an equal," says Rhiannon-Lia. "Ours is more of a religious philosophy. We only conduct spells together when there is a need because of illness or problems. We are much more spiritual than magickal."

The group is very eclectic. Riannon-Lia says that the coven includes three streghans "who practice the old religion of Italy", two Celtics and one Norse pagan. One of their members, Baccianello, is also an initiated santero and an ordained spiritual minister. The group is still debating on whether to accept new members. "We are very selective, but if one or two people stand out, we might consider it," says Riannon-Lia. "They would have to be practicing pagans, who are productive citizens, who are spiritual and not into spells and who are not rigid. Most importantly, they need to be able to add spice to our mix!"

## ZODIAC LOUNGE
*212-724-3750*
In the movie Bell, Book and Candle, the "Zodiac Lounge" was hangout for a fictional group of witches in New York City. The real-life Zodiac Lounge, which formerly occupied a storefront on West 96th Street, fulfills the same function - for real witches in Manhattan. "The Zodiac Lounge began as a social center for the Wiccan community, and evolved into something more," says owner Anthony Russell. The Zodiac Lounge actually began as a series of fund-raising sevents for terminal pediatrics wards and children's hospices

Although Russell closed the storefront in June, 2003, he says that the Zodiac Lounge will still operate as a regular fund-raising event for children's terminal illness programs.

Russell originally opened the Zodiac Lounge in 1997, as a place to purchase "objects of profound transformation and senseless beauty." Many people came to the basement store to get a tarot reading and spiritual guidance from Russell, who has been practitioner of the Craft for more than 35 years. Russell never intended to open Zodiac Lounge, but a near-death experience forced him to re-evaluate his life. He still suffers from a life-threatening illness and was pronounced clinically dead after receiving

YOGA | ESOTERIC GROUPS | **WITCHCRAFT** | OCCULT UNDERGROUND | BOOKS | UFOS | BOTANICAS | TANTRA | ASTROLOGERS & PSYCHICS |

treatment During the death experience, he says that he came face-to-face with the goddess Hecate and was brought to an intersection where three roads met. Russell chose the road which brought him back to life, on the condition that he to care for the "very old, the very young and the very ill."

Russell eventually regained his full health and appearance after conducting a series of rituals to the goddess Aphrodite. Russell kept his part of the bargain and now raises funds and volunteers on a regular basis for children who have terminal illnesses. As part of his soul mission, Russell also guides individuals on their spiritual path.

"I teach people to empower themselves," says Russell. "I can do a spell for someone, but it has much more power if they participate with me, as an interactive experience." As for witchcraft and spells, Russell says that much of the effectiveness from magic comes from psychology and changing the way one thinks. For instance, in the ritual that Russell conducted to Aphrodite, Russell creatively visualized himself with full health, looking fit. He says it was his change in attitude that made the difference. "People come to me when all else has failed," says Russell. "If I can help them change the way they think, they can change their lives. As you see your world, it shall become." Russell also still gives spiritual readings both in Manhattan and at Magickal Realms in the Bronx. He also teaches a Fundamentals of Magic course from his Upper West Side apartment.

# Occult Underground: Secretive New York Esoteric Groups and the Left-Hand Path

When someone mentions the "left-hand path," there is an immediate assumption that the group is involved in black magic. In our current paradigm, we see the right-hand path as "good" and the left-hand path as "evil." However, the truth is much more complex. In a world of spiritual liberation, a Gnostic, for instance, would consider the "monotheistic" God Yahweh as the evil demiurge. And in the underground esoteric community, many (though not all) consider Satan as a great liberator, a role model, if you will, of the new man. As Thelemite Lon Milo DuQuette says, the gods of the past become the demons of today. According to many occultists, Man has become God of the New Aeon.

The left-hand path is all about the celebration of the "self" and a person's individual will. While the Eastern Buddhist would attempt (mostly unsuccessfully) to annihilate the self through spiritual practice, the true Western occultist exalts the self. It takes a spiritually-courageous - and I might add, moral - person to successfully tread a left-hand path. I'm not talking about some teenager who dresses in black, chisels their teeth into fangs and listens to Marilyn Manson. The left-hand practitioner will set himself/herself apart from the "group mind" of conventional society to seek a "higher law," one beyond good and evil. To do this in an ethical way takes incredible determination and intelligence. The true black magicians (though they may not agree) can be found in today's corporate boardrooms, on the trading floor of the New York Stock Exchange and on Madison Avenue, inflicting their will on the world. Hail Satan!

And yet, there is a sensibility that goes along with all of this that defines New York's underground occult scene; it's a dark spiritual current that one knows when one sees it. It's like trying to define what *Chaos Magick* is you just know it and to give it a definition takes away from its intention. So no, some frat-boy who works on Wall Street is not a black magician, because he doesn't know what his true will is. He is simply participating in yet other group mind activity. Mob mentality has inflicted the majority of pain and suffering on the Earth plane. The black magician is often a loner, not buying into the reality that has been handed to them. The black magician will create their own reality, making up rules as they go on, altering their magical world as they see fit. The black magician creates changes in the material world, in accordance with their will, through magical ritual and spells.

And there's the rub. How do a bunch of brilliant, non-conformist loners form magical organizations? Not very well.

**<<<**

The New York occult scene is fragmented and the majority of true magicians work in isolation. The recently formed Yahoo Group NYCMAGICK is attempting to bring these various magicians together Thelemites, chaos magicians, ceremonial magicians, Satanists and Setians. New York has a few left-hand path groups, some of which are listed here. Most of these groups are somewhat private and tend to be selective about their membership. The left-hand path is not for everyone. Yet there are those who need the "shock" of a left-hand experience to bring them to the next spiritual level - whether it is a naked woman on an altar, group sex magic, or evoking an ancient demon whose archetypal energy still exists as an echo on the astral plane. As the great one once said: "Do what thou wilt shall be the whole of the law. Love is the law, love under will."

## ASTRUM ARGENTEUM

*The Cancellarius of A.·.A.·.*
*c/o The EquinoxJAF Box 7666*
*New York, NY 10116-4632*
*www.ordoaa.wolfmagick.com*

The A.·.A.·.(Astrum Argenteum) functions as the "inner school" of English occultist Aleister Crowley's teachings. In general, you need to be an initiate of either the OTO or Holy Order of Ra-Hoor-Khuit in order to be considered for A.·.A.·. training. The training is one-on-one and extremely intensive; the A.·.A.·. is also very secretive and you only get to meet your spiritual mentor, but have contact with no other members. There are those who claim that much of the teachings are conducted on the inner "astral plane," when the aspirant is dreaming.

The ultimate ritual of the A.·.A.·. is the *Knowledge and Conversation of the Holy Guardian Angel.* Students who are ready for this step are usually contacted by a member of the A.·.A.·., and not the other way around. A.·.A.·. members advise aspirants to practice published Crowley rituals like The Star *Ruby* and *Liber v Vel Reguli* daily in order to gain the attention of the "secret chiefs" who oversee the A.·.A.·. from the inner planes. Another rule of thumb: anyone who claims they are a member of the A.·.A.·. usually are not; bona fide members don't advertise.

## CHURCH OF SATAN

*Grotto of the Maninblack*
*c/o Rev. Andre Schlesinger*

*Post Office Box 246*
*Radio City Station*
*New York, NY 10101-0246*
*www.angelfire.com/ny2/maninblack/mani-*
*nblack2.html;*
*www.churchofsatan.com*
*maninblack@nyc.rr.com*

If you have ever flipped through the cable TV channels late Saturday night, you may have come across a startling site - a group of black-hooded New Yorkers conducting a "Black Mass." That would be the Maninblack Grotto, a New York-based group of Church of Satan members, who want to promote Satanism though such media outlets as public access television. "The Maninblack's Grotto's activities are often dictated by its geographical location, that being one of the main media centers of the world," writes Grotto Master Rev. Andre Peter Schlesinger. "We have been often been called upon to represent the Church of Satan in many media forms." Some of the other activities include "Satanic ritual practice, instructional meetings and get-togethers." In order to join the Grotto, you have to be a member of the Church of Satan in good standing. Satanic philosophy holds that man's true nature is that of a "carnal beast," living in a universe that is motivated by the "Dark Force which we call Satan." Satanists consider themselves as their own gods, an ëalien elite' that stands apart from a culture "whose masses pursue solace in an external deity." The Church of Satan was originally founded in San Francisco in 1966 by the late Anton LaVey, and now has its headquarters in Manhattan (see feature article). LaVey claims to have ushered in the "Age of Satan" with the establishment of his church and attracted a great deal of press with his anti-establishment antics, including conducting rituals featuring a nude woman on the altar. Members are quick to point out that theirs is a path of fulfilled desires and they do not believe in violence and do not sacrifice animals. Their brand of Satanism is primarily about the fulfillment of desires and the use of magical techniques to obtain these desires.

## HOLY ORDER OF RAHOORKHUIT
*Children of Zain Lodge*
*PO Box 8140*
*New York, NY 10116*
*www.hoor.org*

When British occultist Aleister Crowley passed away in 1947, his organizations became fragment-

## The Church of Satan: Looking For a Few Good Men (and Women)

New York City is known as the financial center of the world, but now it may become known as the satanic center of the world as well.

In April, 2001, the Church of Satan moved its administrative headquarters from California to New York City - the Hell's Kitchen neighborhood to be exact.

"New York is the perfect city for a Satanist to live in - it is secular, it is Babylon," says Magister Peter Gilmore, who took over the Church in 2001 from founder Anton LaVey's widow Blanche Barton. "It has all the pleasures and wonders of the world; it is the cultural center of the planet."

For a Satanist, pleasure is supremely important. "Satanism is the world's first carnal religion in which each person is his or her own god," says Gilmore, an articulate man who runs the Church with Magistra Peggy Nadramia, the High Priestess of Satanism. "We are basically an epicurean philosophy that accepts man as he really is - a carnal beast. We are pragmatists."

The Church of Satan was established in 1966 by LaVey, a former psychic investigator, musician and police photographer, who lived in San Francisco. Through his occult research, LaVey came up with a unique philosophy that embraced Satan as the symbol of personal freedom and individualism. The Church attracted a great deal of media attention, as well as notable members like Jayne Mansfield, Sammy Davis Jr. and UFO investigator Jacques Vallee.

"One of the biggest misconceptions about the Church is that we worship the devil," says Gilmore. "We don't believe that Satan exists, the same as we don't believe in God. We worship ourselves. Satan is simply an extreme projection of ourselves."

Gilmore says that the Church functions primarily as a means to communicate the concepts and philosophy of Satanism and is not "about fellowship." For that, the Church has established "grottos," like New York's Maninblack Grotto, for "like-minded Satanists" to get together socially and for ritual work.

"We aren't looking to proselytize or convert people; we let them look for us," says Gilmore. "People are either Satanists, or they are not. Frankly, we don't think that everyone could - or should - become a Satanist." Gilmore says that people who join the Church begin by looking at the website, and recognize that Satanism is consistent with their personal philosophy. The typical Satanist is a freethinker who never went along with the group mind of society, part of the "alien elite," as the Church calls its membership.

The Church sees religious fundamentalism as one of the biggest dangers to humanity. This point became apparent after the 9-11 terrorist attack on the World Trade Center. Gilmore made a public statement on the internet calling for vengeance against the perpetrators.

Although the Church does not take a stance on political issues, Gilmore says that he was pleased when the United States went to war in Iraq. "I look at political issues in terms of Machiavellian ideal. Anything that increases our power is good," Gilmore says. "Anyway, the more we spread our secular values in the world, the safer the world will be for people like me."

Gilmore says that he considers the United States the "world's first satanic republic," a secular country that maintains a separation of church and state. "Islamic extremists see us as a great Satan, because we stand for personal freedoms," says Gilmore. "I say, we should be the best Satan there is."

Singer Marilyn Manson is probably the more visible Satanist in popular culture today and Gilmore confirms that Manson is an initiated High Priest in the Church. "The stuff that Manson does on stage has nothing to do with Satanism," says Gilmore. "Manson has basically recycled old orthodoxies - like Alice Cooper and David Bowie - and repackaged it to a forgetful audience. He manipulates his fans, who are nothing but a bunch of sheep. Now that is Satanism."

As for satanic movies? *Willie Wonka and the Chocolate Factory* is one of Gilmore's favorite examples. "In that movie everyone is looking for pleasure and, in the end, everyone gets what they deserve. Willie Wonka is the devil, he is Satan absolutely," says Gilmore.

Under Gilmore's able leadership, the Church of Satan will continue to promote the satanic vision of Anton LaVey. As Gilmore says: "We are in exciting times, so indulge, innovate and celebrate. The world is ours, so go forth and fill your experience with satisfaction."

*You may contact COS through its website: www.churchofsatan.com.*

---

ed. Some Crowley organizations became extremely dogmatic; most groups simply ceased to exist and Crowley's promise of a "new magical aeon" seemed like a distant dream. In 1978, however, a group of Crowley devotees formed the Holy Order of RaHoorKhuit (H.O.O.R) to "teach and fulfill the principles of Thelema." Thelema is the Greek word for "will," which is the cornerstone of Crowley's magical philosophy. Crowley claims to have ushered in the new age, the "Age of Horus," when he received the *Book of the Law* in 1904, dictated to him in Cairo by a supernatural entity known as *Aiwass*. Despite the fact that Crowley's writings are full of references to ancient Egyptian gods who seem to have a certain level of influence over his actions and will, the Book of the Law holds that "every man and every woman is a star," and "doing one's will is the function of each individual star." The New York Children of Zain Lodge holds both first and second degree initiations. The Greater Mysteries are taught in the lodge's "inner triad," and "can only be hinted at," according to the group's published material. The H.O.O.R is an initiatory organization and bases its daily practices on the spiritual exercises *Liber Resh* and *The Star Ruby*. "Thelema is a system of theurgy, a system of initiation and a philosophy for dealing with all aspects of life on earth," according to a H.O.O.R printed statement. "The emancipation of mankind from all limitation whatever is the main precepts of the teachings."

## MAGICAL PACT OF THE ILLUMINATES OF THANATEROS
*www.iot.goetia.net*
Peter Carroll and a dozen or so other magicians from Europe originally formed the Pact of the Illuminates of Thanateros during a *Mass of Chaos* ritual conducted in Germany in the late 1970s, establishing as the Pact as a vehicle for those interested in practicing Chaos Magick. There is an active group of Chaoists (Chaos Magick practitioners) in Manhattan, however you need to go through the main website to get in touch with them. Chaos magicians don't use any one magical system, but rather "pick and choose" from any number of different systems - even fictional systems based on the works the H.P. Lovecraft. Essentially, they use "whatever works," as long as the ritual creates a "change in the universe, according to their will." The motto of the Chaos movement is "nothing is true, everything is permitted," and as they deconstruct magic - as well as the civilizations that created these magical systems. For the Chaos magician, there is no ultimate truth ñ it is whatever you choose to believe in. Chaos is more of a sensibility, than a belief system and its magicians will use ritual, visualization, screaming, meditation and even "extreme states of stress" to achieve that magical state of consciousness necessary to inflict their will onto the universe. They see themselves as a "psycho-historic force in the battle for the eon." Chaos Magick appears to be gaining popularity, perhaps as a response to the chaotic times we are living through. *Or have they caused the chaos?*

## ORDER OF THE THELEMIC GOLDEN DAWN
*Temple of the Star of Babylon*
*www.thelemicgoldendawn.org*

| YOGA | ESOTERIC GROUPS | WITCHCRAFT | **OCCULT UNDERGROUND** | BOOKS | UFOS | BOTANICAS | TANTRA | ASTROLOGERS & PSYCHICS |

The Esoteric Order of the Golden Dawn was founded in London in 1988 by a group of Kabbalists, Freemasons and Rosicrucians as an initiatory order which was designed to serve as the guardian of the Western esoteric tradition. The powerful rituals and lectures of the Golden Dawn were derived from a mysterious document known as the *Cipher Manuscript*. GD founder William Wynn Westcott claimed that he obtained the 60-page manuscript from a "dealer in curios." Westcott deciphered the document, which essentially turned out to be a series of ritual outlines for an occult order. During its early years, the GD was primarily a theoretical school, which performed initiations of the "Outer Order." In 1891, GD member S.L. MacGregor Mathers formed a secret second order, known as the "Inner Order," which was more practical and demanding. The first GD temple in New York City - the Thoth-Hermes Temple - was opened in 1897. Famed occultist Aleister Crowley was initiated into the Second Order in 1899, causing a schism within the organization, by members who felt that Crowley was not worthy of initiation. Because of internal struggles, nearly all GD temples in the United States eventually closed. However, in the past several years, there has been a resurgence of GD activity in the United States. The Order of the Thelemic Golden Dawn combines the teachings of Aleister Crowley, Thelema and the Golden Dawn. Its website proclaims that it is a "magickal order of the New Aeon wherein men and women ... can participate in the Great Work of Thelema." To join, fill out an application on the website. Membership applications are reviewed and accepted only during the Equinoxes and Solstices, so don't expect a prompt response.

## ORDO SUNYATA VAJRA
*Khabs Am Pekht Mahayana Cakra*
*www.ordosv.org* *khabs@ordosv.org*
The Ordo Sunyata Vajra combines the Thelemic ritual and work of Aleister Crowley with esoteric Buddhism. The "mother temple" is located in Portland, Oregon and the New York representation "known as a cakra" is the Khabs Am Pekht Mahayana. The central ritual performed is the *Diamond Sapphire Gem of Radiance* ritual, which is performed publicly in Manhattan the first Saturday of every month. The Order "incorporates aspects of both Western ceremonial magick and Eastern mysticism and ritual," grounded solidly on Crowley's *Book of the Law*. The Order believes that the "stellar gno-

sis" can be found throughout history, as far back as the days of Atlantis and Lemuria. In the modern age, this gnosis can be found in the Western tradition of hermeticism and the Kabbalah and also in the Eastern "non-dual philosophies" of the "Prajna-Paramita traditions of Buddhism, Tao and Vedanta." Contact the group by e-mail in order to find out the location of the monthly public ritual.

### ORDO TEMPLI ORIENTIS (OTO)

*Tahuti LodgeOld Chelsea Station*
*P.O. Box 1535New York, NY 10113-1535*
*www.tahuti-lodge.com*
*tahutilodge@nyc.rr.com*

The Manhattan-based Tahuti Lodge of the Ordo Templi Orientis (OTO) is the oldest OTO lodge on the east coast and the third oldest in the United States. It continues to be New York's preeminent occult organization. The OTO was originally founded in Germany in 1895 by two high-ranking Masons, Karl Kellner and Theodor Reuss. Kellner, who traveled a great deal in the Middle East, claimed that "three Eastern adepts" gave him the "key which opens up all Hermetic and Masonic secrets, namely the teachings of sexual magic and all the secrets of Freemasonry and all systems of religion." Famed English occultist Aleister Crowley took over the OTO in the English-speaking world in 1912 and put his own unique stamp on the organization by reworking the degree rituals according to his Liber Al vel Legis and the Law of Thelema. Founded in 1979, the Tahuti Lodge is one of the most respected OTO lodges in the country. Past lodge masters include James Wasserman, Richard Gernon, Kent Finne and James Strain. The Lodge performs initiations, as well as the Gnostic Mass, which is the central ritual of the OTO. According to the Master of the Tahuti Lodge, the aim of the OTO is to "foster a sense of Thelemic community where true men and women can do their wills." Those interested, can contact the OTO and attend their monthly Gnostic Mass, which is performed publicly.

### TEMPLE OF SET

*Black Sun Rising Pylon*
*www.xeper.org*
*sirHarlequin9@aol.com*

The Black Sun Rising Pylon is one of the more active Temple of Set pylons and was founded in 1999 to "fulfill the needs of New York area Setians." The TOS itself was founded by former Church of Satan member Michael Aquino, who resigned from the church in 1975 after "invoking the Prince of Darkness" and receiving a new mandate. Aquino considered the Egyptian God *Set* as the most ancient form of the Prince of Darkness, whose priesthood can be traced back to predynastic times. The TOS does not consider itself a Satanic group, but rather a "left-hand path" organization that practices black magic. Black magic, according to TOS, is "my will be done," as opposed to the "thy will be done" philosophy of white magic. TOS operates as an initiatory organization and each "Setian" is expected to affiliate with at least one "pylon" (the name for the unique gates of ancient Egyptian temples) within a year of admission. Sir Harlequin, the head of the Black Sun Rising Pylon, says that his pylon meets twice a month and includes "workshops and workings of a Setian nature." The type of individual that TOS would consider accepting as a member would be "a well-educated, well-traveled individual dedicated to their personal transformation and initiation and the pleasure's that such a quest will bring," Harlequin says. "In addition, a prospective member should have a good sense of humor and an eye for how magic and initiation integrate into the totality of experience." The TOS warns the "the black arts are dangerous in the same way that working with volatile chemicals is dangerous. This is most emphatically not a field for unstable, immature or otherwise emotionally or intellectually weak-minded people."

YOGA | ESOTERIC GROUPS | WITCHCRAFT | **OCCULT UNDERGROUND** | BOOKS | UFOS | BOTANICAS | TANTRA | ASTROLOGERS & PSYCHICS |

# Esoteric Bookstores & Libraries

At one time, New York City was the center of universe as far as bookstores go. Weiser Books and Magickal Childe were among the best bookstores in the world for occult and spiritual titles. However, both bookstores closed in the mid-1990s, victims of rising rents in Manhattan, among other reasons.

"It is difficult for an independent bookstore to survive in Manhattan. The rents are very high and the bigger chains simply took away many of our customers," says Donald Weiser, who now runs Weiser Antiquarian Books in York, Maine.

Weiser says that when his father, Samuel, began selling esoteric books in the 1930s, his store was the first in Manhattan to do so. "We used to sell the esoteric books in the basement of the store and the regular books on the main floor," recalls Weiser.

When Donald Weiser joined the family business in 1951, he put an emphasis on the spiritual and occult book side of the store, since he was deeply interested in the esoteric. Under his supervision, Weiser Books began reprinting many out-of-print occult titles like *Kabballah* by Isaac Meyer and *Book of Thoth* by a then-obscure occult writer named Aleister Crowley. Weiser Books played a big role in the 1960s Crowley revival, by reprinting Crowley's major works. At the time, most of Crowley's works were in the "public domain" and not under copyright protection.

>>>

**ASSOCIATION FOR RESEARCH AND ENLIGHTENMENT (A.R.E.) OF NEW YORK BOOKSTORE**
*150 West 28th Street between 6th and 7th Streets, suite 1001*
*212-691-7690*
*www.mindspring.com/~areofnyc/bookstore.htm*
*Hours: M-Fri: 6:30-9:30 pm; Sat: 2-6pm*
*Closest subway: 1/9/N/R to 28th Street*
The A.R.E. Bookstore is an all-volunteer run store, devoted to the works of the "Sleeping Prophet" Edgar Cayce, a psychic who would go into a sleep-like state and give discourses on health and various metaphysical topics. The bookstore stocks numerous books on Cayce, as well as books by Cayce students. Many of the books are based upon the voluminous Cayce readings, including a fascinating book on the past lives of famous people. The store also stocks rare health products prescribed in his readings, like lotions and oils, skin care treatments, castor oil treatments, Atomic Iodine, and even Carbon

<<<

"We printed what the customers came in looking for," says Weiser. "It was a very interesting time in New York. There were a lot of characters who would come into the store."

At the time, the other esoteric stores included "Orientalia" and "Gateways," both of which were closed by the late 1960s and early 1970s.

In the 1970's and 1980s, Herman Slater opened the Warlock Shoppe in Brooklyn Heights and later the Magickal Childe on West 19th Street, selling and publishing books on ceremonial magic and Wicca, creating the modern New York Wicca movement in the process. Slater passed away in 1992. Although his bookstore continued operation for a year or so after his death, it eventually was forced to close.

After leaving New York, Weiser moved his entire operation to Maine. He eventually sold his publishing house to Red Wheel and now concentrates on selling rare and hard-to-find occult books. His Maine warehouse features two floors of new and used esoteric books, one of the largest occult collections in the world.

"The internet was both good and bad for the esoteric book business," says Weiser. "It really hurt us when we were in Manhattan, but now we survive on our internet sales." Weiser says that he misses his days in New York City, particularly the people who would come into the store on a regular basis. "It was a magical time," says Weiser. "Everything was new and exciting."

New York still has some of the best esoteric bookstores and libraries in the world, each with its own unique specialty.

Ash. The store has a section for writers who have given programs at the A.R.E center, including Budd Hopkins, Hans Holzer and Dolores Cannon.

### ASTRO GALLERY
*185 Madison Avenue at the corner of 34th Street*
*212-889-9000*
*Hours: M-Fri: 10am-7pm; Thu: 10am-8pm; Sat: 10am-6pm; Sun: 11am-6pm*
Astro Gallery collects magic stones, spiritual crystals, gems, crystal balls, pyramids and even crystal skulls from around the world. The staff is knowledgeable and can guide you to what you need. They have listed the gems according to their healing properties. For instance, Amazonite "aligns the etheric and mental bodies"; Citrine "breaks up energy blocks in the body," and Tourmaline "dispels fear, negativity and grief." Michael, a long-time staffer,

told me that he became a "true believer" in crystal healing after he used a crystal to heal a chronic back problem. He said that he fell asleep with the crystal on his back and when he woke up in the middle of the night, the crystal was "red hot," and his back pain was gone. Michael. The staff at Astro Gallery is passionate about crystals - they believe that everyone should have several personal crystals for healing and meditation. The day I was there some of the more stunning pieces included a three-foot tall Amethyst crystal cluster, perfect for an altar. Healers, reiki masters, feng shui consultants and meditators flock to Astro Gallery for their crystal supplies.

## AURORA

*43 Clinton Street between Rivington and Stanton*
*212-477-0101*
*www. Aurora-usa.net*
*Hours: daily from 12-8pm; Saturday 12-7 pm*
*Closest subway stop: F train to Rivington*
At one time, Angela Babekov worked as a high-powered CEO for a Wall Street financial services company. Her life was transformed, however, after she met her spiritual teacher, an Agni yoga master living in New York City. Babekov, a Russian native who moved here when she was four years old, made a profound life decision. She quit her high-paying job and, in March, 2001, opened the Aurora Bookstore in the Lower East Side. Babekov, who exudes a deep spiritual energy, says that she was guided to the location. "This neighborhood is transforming itself," Babekov says. "We are drawing in some very interesting people and it is changing the entire area." Aurora stocks an eclectic selection of books; many reflecting Babekov's spiritual lineage. Aurora features the works of Omraam Mikhael Aivanhov and Nicholas Roerich, in English, Russian and Spanish editions, along with books on Theosophy, the ascended masters, higher consciousness and conspiracy. Much of the collection includes rare and out-of-print books. Roerich, who lived in New York City in the early 20th century, is the spiritual master of Agni yoga, a mystical mixture of Eastern and Western philosophy. Walking into Aurora feels like walking into a sacred space. Every afternoon a small group of Aurora students gather for tea and spiritual fellowship. The day I visited, Arabic Sufi music was softly playing. The bookstore also stocks jewelry, unique world music, healing tools and herbal remedies. Aurora is named after Babekov's mysteri-

YOGA | ESOTERIC GROUPS | WITCHCRAFT | OCCULT UNDERGROUND | **BOOKS** | UFOS | BOTANICAS | TANTRA | ASTROLOGERS & PSYCHICS |

ous spiritual teacher, who works only with a small, select group of students. "I can't say much about her, but I can say that she is an ascended master," says Babekov. "In order to do her work, she does not want to be revealed. But someday, she will make her presence known."

## BUTALA EMPORIUM
*37-46 74th Street in Jackson Heights*
*718-899-5590*
*www.indousplaza.com*
*Hours: daily from 10am-9pm*
*Closest subway: 7 to 74th Street/Roosevelt Avenue*
Located in "Little India" Queens, Butala is a must-stop for those interested in esoteric Hinduism. It also has one of the most intriguing bookstores in the city with titles on Hindu deities, tantra, astrology, yoga and even Western occultism. I was amused to find an Indian-published edition of Tantra Without Tears by Christopher Hyatt and S. Jason Black. This is one-shopping for all of your puja needs - jyoti lights, incense, statues of deities, incense holders and even a large brass Om candle holder. The neighborhood is also very cool and you could spend an entire day poking through the stores. The Jackson Diner, located across the street, is in my opinion, the best Indian buffet in the city. Strolling through the neighborhood, you will feel as though you are in India. And you may even find that perfect "sari" you have been looking for.

## EAST-WEST BOOKS
*78 Fifth Avenue between 14th and 13th Street*
*212-243- 5994*
*www.himalayanyoga.com*
*Hours: M-Sat: 10am-7:30pm; Sunday: 11am-6:30pm*
*Closest subway: 4/5/6/N/R/L to 14th Street*
Run by the Himalayan Institute, East-West Books has one of the best collections of books in the city, geared toward "Eastern" spirituality. Swami Rama opened the bookstore in the early 1970s, to serve the yoga community. Their astrology section is really strong, along with the Eastern yoga section. They are heavy with the works of Eastern gurus and also have a good collection of wind chimes, candles, fountains and meditation pillows. A lot of interesting characters hang-out there. The basement of the bookstore is used for yoga classes by the Himalaya Institute. It is a nice place to spend a Saturday afternoon, and right down the street is the wonderful Vege-City Diner, for a complete, enlightened day.

## EILEEN J. GARRETT LIBRARY

*Parapsychology Foundation*
*228 East 71st Street between 2nd and 3rd Avenues*
*212-628-1550*
*www.parapsychology.org*
*Hours: M-F: noon-5pm; closed July and August*
*Closest subway: 6 to 68th Street*

Many consider the library at the Parapsychology Foundation the finest in the world for psychic research, occultism, spiritualism and mysticism. The library contains a collection of more than 10,000 volumes, along with hundreds of related videotapes. An esotericist could spend days browsing through the rare volumes from authors like spiritualist Allan Kardec, and newer authors like Hans Holzer. While there, I spied books on ceremonial magic, voodoo, along with a huge section on ghosts and poltergeist activity. Although the library does not lend books, researchers can spend the day taking notes and making copies in the library's photocopy room. Eileen J. Garret was a famous medium and the founder of the Parapsychology Foundation. The Foundation also has its own publishing house and recently re-released Garret's ground-breaking book Adventures in the Supernormal, and Tony Cornell's Investigating the Paranormal. Folks at the Foundation consider themselves scientists and seek to investigate psychic phenomena through laboratory methods. The library has served New York City for more than 50 years through several different incarnations. The Foundation may be changing locations, so check the website before making the trek there.

## ELYSIAN FIELDS

*1884 McDonald Avenue between Avenue P and*
*Clinton Street in Brooklyn*
*718-627-8442*
*Hours: daily from 11am-7pm*
*Closest subway: F train to Avenue P*

Alice Stuart and her daughter Julie are a perfect team, Alice is a tarot reader and Julie specializes in ritual baths and soap making. Together they operate Elysian Fields, an eclectic Brooklyn store which stocks everything from Wiccan and Santeria supplies to Buddhist and Hindu goods. "We have an eclectic spirituality," says Julie. "We add a personal touch to what we sell." The Stuarts have been working in the magical field for a number of years, but only opened their store in 2001. They sell a wide selection of incense, magical oils, dried herbs and blessed candles, along with the magical soaps and baths that Julie custom makes for her clients. In Greek mythology, the Elysian Fields were a place where the gods went to gather and be safe. In Brooklyn, Elysian Fields is a magical gathering place for like-minded individuals who want a spiritual boost.

## EMILY SELLON MEMORIAL LIBRARY OF THE THEOSOPHICAL SOCIETY

*240 East 53rd Street between 2nd and 3rd Avenues*
*212-753-3835*
*www.theosophy-ny.org*
*Tues-Wed-Fri: 11am-6:00pm; Sat: 12noon-5pm*
*Closest subway: 5/6 train to 53rd Street*
Theosophical Society librarian and historian Michael Gomes has turned the Theosophical Society Library into an eclectic and vitally important library for the esoteric community in New York. Gomes has collected a number of rare and out-of-print metaphysical and spiritual books. Gomes is a fountain of information, not only about Theosophy and Helena Petrovna Blavatsky (HPB), but also Western hermeticism and occultism. He is considered one of the world's foremost authorities on the history of the Theosophical Society. The library reflects Gomes' well-read metaphysical interests. In addition to works by and about HBP, the library has diverse and rare titles on metaphysics, ceremonial magic, Kabbalah, Sufism and even sex magic. Anyone can visit the library to conduct research. In order to take out a book, you can join the library for $20 a year, or simply become a member of the NY Theosophical Society. The library is names after Emily Sellon, a former New York Theosophical Society member and benefactor of the library.

## ENCHANTMENTS

*341 East 9th Street between 1st and 2nd Avenues*
*212-228-4394*
*www.enchantmentsinnyc.com*
*Hours: M-Sat: 12:30-8:30pm; Sun: 1-7:30 pm*
*Closest subway: 6 to Astor Place; R to 8th Street*
For the past 20 years, Enchantments has been Manhattan's best store for witchcraft and goddess supplies. Carol Bulzone, who originally opened the store with Lady Rhea in 1982, still runs the store and is one of the elders in the New York Wiccan community. Enchantments has an amazing collection of herbs, incense and oils for "every magickal need," along with candles, magical baths and talis-

mans. The store also rivals many botanicas as well, carrying Santeria supplies like Florida Water, Blue Balls "anil" and even Eleggua heads "it will save you a trek to Spanish Harlem". The staff is knowledgeable and seems passionate about paganism and Wicca. Joe Zuchowski, who runs the Enchantments Grove with his partner Jezibell, can be found at the store nearly every day, giving advice and sharing his experiences in the occult. You never know what subject will be discussed when you walk into Enchantments. The day I was there, the discussion ranged from the history of Chaos Magick, to the occult involvement of the Third Reich. Enchantments has a great occult book selection, heavy on witchcraft, Thelema and Western magic. Joe is also an excellent tarot reader and is available most days for consultations.

## LIVINGSTON MASONIC LIBRARY
*71 West 23rd Street between 6th and*
*7th Avenues, 14th floor*
*212-337-6620*
*www.livmalib.org*
*Hours: M, W-F: 9am-4:30pm; Tue: 12-8pm*
*Closest subway: 1/9 to 23rd Street*
The Livingston Masonic Library has one of the best collections of Masonic books in the world, including rare letters and correspondence. The library shares space with the Masonic Museum, featuring Masonic art works, along with items like Norman Vincent Peale's personal desk. The library has more than 60,000 volumes in a temperature controlled room. Only lodge members can take out books; however the general public is allowed to use the library for research purposes. In addition to nearly every book that has been printed about Masonry, the library also has a large selection on occultism and esoterica. The occult section includes books by Manly Hall and volumes on the "Golden Dawn" and Western mystery teachings. Library director Tom Savini says that the library has a number of rare volumes, and also keeps up with recently released materials.

## LUCIS TRUST LIBRARY
*120 Wall Street between Front and*
*South Streets, 24th Floor*
*212-292-0707*
*www.lucistrust.org*
*Hours: M-Fri: 9:30am-4:30pm*
*Closest subway stop: 1/9 to Wall Street*
*(walk east on Wall Street)*
Lucis Trust Library has one of the more unique col-

| YOGA | ESOTERIC GROUPS | WITCHCRAFT | OCCULT UNDERGROUND | **BOOKS** | UFOS | BOTANICAS | TANTRA | ASTROLOGERS & PSYCHICS |

lections of metaphysical, world religion and meditation books in the city. The Library is run out of the
office of the Lucis Trust, the occult organization
founded by mystic Alice Bailey. Bailey wrote twen-
ty-four books on behalf of her teacher, known only
as the "Tibetan." The books laid out a new "spiritual
hierarchy of the planet" and set the foundation for
the New Age movement. The primary focus of the
library, of course, is the work of Bailey. The library is
also heavy on Theosophy, new world religion, world
government and philosophy. It is free to join the
library - you simply need to fill out a library card and
provide two references. You can take out two books
at a time and keep the books for a month.

## MAGICKAL REALMS/ENCHANTED CANDLE SHOPPE

*2937 Wilkinson Avenue between Westchester
and Hobart Avenues in Bronx*
*718-892-5350*
*www.magickalrealms.com*
*Hours: M-Sat: 11am-7pm*
*Closest subway stop: 6 train to Pelham Bay
(last stop) and walk three blocks*
Magickal Realms is a charming store, specializing
in witchcraft, run by Lady Rhea (see feature article)
and her partner, Lady Zoradia. The store stocks a
full supply of candles, oils and supplies for spells.
Lady Rhea has been in the business for more than
30 years and was one of the original owners of
Enchantments in the East Village. After she left
Enchantments, Lady Rhea opened her own store in
Greenwich Village in 1992, and later moved to the
Bronx in 1995. Lady Rhea is often on hand to give
tarot and spiritual readings. The store itself reflects
Lady Rhea's eclectic spiritual tastes. Statues of
Catholic saints, Hindu deities and Wiccan goddesses
all occupy the same space. The store's specialty is
candle magic, since Lady Rhea developed the candle
magic spell system with her book Enchanted Candle
Spell Book. Magickal Realms also has excellent
training classes for those interested in witchcraft
and paganism.

## MORGANA'S CHAMBER

*242 West 10th Street between Hudson
and Bleecker*
*212-243-3415*
*www.members.tripod/com/morganaschamber*
*Hours: T-Fri: 2pm-8pm; Sat: 1pm-8pm;
Sun: 1pm-6pm*

*Closest subway: 1/9 to Christopher Street*
Morgana's Chamber bills itself as a "Cauldron of Transformation." Located in the heart of Greenwich Village, the store offers a nice collection of incense, oils, herbs and ritual tools for the Wicca and pagan community. The store is cramped with books on various aspects of witchcraft and even has an "occult fiction" section. What makes the store special, however, is the presence of the owner, Morgana SidheRaven. Morgana - a practicing witch since the late 1970s - gives tarot and psychic readings and teaches a number of workshops. Morgana gained national prominence recently after her "cruelty-free" incense blends were featured in several books by Silver RavenWolf. Morgana is a member of the Black Forest Clan. Her store regularly hosts other witches and pagans for book-signings and workshops. Astrologer/tarot master Lexa Rosean also gives readings every Wednesday and Friday.

### MYSTICKAL WONDERS
*451-A Jewett Avenue at Forest Avenue*
*in Staten Island*
*718-816-1234*
*Hours: M-Fri: noon-7pm; Sat: noon-5 pm*
*Closest subway: From Manhattan, take the Staten Island Ferry and then the 66 Bus to Jewett Avenue*
Mystickal Wonders has been dubbed the "Witchcraft store of Staten Island." Long-time psychic and witch Adele Basile took over the store, formerly known as Wizards Wonderland, in 2001. Basile has increased the stock of Wiccan supplies and carries one of the largest selections of wands, chalices, altar items, tarot cards, herbs and oils in the Tri-State area. Basile also teaches workshops nearly every Sunday, like Witchcraft 101 and Fundamentals in Tarot. Basile also organizes the yearly Halloween Witches Ball in Staten Island. Basile's spiritual path is eclectic. She is a reiki master, channeler, spiritual counselor, and an ordained minister. However, she is best known for her tarot readings; for the past 40 years she has been giving readings in Staten Island. "Many people come into the store out of curiousity," says Basile. "But in reality, they have been guided here because there is something they need to learn. My role is as a teacher. I am one of the white light healers."

### NEW YORK ASTROLOGY CENTER BOOKSTORE
*370 Lexington Avenue between 40th and*
*41st Streets, suite 416*
*212-949-7211*

YOGA | ESOTERIC GROUPS | WITCHCRAFT | OCCULT UNDERGROUND | **BOOKS** | UFOS | BOTANICAS | TANTRA | ASTROLOGERS & PSYCHICS |

www.afund.com/store
Hours: Mon: 10am-6pm; Wed: 10am-7pm;
Fri: 10am-5pm
Closest subway: 4/5/6/7/S to Grand Central/
42nd Street

The New York Astrology Center Bookstore has been referred to as the "world"s astrology bookstore." It has the best astrology collection in the city - everything from old classics by Sephariel to the latest works by Steve Forrest. For astrology students, you can find great out-of-print and rare gems here. The bookstore has been around since the late 1960s and is part of noted financial astrologer Henry Weingarten"s Astrology Center. The center itself now offers astrology seminars with Mitchell Scott Lewis. Both Weingarten and Lewis are often around and are extremely gracious if you have any astrological questions. For the serious astrologer, a stop at this bookstore is a must.

## NEW YORK OPEN CENTER BOOKSTORE

83 Spring Street between Broadway and
Lafayette Street
212-219-2527, ext. 5
www.opencenter.org
Hours: M-Sat: 12-10pm; Sun: 12-6pm
Closest subway: N/R to Prince Street;
6 to Spring Street

The Open Center Bookstore specializes in books related to the numerous spiritual classes held at the center. The store as a section devoted to course books on Polarity Therapy, Reflexology, herbology, massage, yoga - and even Coyote Healing. The center is particularly strong on Native American, African and Latin American diaspora religious books, and has a section for Spanish-language esoteric titles. Keeping with the Open Center philosophy, the store carries an excellent selection of books on the Western esoteric tradition, Kabbalah, as well as Hindu and Buddhist philosophy.

## OTHER WORLDLY WAXES ... AND WHATEVER

131 East 7th Street between Avenue A
and 1st Avenue
212-260-9188
www.candletherapy.com
Hours: M-Sat: 1pm-10pm; Sun: 2pm-10pm
Closest subway stop: 6 to Astor Place;
R to 8th Street

Other Worldly Waxes owner Dr. Catherine Riggs-Bergesen has helped popularize this powerful white magic self-help technique with her Candle Therapy. This ancient technique merges psychology and magic. By ritualistically carving a seven-day candle with the appropriate sigil and magical oils, Dr. Bergensen claims that you can get a new job, find love, expand your business and increase your prosperity  Dr. Bergensen, a psychotherapist, also teachings classes on candle carving, tarot and oils and incense blending at her East Village store. The store has an excellent collection of candles, oils, incenses, tarot cards, along with books on witchcraft and white magic. The store also sells Candle Therapy Kits, for specific intentions, such as healing, passion, success and love. While many occult stores offer their own "candle carving" services, Dr. Bergensen contends that the magic is more powerful if you carve the candle yourself.

## PASTIMES
*5 Continental Avenue between Queens Boulevard and Austin Street in Forest Hills*
*718-263-4747*
*Hours: M-Sun 10:30am-7:30pm*
*Closest subway: E/F/V/G/R to 71st Street*
ContinentalPastimes bookstore has been described as an "escape from every day stress." Pastimes is one of the only metaphysical bookstores in Queens. "A lot of people are surprised when they find us," says Dino, an employee. "They are walking next to the noisy traffic on Queen Boulevard and suddenly they turn a corner into an alley and here we are. It is like walking into another world." Opened in 1986 by Shelly Wollensky, the small, eclectic store is described as a "serenity shop" and offers books, meditation tapes, and self-help products. "We have a little bit for everyone," says Dino. "We have products for Buddhists, Wiccans, Christians and even Muslim products." The store operates by word of mouth and is "like a family." "Our customers become our friends," says Dino.

## PHENOMENATURE
*9 St. Mark's Place between 2nd and 3rd Avenues*
*917-744-8721*
*Hours: M-Sat: 11am-7pm; Sun: 1-7pm*
*Closest subway: 6 to Astor Place; N/R to 8th Street*
Phenomenature specializes in rocks, crystals and minerals for esoteric use. Phenomenature is located inside the store "In the Woods," and has developed a loyal following of healers, massage therapists and metaphysicians. "I was guided here by my spirit

guides," says "chakra balancing" healer Shirley Gilbreath, who is a regular customer. "I come back regularly because the staff is so knowledgeable about the metaphysical qualities of the stones." Indeed, on a recent afternoon, Phenomenature employee Meredith Genin was demonstrating to a customer how to "seal her aura," every morning before going out into Manhattan streets. "You simply have to protect yourself in this city through metaphysical means," says Genin, who uses crystals and herbs in her own healing practice. Genin says that the human body "resonates" to certain crystals and minerals because there are crystals and minerals in our bloodstream and bone structure. "We are carbon-based creatures, but there is a theory that someday we will become crystal-based beings, much in the same way that many extraterrestrials are crystal beings," she says. Phenomenature categorizes each stone with its "healing property," and the staff can often advise what stones are appropriate for a specific case. "Many people think that the use of crystals and minerals for healing is New Age," says manager Eva Zucker. "But in reality, it is an indigenous practice. Every culture has its own use of minerals. There is a lot we can learn from these ancient practices."

## QUEST BOOK SHOP
*240 East 53 Street between Second and*
*Third Avenues*
*212-758-5521*
*www.questbookshop.com*
*Hours: M-F: 11am-8pm; Sat: noon-8pm;*
*Sun: noon-5pm*
*Closest subway: 6/E/F to 51st Street*
Quest Bookstore offers a "tranquil oasis in the heart of midtown." "A lot of people are surprised to find us here in mid-town," says manager Lynn Trotman. "We are the only esoteric bookstore in this area." The New York Theosophical Society runs the bookstore, and its influence shows; Quest has the definitive collection of works by Theosophical Society founder Madame Helena Blavatsky, Alice Bailey and Annie Besant. The staff is knowledgeable and eclectic, and they don't mind if you spend your time browsing its excellent selection of books on astrology, Kabbalah, yoga and Eastern and Western esoterica. During the past two years or so, the selection at the bookstore has really grown, particularly the section on Western magic and paganism. The store usually has a tarot reader on hand for those who want their

future known, but call in advance to reserve a reading. Quest is a great place to browse, particularly before the nightly lectures at the Theosophical Society next door.

## ROCK STAR N.Y.C.
*150 West 28th Street between 6th and*
*7th Avenues, suite 201B*
*212-675-3065*
*Hours: W-Sat: 1-6pm*
*Closest subway: 1/9 to 28th Street*
"If someone is buying a metaphysical tool made out of a crystal or mineral in New York City, they are buying it from me," says Walter Streng, co-owner of Rock Star NYC. Rock Star NYC has one of the best and most inexpensive collections of rocks and crystals, specifically geared toward metaphysical use, in the city. Streng has been in the business for 17 years and travels throughout the world looking for high-quality crystal products. For instance, Rock Star NYC has 17 different kinds of massage wands made out of crystals and minerals. It also stocks crystal pendulums, crystal skulls, inexpensive Amethyst "cathedrals," and even rare Scolecite, which "opens communication with other worlds, ancient civilizations... and extra-terrestrial communication." "It is our belief that the crystals are alive and that they have energy as part of their being," says Streng, who wholesales crystals to more than 200 New Age shops around the country. Streng passionately points out that many of his crystals are more than 20 million years old. He holds up a rare double-terminated quartz crystal from China, which has droplets of water inside. "Just think. This water is ancient. It is an amazing combination of fire and water energy," says Streng. Rock Star NYC has become a favorite of architects, interior designers, healers and feng shui consultants in the city. "One of the best feng shui cures for a dark corner in a home is a crystal," says Streng. "They generate a great deal of light - as well as positive energy."

## RUDOLPH STEINER BOOKSTORE
*138 West 15th Street at Avenue of the Americas*
*212-242-8945*
*Hours: T-W-Fri: 5pm-7pm; Thu: 5pm-7:30pm;*
*Sat: noon-3pm*
*Closest subway: 1/9/2/3 to 14th Street*
During his prolific life, Austrian mystic Rudolph Steiner wrote 40 books and gave more than 6,000 lectures. The Rudolph Steiner Bookstore has nearly

every book and lecture that Steiner ever gave. It
also stocks authors who have written about Steiner
or who are consistent with his philosophy of
Anthroposophy, like Emmanual Swedenbourgh
and contemporary writer Marko Pogacnik. The
bookstore is run by the New York Anthroposophy
Society, the spiritual group that Steiner founded.
The small, tidy store has the feel of a salon. Patrons
are invited to sit and read in the store's chairs and
sofa. When I was there, there was a lively discussion
on the esoteric implications of the World Trade
Center attack. "One Anthroposophist claimed that
the falling towers activated a "ley line" that runs
through Manhattan, awaking the elemental beings
that live in Central Park." Steiner was a colorful,
magical personality and his spirit certainly lives
on at the bookstore that shares his name.

### STICK, STONE AND BONE
*111 Christopher Street between Bleecker
and Hudson Streets*
*212-807-7024*
*Hours: Sun-Thu: 12-10pm; Fri/Sat: 12-midnight*
*Closest subway: 1/9 to Christopher Street*
Stick, Stone and Bone is "not just a store, but a
place to where people come to get spiritual assistance from books and the mineral kingdom." Opened
in 1990, the Greenwich Village store combines co-
owners Linda Curti's interest in metaphysics with
Yolanda Miller's interest in Native American spirituality and crystals. "The marriage of the two interests has created a very special place," says store
employee Lee Newton.  The store has a wonderful
collection of crystals, dream catchers, tarot cards,
drums, rattles and Native American jewelry. It has
a nicely displayed book section, with titles like
Michael Harner's Way of the Shaman, and other
books devoted to indigenous beliefs. The store
has a very clear, bright energy and attracts an equal
number of spiritual seekers and tourists who have
come to Christopher Street.

### SUFI BOOKS
*227 West Broadway between Franklin
and White Streets*
*212-334-5212*
*www.sufibooks.com*
*Hours: T-Sat: 1-7:30pm*
*Closest subway: 1/9 to Franklin Street; A/C/E to
Canal Street*
For more than ten years, Sufi Books in lower

Manhattan served the Islamic esoteric community. Lex Hixon originally opened the bookstore and turned the Tribeca hide-away into one of the best bookstores in the world catering to the mystical path of Islam. From Rumi to Ibn Al-Arabi, Sufi books had the largest selection of mystic Islamic books and Sufi music anywhere. However, as of early 2003, the management decided to convert the bookstore into a reading room. Although it still offers a decent selection of books for sale, the shelves have thinned considerably. The Nur-Ashki Al-Jerrahi order of Sufis - which was founded by Hixon - still calls Sufi Books its home. The organization now concentrates more on the lectures, talks, classes and workshops at its space, located next to the bookstore. "Most of our books are still available," says an employee of the store. "The store remains a peaceful place where you can gain clarity on your life."

## THREE JEWELS OUTREACH CENTER AND BOOKSTORE

*211 East 5th Street between Bowery and 2nd Avenue*
*212-475-6650*
*www.threejewels.org*
*Hours: daily from noon-7pm*
*Closest subway: 6 to Astor Place; R to 8th Street*
You'll get more than a caffeine buzz when you walk into the Three Jewels Center in the East Village. The coffeehouse/spiritual center has a unique, edgy spiritual vibe. On any given evening, you may find a meditation going on, a spiritual reading or class. The center was founded by students of Geshe Michael Roach, director of the Asian Classics Institute of New York and is now run by volunteers. The director, Debra Ballier, is one of the few women in the West to have studied in a Tibetan monastery. The students at Three Jewels follow the Gelukpa order of Tibetan Buddhism, which began 500 years ago and is the tradition of His Holiness the Dalai Lama. The center sponsors daily meditations and classes in the evening. The front of the center includes a "health café" with coffee, tea and sandwiches, along with tables and free internet access. The back room of the center has a small lending library of Buddhist books and cushions for seated meditation.

## WEISER BOOKS

*York, Maine*
*207-363-7253*
*www.Weiserantiquarian.com*

YOGA | ESOTERIC GROUPS | WITCHCRAFT | OCCULT UNDERGROUND | **BOOKS** | UFOS | BOTANICAS | TANTRA | ASTROLOGERS & PSYCHICS |

For those who miss browsing at Weiser's Books, formerly located on East 24th Street, you can still find Donald Weiser at the latest incarnation of his bookstore in York, Maine. Many faithful customers now make the trek to the Weiser warehouse, located just off the Route 95 York exit, on Raydon Road. The store is open 10am-5pm during the weekdays and still offers the world's best selection of hard to find, out-of-print, used and rare esoteric books. Since selling his publishing house to Red Wheel Books, Donald Weiser has concentrated on building stock, and now has two floors filled with metaphysical and occult titles. Weiser has a very strong collection of Aleister Crowley and Kenneth Grant works, and rare editions by writers like Austin Spare. Weiser also specializes in limited edition esoteric works you name it and Weiser has it. "We have one of the strongest esoteric collections in the world now," says Weiser. "It is surprising how many of our former customers from New York have visited us in Maine."

# UFO Groups:
# There are Aliens Among Us

New York City is not exactly Area 51, but it has had its share of UFO encounters and strange events. The most famous UFO incident occurred on November 30, 1989, when Brooklyn resident Linda Cortile - a mother of two - was allegedly abducted by a UFO from her bedroom window. What made this case unusual was that it was witnessed by two police officers sitting in their patrol car on FDR Drive, as well as the former Secretary General of the United Nations, Javier Perez de Cuellar, who happened to be looking out of his window as the UFO abduction occurred.

Dubbed the "Brooklyn Bridge Abduction," the witnesses described how Cortile was suspended in a "blue beam of light" and lifted into the UFO, accompanied by "three alien figures." New York native and UFO investigator Budd Hopkins made the case famous with his acclaimed book *Witnessed*.

Despite the fact that Manhattan is one of the most densely populated areas in the world, UFO sightings abound. There are those in the UFO community who claim that the mysterious Men in Black are active in Manhattan, along with aliens who have taken human bodies and inter-mingle with humans.

For those who believe that they have had an alien encounter, New York City has plenty of support groups. Some are mainstream groups, like Budd Hopkins' Intruders Foundation, while others have veered into the world of conspiracy theory, like Francine Vale's Millennium Group.

Interestingly, many in the UFO community have approached the interaction between human and aliens in terms of religious experience. New Jersey native Ashayana Deane, formerly known as Anna Hayes, has founded her own religious organization called the Azurite Temple, based upon the teachings of the "ETs (Extraterrestrials)" known as the "Guardian Alliance." She claims that the aliens taught her a spiritual development system called *Keylontic Science*, which she now teaches to others. Similarly, the Raelians, who have a New York Chapter, founded a religion on the teachings of claimed UFO abductee Claude Voirlhon, who became known as "Rael."

Many occultists believe that most UFO experiences are nothing but the interactions between humans and astral entities that exist on the "inner plane." Are UFOs extra-terrestrial - or are they "inter-dimensional"? This is a question which will be debated in the UFO community for years.

## DISCLOSURE NETWORK/NEW YORK
*www.dnny.org; www.disclosureproject.com*
*917-701-9033*
*coordinator@dnny.org*
*Meets: first Sunday of every month from 2-5pm*
*at the LGBT Community Center at 208 West 13th*
*Street, Room 410, Greenwich Village*
Did you know that former President Ronald Reagan
had two UFO experiences? According to Dr. Stephen
Greer, Reagan was one of many US government officials who have had contact with or witnessed UFO
phenomena. Greer began the Disclosure Project in
1993 to "identify first- hand military and government witnesses to UFO events." Greer's goal is to
have the US government hold open, secrecy-free
hearings on the UFO/Extraterrestrial presence on
and around Earth. Greer also wants the government
to publicly release its "alien technology," like
advanced energy and propulsion systems, to provide "solutions to global environmental challenges."
Disclosure Network/New York (DN/NY), an unofficial affiliate of Greer's Virginia-based organization,
meets once a month in Manhattan to discuss government UFO cover-ups and listen to guest speakers. Recent lectures have included Shawn and Clay
Pickering's presentation on The Zepruder Tape
and the Occult Significance Behind the
Assassination of JFK. DN/NY was formed in 2001
by a group of New York City volunteers involved
with Greer's Center for the Study of
Extraterrestrial Intelligence (CSETI), an organization that works to initiate contact with ETs
through high-powered transmitters. DN/NY is a
"grass-roots" organization that also seeks to publi-
cize the 400 hours of videotaped testimony of
government and military witnesses who have been
"first-hand observers of UFO activity."

## EARTH MATTERS
*177 Ludlow Street between Orchard and*
*Essex Streets*
*212-475-4180*
*www.earthmatters.com*
*Closest subway: F to 2nd Avenue*
Isaac Tapiero opened Earth Matters in 2001, as a
health food store, holistic food cafe, and spiritual
center. The three-level store opens up into a roof-
garden and has a neon Kabbalistic "Tree of Life"
sign on the ceiling of the cafe. Tapiero was an
accomplished dancer with the Israeli Ballet
Company, but a little more than 8 years ago his life

began to transform after he began studying at the Kabbalah Center in Jerusalem. His spiritual studies led him to study crop circles, the giant designs found in fields, primarily in England. When he is not in his lower East Side store, he spends much of his time in the field researching crop circles and UFO phenomena; he travels to England regularly to visit the newest sites. Once a month he gives lectures on his latest findings.

His conclusion: many crop circles are of human origin, but there are a significant number which are of non-human origin. He bases this conclusion on his studies of the grass in crop circles. Man-made crop circles have grass that has clearly been broken by manual means; but the grass in "genuine" crop circles has internally been bent, as if the molecules of the grass themselves have altered. Tapiero contends that it does not really matter if some of the crop circles are from humans with planks and giant rolling pins, he contends they all are ritualistic communications aimed at altering the consciousness of the human race. "I know people who have made crop circles in England," Tapiero says. "They get into a very meditative state and channel a higher force when they are making the designs. Many times they are surprised when they see the final result." Tapiero contends that crop circles are "signs of awakening." Check the Earth Matters website to find out when Tapiero's next lecture is. Earth Matters also hosts the Millennium Group, a UFO group also reviewed in this section. Both the roof garden and second-floor internet cafe are open to the public and feature an extensive spiritual and UFO book collection. The store also offers daily yoga classes, as well as special workshops on healing, nutrition and spiritual growth.

### FLYING SAUCER CAFÉ
*494 Atlantic Avenue between Third Avenue and Nevin Street in Brooklyn*
*718-522-1383*
*Hours: M-F: 7:30am-7pm; Sat/Sun: 8:30am-7pm*
*Closest subway: B/N/R to Pacific Street; 2/3/4 to Atlantic Avenue*
Julie Ipcar and her husband John Brien opened the Flying Saucer Café in 1999 to offer an "alien-friendly" cafe in their Borum Hill neighborhood. They both are UFO-enthusiasts and science fiction fans. Ipcar's father, Robert, wrote the science fiction series, Children of Orion. The café is decorated with alien memorabilia, including numerous UFO related items that customers have brought in. The café has also

# Dr. James Graves: UFOs and the Dalai Lama

Dr. James Graves is well-known in New York City to thousands of students for his 26 years of service as a teacher at the Art and Design High School on 57th Street.

However, since his retirement he has become a familiar face in the New York esoteric community as a healer, UFO-ologist, and spiritual adept.

"When I was growing up, I always felt different," says Graves, who was raised by his grandparents in Virginia. "I had a difficult time relating to anyone. I literally felt like an alien, before I knew what the term really meant."

After years of metaphysical study and meditation, Graves has come to the conclusion that he literally is an alien, from the planet Arcturus to be exact.

Graves is part of a growing number of people who believe that they are "walk-ins," that is beings from a higher dimension who take over a person's body after the person's soul decides to "check out."

One of the more famous walk-ins is Drunvalo Melchizedek, who developed the *Flower of Life* workshops. Melchizedek claims that the Egyptian deity Thoth gave him a meditation technique of the New Age called the Merkaba Meditation.

"I never felt comfortable in my body, I always felt like a fish out of water," says Graves. "A walk-in is a soul being from a higher consciousness who inherits the body and also takes on the karma of the soul which previously inhabited the body."

As a result of his awakening, Graves has come into contact with other "walk-ins," as well as angelic beings that have incarnated and are walking the streets of Manhattan. Like UFOs, they are visible to the naked eye, but most people simply don't notice them, he says.

For instance, in 2002, he says that he was approached by the Archangel Metatron in a Burger King on Canal Street. Graves had just been initiated into Kriya Yoga at the Sufi Bookstore by Swami Hariharanda's group and was unwinding with a Diet-Coke at the restaurant. He said that a "well-dressed African man, with a tiny head and large shoulders" sat down next to him. The mysterious man engaged Graves in a discussion about the time-coding of the Giza Pyramids.

As the man got up to leave, he walked over to Graves and told him: "I was sent to tell you that you are on the right path." Graves said several psychics and adepts had confirmed that Metatron was, indeed, walking the streets of New York City and had spoken to Graves.

Many walk-ins feel that they have a special mission to complete while on Earth, as teachers and light-workers.

Graves is an adept, teacher and healer with the Rocky Mountain Mystery School (RMMS), located in Utah, reportedly one of seven mystery schools active on the planet. He is also a student of the Dalai Lama and the head of the local Nechung Foundation, a Tibetan foundation affiliated with the Dalai Lama. He recently spent two weeks in Dharmasala, studying directly with the Dalai Lama.

"I have always felt very close to the Tibetans," says Graves. "They have an ancient culture. They just don't talk spirituality, they live it."

As a healer, he does the *22-Strand DNA Activation*, a mystical technique that allows the client to access higher energy from the cosmos. Graves says that the Earth is about to enter the photon belt, which will increase the consciousness of the planet. The Earth will be bathed in "liquid light," which will create a "new spiritual vibration." Light workers have been creating new templates on the planet to anchor this light.

As the consciousness on the planet is raised, many people may not be ready for the increased energy. As their awareness is increased many people "will think they are losing their minds," says Graves.

Part of his work is to prepare people for this upcoming paradigm change, by teaching meditation techniques and working with local groups to educate people about the changes. He says that he is also working with "Indigo Children" and "Crystal Children," highly-evolved beings who have incarnated onto the planet to assist in the transition.

"People are feeling the energy shift on the planet and it is causing a great deal of stress," says Graves. "We are on the verge of becoming the paradise that we always dreamed the Earth would be."

As a result of the changes, Graves says that extraterrestrials "ETs" have taken a renewed interest in the Earth and are carefully studying what is happening, to see if we will actually evolve sufficiently to become part of the "Galactic Federation."

"We (the Earth) are actually the third-world, as far as planets go. The Earth was destroyed twice by nuclear holocaust, once in Atlantis and also during the ancient civilization of Mu," says Graves. "However, particularly after millions of people recently came together against the latest Iraq war, the hierarchy of light believes that the Earth is now ready for the next step. We have a chance to get it right."

However, to complicate matters, Graves says that there is an inter-galactic war being fought on Earth by good and bad aliens from

>>>

**<<<**
the star system Draconis, a battle which began far from the Earth.

Graves says that he has been involved in UFO research ever since his first encounter with an ET in France in the early 1970s. He was on a teaching sabbatical and witnessed a UFO near the village of St. Germaine LeBelle. The encounter left him nearly blinded - he woke up the next morning with a gray film over his eyes.

Since then, he sighted many UFOs, particularly in Utah, near the headquarters of the RMMS. Unlike many UFO researchers, he believes that there are both good and bad aliens who are interacting with the human race.

"It is all part of the divine plan," says Graves. "God created these alien intelligences, just as God created us."

He says that the number of people having ET experiences is increasing - and will increase more during the next few years - given the number of "stargates" and "portals" which are being activated on the Earth.

He also says, as a walk-in, it is no coincidence that he chose to live in New York City.

"New York is playing a key role in this," says Graves. "Everyone is here - ETs, angels and light-workers. This is where the drama is being played out."

*Dr. Graves can be reached for healing and consultations at (212) 644-8345.*

---

sponsored Howard Elgin's UFO group SPACE, and holds a Friday night "alien film festival" in the outdoor garden. "This neighborhood is very unique, it reminds me of the television show Sesame Street," says Ipcar. "Everyone knows everyone and we have a number of regulars who come in everyday." The cafe has sandwiches, pastries and coffee that "is out of this world," the café advertises. "We have also had a few aliens come in for coffee," jokes Ipcar. "I think extraterrestrials like to visit Brooklyn for vacation."

### PHIL GRUBER
*212-462-9257 (voice mail)*
*happynoodle1728@hotmail.com*
Attending a Phil Gruber lecture is a mind-expanding experience. When I first met Gruber, he was giving a talk on the Kathara Healing System, which was developed by his former wife, UFO contactee Ashayana Deane, the author of the Voyager series of books. Gruber pulls together diverse streams of history into one grand conspiracy theory, pitting the so-called alien "Guardian Alliance" (the good aliens) against the "Zeta Reticulans" (the bad aliens). It is an exhilarating and mind-bending cosmology that spans from the days of Atlantis to our present day

political system. Some of Gruber's observations: the movie The Wizard of Oz? An occult mystery play embedded with secret messages. The US-led attack on Iraq? A battle over a star gate. Gruber contends that humanity is about to take a quantum leap forward in consciousness - with a little help from our ET friends. One of the main helps that the ETs have given us, Phil says, is Keylontic Science, an elaborate meditation system that Gruber claim dates back to the days of Atlantis.

Gruber himself has a very interesting background. Gruber was initiated into the Ordo Templi Orientis (OTO), by famed occultist Grady McMurty. Gruber also became a member of the A.: A.: (Astrum Argenteum), the secretive occult training group developed by Aleister Crowley, and spent many years studying Crowley's Thelemic magic system.

Gruber, however, says that he found the keys to all truths when he met Deane - then known as Anna Hayes - at a Drunvalo Melchizadek workshop in New York City in 1999. Deane asked several questions to Meclchizadek during the question and answer period that Melchizadek reportedly could not fully answer. Gruber says that the crowd was so impressed with her that they crowded around her after the workshop. At the time, Deane was living in a trailer park in New Jersey, and had not yet published her Voyager series of books.

Deane claims that, as a young girl, she was being prepared by the Zeta Reticulans to become a "breeder" for them, to create a hybrid alien race on the Earth. She says she was "rescued" from the Reticulans by the "Guardian Alliance," who taught her the true history and future of the human race, along with a series of spiritual techniques for "spiritual ascension." Part of the master plan for the "ascension" of the planet includes groups of highly developed souls incarnating onto the earth at this time known as the "Indigo Children," because of the indigo color of their auras. Although no longer married to Deane, Gruber remains a believer and promoter of her system. Gruber considers New York City his home base, though spends much of the year overseas, primarily in Asia, lecturing. He comes through the city several times a year to give weekend workshops and conduct Kathara Healing sessions. To get on his e-mail list, write him at the above e-mail or leave a voice message on his New York phone.

**INTRUDERS FOUNDATION**
*PO Box 30233*

*New York, NY 10011*
*212-645-5278*
*www.intrudersfoundation.org*
*Meets: one Saturday a month at the A.R.E. New*
*York Center, 150 West 28th Street, Suite 1001.*
New York native Budd Hopkins' life changed in
1964, when he and two friends witnessed a UFO
while hiking in the sand dunes near Truro, Mass. The
incident haunted Hopkins, propelling him into the
world of UFO investigation. Hopkins has written a
series of books on the UFO abduction phenomena,
including Missing Time, Intruders and Witnessed,
which details the NYC "Brooklyn Bridge Abduction."
Hopkins was the first to use "hypnotic regression"
techniques to investigate cases of "missing time,"
when abductees cannot recall all the details of their
experience, and have large amounts of time that
they cannot account for. His investigations are done
in an "objective, scientific and dispassionate" way.
Hopkins began the Intruders Foundation in 1989, as
a non-profit organization devoted to "research and
public education" about UFO abductions. The group
meets publicly once a month at the Association for
Research and Enlightenment (A.R.E.) Center in
Chelsea. The meeting that I attended featured a
video tape shot by a New York Corrections Officer
of a UFO that appeared near his home in Long
Island. The correction officer and his wife "also a
law enforcement officer" both claim that they were
abducted in the middle of the night by a group of
aliens who "walked through their bedroom wall."
They claim that they were then taken up into a
spaceship where the aliens took tissue samples
from them and conducted "some type of examination." During part of the evening, Hopkins played
the hypnotic regression tape in which the officer
"recalled" his harrowing abduction.

The audience members were, for the most part,
middle-class and conservative, like the type you
would find at a church function, though nearly all
had paranormal experiences which drew them to the
group. Hopkins has the gentle demeanor of a parish
priest, and appears to have taken on that role as
well. During the break, many of the attendees gath-
ered around him, trying to make sense of their
unusual experiences. Hopkins has no patience with
some of the newer UFO groups which combine conspiracy theory with extraterrestrial research. "This
is a science," says Hopkins. "People are experiencing
real and terrifying events and it is up to us to figure
out what happened to them."

## MILLENNIUM GROUP

*Francine Vale*
*917-405-1070*
*Meets: once a month at Earth Matters,*
*177 Ludlow Street*

Healer and UFO contactee Francine Vale formed the Millennium Group two years ago as a type of Native American "spirit circle" for people to share their experiences and analysis of UFO contacts. The group has evolved to include conspiracy theories and government cover-ups. At the meeting I attended, Vale began with a guided meditation and hands-on healing with each of the 20 or so people who attended. Vale then opened the floor by posing the question: "How is what is happening today similar to George Orwell's 1984?" This opened a floodgate of UFO-related conspiracy theories, including: Walt Disney was a Satanist and CIA agent who was paid by the US government to "make fun of aliens," the American government is spreading Wahhabi Islamic fundamentalism to create a "new communism," and that President George Bush was caught having sex with a 2 year old in the Oval Office (not sure what the UFO connection to this one was). Members of the group see a far reaching conspiracy, with UFO entities at the top, controlling events on Earth. Several members of the group said they believe that all world leaders are in cahoots with the aliens and wars were nothing but staged events to keep humans' attention off the alien conspiracy. One woman announced to the group that she had done a "remote viewing" session earlier in the day and factually reported: the US "was up to something in Iraq. I saw a lot of activity. They were building tunnels under Baghdad, looking for the star gates." Some members said that they feared for their lives because they were "exposing the truth." Vale assured the group that THEY (the UFO/government cabal) weren't interested in the group. "We are too small. Most people think we are crazy. I mean, who else would spend a Saturday night talking about this stuff?"

## NEW YORK MUTUAL UFO NETWORK "MUFON"

*James Bouck, Jr.*
*State Director*
*1225 Paul Avenue*
*Schenectady, NY 123065*
*www.mufon.com*

The Mutual UFO Network (MUFON) is the largest civilian UFO investigation group in the world. The

YOGA | ESOTERIC GROUPS | WITCHCRAFT | OCCULT UNDERGROUND | BOOKS | **UFOS** | BOTANICAS | TANTRA | ASTROLOGERS & PSYCHICS |

New York group meets once a month in Yonkers.
Members tend to approach UFO investigation in a
very scientific way. The Yonkers MUFON meetings
usually feature a guest speaker and discussion with
"like minded people" interested in the UFO phenomenon. The New York chapter also investigates reported
UFO events in the area from "genuine, on-site investigations." Founded in 1969, MUFON was founded
as a non-profit corporation dedicated, through its
volunteers, "to resolving the scientific enigma known
collectively as unidentified flying objects."

## RAELIANS
*1-866-895-4202*
*www.rael.org*
*mparent1@bellsouth.net*
*Meets: Second Sunday of every month at 250 West
54th Street, 11th Floor (studio C) at 10am*
I went to the monthly New York meeting of the
Raelians hoping to partake in the "sensual meditation" that the group founder "Rael" "former French
race car driver Claude Voirlhon' claims that aliens
gave him in 1973. Rael claims that he was taken up
into a spaceship by a group of entities known as the
"Elohim," who taught him the "real history of humanity." Turns out, we've gotten things all wrong. That
Yahweh character? - an extraterrestrial. And Jesus? -
a cloned "test-tube" baby.
    Rael claims that all life on Earth, human includ-
ed, has been scientifically created by the Elohim,
who have developed a mastery of genetic engineering and DNA synthesis, he says. Raelians point out
that the word "Elohim" - which appears in the Old
Testament - means "those who came from the sky."
The Rael movement has grown to an estimated
30,000 members worldwide and is now based near
French-speaking Montreal. Rael claims that the
Elohim have entrusted him with the mission of
spreading their message and to build an embassy,
where the Elohim will return. The Raelians picture a
world in which "science replaces religion," to make a
paradise on Earth through cloning, nanotechnology
and artificial intelligence.
    The Raelians practice a nude "sensual medita-
tion," part of the Elohim's "instruction manual for
happiness" - probably one of the reasons the
Raelian religion has so many adherents. "It is an
amazing feeling, you must try this," one Raelian
told me just before the monthly meeting of the

Manhattan group. "We also massage each other." Pierre, a long-time Rael member from Montreal, led the New York group. Handsome and fit, with a pony-tail and large "Raelian" medallion (a variation of a swastika) hanging over his chest, Pierre looked like a New Age fitness instructor. He showed a videotaped television interview with Rael, and then he opened the floor up to questions. The group consisted of about ten Rael members, along with an assortment of odd curiosity seekers. One man with thick glasses and a poorly-fitting wig peppered Pierre with questions, mentioning that he was also in contact with UFO aliens.

"No, no. There is only one human being who has had contact with aliens - and that is Rael," says Pierre. "Others who claim to have extraterrestrial contact are either imagining it, or are liars. So it is impossible for you to have had interaction with aliens." Pierre explained that the Elohim aliens would soon be coming back and that the group needed support to build an "embassy" for the aliens in Israel, since this is what the Elohim asked of Rael. He asked if anyone had any contacts within the Israeli government. "For some reason, the Israeli government has not been open to this idea," says Pierre. "I'm confident that one day the Israelis will accept our idea of putting an embassy for the Elohim in Jerusalem." As for the sensual meditation? "Maybe next time," says Pierre. "It is good to understand what we are about first. Then, you come back, and we'll do the meditation."

## ZECHARIA SITCHIN

*P.O. Box 577*
*New York, NY 10185*
*www.Sitchin.com*

No UFO guide would be complete without mention of New York's favorite son, Zecharia Sitchin. Sitchin is the godfather of the UFO movement, the first to promote the idea that aliens founded Sumerian civilization and "seeded" the human race (meaning we all have the "alien" gene in us).

Sitchen says that he became interested in UFO phenomena back when he was a young boy, growing up in Israel. During a religion class, while studying the Old Testament, Sitchen became obsessed with the story of the Nephilim, the "giants on earth," who "married the daughters of men." Sitchin noted that in Hebrew, Nephilim means "those who have come down," and not giants.

YOGA | ESOTERIC GROUPS | WITCHCRAFT | OCCULT UNDERGROUND | BOOKS | **UFOS** | BOTANICAS | TANTRA | ASTROLOGERS & PSYCHICS |

"I tried to point this out in my religion class, but I was told not to question the bible," recalls Sitchin, who now lives on the Upper West Side of Manhattan.

Sitchin has spent his entire archeological career questioning history as we know it. He is one of only 200 people in the world who can read Cuniform, the language of the Sumerians.

His conclusions about Sumerian history, however, have put him at odds with the academic community. He claims that the Nephilim - also known as the Annunaki - were actually astronauts from the planet "Niburu," who originally visited the earth to mine for gold. Niburu, the enigmatic "12th Planet," passes very close to earth every 3,600 years, causing natural catastrophes, the "great flood" being the last time the planet passed. We are due for another pass any year now, according to many Sitchen followers.

The Nephilim first came to earth about 450,000 years ago, according to Sitchin, first "splashing down" in the Persian Gulf. They established "space bases" throughout the Middle East, most notably in the Sinai and in Iraq, where they ended up settling. The Nephilim "created" the human race about 300,000 years ago by genetically engineering the "beautiful animals" they found on Earth, making them more intelligent to work as their "slaves" in the gold mines. Sitchin claims that the Nephilim began having sex and babies with the "humans" that they created, starting a feud that turned into a nuclear war, which ultimately resulted in the destruction of the Sumerian civilization in 2024 B.C. The abrupt end of their civilization was caused by an "evil wind," according to Sumerian texts.

Sitchin gives regular lectures and workshops throughout the United States and offers a Sitchin Studies Certification Seminar. "History clearly shows that we are not alone in the universe," Sitchin says. "But if the past is the key to the future, has the future begun?"

# Botanicas:
# May the Orishas Be With You

At one time, Miami was the Santeria capital of the world. However, New York City is catching up and may soon take the title. New York City has more than 80 *botanicas*, stores that cater to the Santeria, Voudon and *esperita* community, selling magical herbs, incense, candles, statues of saints, oils, baths and other esoteric products.

The first *botanica* in the United States is believed to be Otto Chicas Rendon's store on East 116th Street, which first opened in the 1920s, originally selling herbal formulas, oils and incense to the West Indian and African-American community. When the demographics changed, Rendon's uncle began focusing on the growing Hispanic community.

While many *botanicas* outwardly seem devoted to selling Catholic products like statues and religious candles, look a bit closer. That statue of Saint Barbara, well, it does represent Saint Barbara, but it also represents the African deity *Shango*, who controls fire and lightning. That statue of St. Peter actually represents the deity *Oggun*, the African god of iron and of war. Santeria literally means "saint worship" - but the "saints" that are worshiped are also African deities.

Practitioners of Santeria worship the pantheon of deities collectively known as the *Orishas*, the gods of the West African Yoruba tribe. Many believe that the *Orishas* represent a certain archetype of human personality. There are eleven major *Orishas*, which correspond to specific Catholic saints, along with hundreds of minor deities.

*Orisha* worship was introduced to the Western hemisphere through the slave trade; many Africans practiced the "old ways," hiding their native religion under the veneer of Christian worship. *Orisha* worship eventually spread to Latin American culture through the slaves who were brought to Cuba. In Haiti and the Dominican Republic, African religion forms the basis of the Voudon religion, and the African deities worshiped there are known as the *Loas*. There are some in the *Orisha* community who believe that slavery was somehow part of the "divine plan" to bring *Orisha* worship to the West.

In the past, *Orisha* worship was always conducted in secret; altars were usually hidden in the back room of a house. Now, thanks to the religious freedom in the United States, *santeros* (Santeria priests) have come out of the closet and have become respected members of the community. *Orisha* worship is now spreading outside of the Latin and African communities. More and more Anglos are now learning about *Orisha* worship, particularly in the New York Wiccan community.

Santeria is a living religion that speaks to many people

<<<
very deeply, as people reconnect with their indigenous past. When an initiate forms a relationship with a particular *Orisha*, the *Orisha* lives through that initiate. It is a profound and comprehensive magico-religious system, complete with its own unique form of herbal healing, spell craft, divination and spiritual healing.

Some have criticized Santeria because of the use of animal sacrifice during initiation rituals. There are some *santeros* who are vegetarian and only "feed" the *Orishas* with vegetarian foods. However, many *santeros* says that *Orishas* simply "cannot be born" without the blood of an animal. They point out that the animal is eaten after the initiation and that it is no different from Christians who eat turkey on Thanksgiving.

"Santeros give life, they don't destroy it," says Anthony Perrone, who has been a santero for 22 years. "The *Orishas* are all about giving life and extending life. It is a profound mystery."

Botanicas in New York City serve both the Santeria and spiritualist communities in the city. In Hispanic neighborhoods, there is a *botanica* on nearly every block, where you can get a spiritual reading or pick up some sacred incense. Many are run by genuine *santeros*, and it would be difficult to list them all. The following are the most established *botanicas* in the city.

## ALMACENES SHANGO
*1661 Madison Avenue between East 110 and*
*East 111*
*212-722-4275*
*Hours: T/Thu/Fri/Sat: 10am-5:30pm*
*Closest subway: 2/3 to Lenox/110;*
*6 to 110/Lexington*
*Spiritual readings: no*

Almacenes Shango has been serving the Hispanic and Santeria community in New York since 1960. It has been described as a "one-stop shopping" for Orisha worship supplies, as well as Catholic statues, candles, oils and incenses. Originally opened by late Artemio Rivera, the store is now run by Rivera's daughter Carmen and her husband Kenny Nash. Carmen and Kenny are well respected in the Santeria community for their knowledge and ability to obtain hard-to-find products. "Most people come in here for the love, luck and money," says Carmen. "Most of our customers are older, who grew up with the worship of saints." The shop is named after the deity Shango. Carmen and Kenny are extremely friendly and will gladly assist even the most puzzled neophyte.

## BOTANICA ANAISA Y SUS 7 VUELTAS

*1175 Jerome Avenue in Bronx*
*718-588-1407*
*www.elninoprodigio.com*
*Hours: M-Sat: 10am-8pm*
*Closest subway: 4 to 167th Street*
*Spiritual readings: yes (by appointment)*
Victor Florencio became known as El Niño Prodigio (The Child Prodigy) after he began telling the future for his classmates and teachers when he was seven years old, while living in the Domincan Republic. Florencio was recognized as being "born with the light," a child sensitive to spirits. He was eventually initiated as a houngan (priest) in the Loa religion, the Dominican form of Voudoun. "We have the same gods as in the Haitian Voudon religion, however we do not sacrifice animals," says Florencio. "Our religion is based upon water, candle and flowers." His Botanica Anaisa y sus 7 Vueltas caters to the Haitian, Dominican and African communities in the city, offering statues, herbs, incense, candles, magic baths and floor washes. Florencio also blends special herbal formulas for his customers, including a popular blend that increases the fertility of women who want to conceive a child. As a hougnan, Florencio's role is to "bring good fortune and healing" to his community. He gives readings at his store on Tuesdays, Thursdays and Fridays after 5 p.m. (you need to call that morning, between 10-11 a.m., in order to make an appointment). Florencio specializes in astrology, tarot readings and spiritual advice. His psychic abilities are in great demand from both his customers and the police department. He has assisted the police in several unsolved cases, using his psychic skills. Still known as El Niño Progidio, Florencio has clients from around the world, who are drawn to him for his natural ability and spiritual approach to life issues. "I was born very sensitive to things, with the ability to predict the future," says Florencio. "Since I was a child, I could feel the spirits and have been a guide for others."

## BOTANICA YEMAYA

*1645 Woodbine Street off Wyckoff Avenue*
*in Ridgewood*
*718-386-9345*
*Hours: M-Fri: 11am-7pm; Sat: 10am-6pm*
*Closest subway: L to Myrtle Avenue;*
*J to Wyckoff Avenue*

## Anthony Perrone:
## A Life Devoted to the Orishas

Anthony Perrone wanted to become a Catholic priest when he grew up.

But his introduction to the *Orisha* religion - known as Santeria - gave him a new calling. Anthony - known by his spiritual name of *Okan l'Osha* - instead became a Santeria priest of Obatala, the deity who is the father of all *Orishas*.

"We don't choose the *Orishas*, the *Orishas* choose us," says Anthony, the owner of *Botanica Yemaya* in Queens. "I discovered spiritualism and the *Orishas* at age six through family and friends and things changed. A new calling was awakened."

The *Orishas* are the pantheon of deities of the Yoruba of West Africa, which traveled to throughout the world with the slave trade. The deities - like *Chango*, *Elleggua*, *Oddudua*, *Yemaya* and *Oshun* - all have their own unique personalities and attributes. The *Orisha* tradition came to be known as *Candomble* in Brazil, Santeria in the Cuban communities, and the *Loa* religion in Haiti and the Dominican Republic.

While Miami has unofficially become the world headquarters of *Orisha* worship, New York is catching up; Santeria has become the fastest growing religion in New York City.

"There will be a time when *Orisha* worship will be an acknowledged religion like the Catholic and Jewish faiths," says Anthony. "*Orisha* worship is traveling throughout the world and interest in the religion is growing. You also don't have to be Latino or of African descent for the *Orishas* to work in your life."

As an initiated *santero*, Anthony has become a channel for "divine grace," known as ashe. Anthony can use his *ashe* to both heal and divine the future. Anthony says that he has seen healing miracles occur through the intercession of the *Orishas*; he has seen cancer go into remission when the *Orishas* are invoked.

Anthony's most sought-after role, however, is as a divinator. He uses both cards and cowrie shells to give spiritual advice.

Anthony will only do a cowrie shell reading for someone who is sincerely looking for spiritual guidance, as well as people who are interested in becoming initiated into the Santeria religion.

"The shells are very sacred. They are not for the general public," says Anthony. "It is not good to bother the *Orishas* for mundane questions." For day-to-day matters, like relationships and jobs, Anthony uses his cards.

Anthony notes that there has been a profusion of books on Santeria during the past few years. However, he says that there is only one way to become a *santero* - and that is through initiation from another *santero*. Only in this way can the ashe be passed down through the lineage of priesthood.

Anthony was initiated as a *santero* when he was 17 years old by his "godmother," Nancy Rivera, known by her spiritual name of *Omi Yomi Omo Yemaya*. To become a *santero* is a long and arduous process that takes a big commitment; initiates must shave their heads and wear white for a year and seven days after the initiation ceremony. As part of this year-long purification process, initiates cannot shake hands with people, attend funerals or visit hospitals unless they are sick, and they can't take money directly from a person - the money must be placed on the counter.

"It is all about rebirth and purification, so that the initiate does not pick up negativity," explains Anthony.

As a *Baba l'Orisha* (father of the *Orishas*), Anthony is the head of his own "house" and has initiated nearly 100 people into the *Orisha* tradition. A *Baba l'Orisha* has the responsibility of bringing people into the *Orisha* religion, and the added responsibility of being a "godparent" to the initiates. Some of his Anthony's initiates include police officers, commodities brokers and business people, "as an example of people from all walks of life looking to the *Orishas* to help in improving their lives and the lives of their families."

Not every initiate is destined to become a Santeria priest. Some are initiated because of a life-threatening illness. Likewise, not every Santeria priest is destined to become a Baba l'*Orisha* or *Lya l'Orisha* (mother of *Orisha*) for women". Anthony says that it is the "*Orishas* who choose."

"Everything begins with divination," says Anthony. "The *Orishas* will let it be known who is destined for priesthood. Being a responsible godparent is a lot of work and responsibility. Not everyone is prepared, even after initiation, to carry such a weight."

Anthony says that those interested in *Orisha* worship should begin their journey by getting a divination from a respected *santero*.

"I can't describe how wonderful it is to have the *Orishas* working in your life," says Anthony. "*Obatala* is everything to me."

| YOGA | ESOTERIC GROUPS | WITCHCRAFT | OCCULT UNDERGROUND | BOOKS | UFOS | **BOTANICAS** | TANTRA | ASTROLOGERS & PSYCHICS |

*Spiritual readings: yes (by appointment)*
Botanica Yemaya is an excellent and friendly
botanica, which is run by a practicing santero.
Anthony Perrone (see feature article) opened the
botanica seven years ago as a place for practicing
santeros to purchase genuine and high-quality
tools and implements for Orisha worship. Anthony
has commissioned a number of initiates in the
New York area to make such items as crowns and
toureens, which are used in Santeria rituals and ceremonies. He also obtains hard-to-find products from
Miami, including fresh herbs for spiritual work and
Orisha ceremonies. Many people come in for a reading and spiritual advice from Anthony, a popular
reader in the Santeria community. Anthony is a
priest of Obatala, as well as a Baba l'Orisha (father
of the Orishas). He has the ashe (spiritual power) to
conduct genuine cowrie shell readings and healings.
The store also offers a full selection of statues,
candles, oils, incense, perfumes and books for the
lay person. Anthony is proud and passionate about
the Orisha tradition, and is a generous teacher,
particularly for those who feel they may have a
"calling" to become an initiated santero.

### EL CONGO BOTANICA INC.
*1787 Lexington Avenue between East 110 and
East 111 Streets*
*212-860-3921*
*Hours: M-Sat: 10am-6pm*
*Closest subway: 6 train to 110th Street*
*Spiritual readings: no*
El Congo is one of the oldest and most dependable
botanicas in Manhattan. But Anglos beware; it is
one of the few botanicas listed in which the owners
do not speak English. When I walk in, owner Ernesto
Santana points to the tiny nail on his baby right
hand finger, indicating how much English he speaks.
The neighborhood's a bit dicey too - I had to wade
through a group of gang-bangers at the corner to
get to the store. But the trek may be worth it, particularly if you like fresh herbs. El Congo has a full
selection of saint statues, incenses, candles and
some books, most of which are in Spanish. Most
of the products are behind the counter, so you
generally need to know what you are looking for.

### ORIGINAL PRODUCTS
*2486-88 Webster Avenue in Bronx*
*718-367-9589/9591*

*www.originalprodcorp.com*
*Hours: M-Sat: 9:30am-5:45pm*
*Closest subway: D Train to Fordham Road*
*(walk 5 blocks)*
*Spiritual readings: yes*

Original Products is both one of the "original" botanicas in New York City, as well as the "king" of botanicas. Original Products has been serving the Santeria and occult community in New York since 1959 and has grown into one of the largest and most respected botanical supply companies in the world. Original Products is the primary supplier to the 80 or so other botanicas in the New York area. Employees work overtime in the back and basement of the store, mixing the hundreds of oils, incenses and waters that bear the Original Products logo. Original Products looks like a small supermarket and stocks more than 250 fresh and dried magical herbs, along with one of the largest selections of religious statues in the area. Customers include many neighborhood people who come to the store for readings, as well as for the many products designed for the layman, such as the Go Away Evil incense, Mister Money cologne, and Court Case floor wash. If you can't find an occult supply at Original Products, most likely you won't find it. In addition to having the most complete selection of Santeria supplies, Original Products has expanded into Western occult supplies, like tarot cards and books. Unlike many of the botanicas in Manhattan, Original Products also supplies spiritual products geared to the African-American "Hoodoo" community. The store is now run by Jason Mizrahi, the son of co-founder Jack Mizrahi (see feature article). For the practicing occultist, a trip to Original Products is a must; it will open up a new world. Many in the witchcraft and pagan communities have also discovered the store. Lady Rhea, godmother of hundreds of witches in New York, offers tarot readings there on Fridays. Readers are available daily and walk-ins are welcome.

### OTTO CHICAS-RENDON

*60 East 116th Street between Park and*
*Madison Avenues*
*212-289-0378*
*Hours: M-Sat: 10am-6pm*
*Closest subway: 6 to Lexington/116th Street*
*Spiritual readings: no*

Otto Chicas Rendon is one of the most well-known botanicas in the city - and one of the oldest. It was

YOGA | ESOTERIC GROUPS | WITCHCRAFT | OCCULT UNDERGROUND | BOOKS | UFOS | **BOTANICAS** | TANTRA | ASTROLOGERS & PSYCHICS |

## *Original Products: Botanica to the World*

Jason Mizrahi spent his childhood playing among the *santeros*, witches and Voodoo
priests who came into Original
Products, his father's *botanica*, located on Webster Avenue
in the Bronx.

Now, at age 27, Mizrahi is
running the store, which has
become one of the largest and
best known *botanicas* in the
world.

Mizrahi took over the
store in 1999, from his father
Jack and co-founder Milton
Benezra, who opened the
*botanica* in the Bronx in 1959.
The Mizrahi family has been in
the *botanica* business for the better part of the last century; in the
1920s, Mizrahi's great-grandfather opened one of New York City's
first *botanicas* in Harlem, which catered to the recently arrived
Hispanic community.

"My family is originally from Spain, way back. We are Sephardic
Jews," says Mizarahi, from his office in the back of Original
Products. "We all speak Spanish and have a close connection to the
Hispanic community."

Mizrahi, who graduated from the University of Richmond with
a degree in Finance, says that, like his father, he does not practice
Santeria.

Mizrahi says that Original Products has been so successful
over the years because, if a customer came in looking for a product, his father would find a supplier to get this product. As a
result, Original Products has one of the largest selections of magical herbs and oils in the world.

"If we don't have the product you are looking for, we will track
it down for you," says Mizrahi. "Our business has grown and
changed over the years. When we first started, we catered mostly
to the Hispanic community. But this has shifted more to the
African-based religions, like Santeria."

Mizrahi says that the *botanica* business has blossomed during the past few years, primarily due to the intermingling of spiritual paths in New York City.

"In the past, Santeria was extremely inclusive and secretive,
but there is much more openness now," he says. "We are seeing an
incredible mixing of spiritual traditions. Santeria, Wicca and
white magic are all represented in the store now."

The pagan and Wicca communities in New York have embraced
many Santeria beliefs and practices. For instance, Lady Rhea, a

High Wiccan Priestess and co-owner of Magickal Realms in Bronx, conducts spiritual readings at Original Products every Friday.

With the growth in the interest in Santeria, Mizrahi's business has expanded overseas. In the back of the store, boxes of incense and oils were waiting to be shipped to stores as far away as Holland and Spain.

The basement of Original Products, workers mix incenses and oils, according to ancient, and sometimes secret, formulas that the Mizrahi family has been collecting since they began in the business. During a tour of the workshop, Mizrahi shows off his prized possession an *anil* mixer in a small room covered in blue powder. Original Products is the only company in the United States producing "Blue Balls," the round anil balls which *santeros* use for purification in baths and floor washes, and housewives use to get their clothes white. The secret recipe has been handed down for generations and Mizrahi supplies the "Blue Balls" to *botanicas* throughout the country.

"We have customers who come from all over to shop here," says Mizrahi. "This is a great business, because you can meet so many different and interesting people. All types shop here, from witches to people from the Church who want to buy our candles and statues."

originally opened in 1921 by Alberto Rendon, the uncle of current owner Otto Chicas Rendon. The store has one of the best supplies of fresh herbs, spiritual oils, incense, spiritual baths and statues in the city, catering to the Spanish and West Indian communities (its original name was West Indian Botanical). Chicas Rendon is an expert herbalist and spiritualist who is often on hand to answer customer questions. The store imports many of its herbs fresh from Puerto Rico and other Latin American countries and often supplies to the smaller botanicas in the area. The store caters to the lay person and the staff is known in the Latino community for being helpful and knowledgeable. "Most people come in here looking for love or money," says Rose, an employee at the store. "The staff can usually guide a person in the right and get them the extra spiritual help they need."

### PACOS BOTANICAL PRODUCTS
*1864 Lexington Avenue between East 115*
*and East 116*
*212-427-0820*
*Hours: M-Sat: 9:30am-6:30pm*
*Closest subway: 6 train to 116th Street*
*Spiritual readings: no*

# *Florida Water: The New York Cologne "Pleasing to the Spirits"*

When New Yorker Robert Murray first introduced his cologne "Florida Water" to the public in 1808, he advertised that the floral-scented water had "more than 20 uses," among them, "to freshen rooms," "for boudoir daintiness," and "for the hair, a sprinkling gives an enchanting fragrance appropriate to a party or dance."

However, Murray probably never imagined that his humble cologne would eventually become a key ingredient in Santeria and Voodoo rituals, known worldwide for being "pleasing to the spirits." Florida Water is considered the best "aura cleanser" on the market by spiritualists and santeros, who spray it on themselves during rituals, and use it in baths and floor washes for "spiritual cleansing."

"It really surprised us when we learned that our cologne was being used in this way," says Daisy Villegas, general manager of Lanman and Kemp-Barclay, the New Jersey-based company that now makes Florida Water.

Villegas says that *botanicas* and spiritualist store now account for nearly 50 percent of Florida Water sales. Villegas says that her company still advertises Florida Water's "20 uses," but the company only makes vague references to the cologne's "spiritual powers."

"As long as I can remember, Florida Water has been used in the Hispanic community for medicinal purposes and as a spiritual cleanser," says Villegas. "But its use in the spiritualist community definitely grew through word of mouth."

Florida Water's ingredients are a "closely-held secret," however the cologne seems to have cloves, cinnamon and lavender in it - herbs traditionally used by ceremonial magicians for cleansing and to "attract high astral entities."

*Botanica* owner Victor Florencio, also known as *El Niño Prodigio* (the child prodigy) for his divination abilities, says that every spiritualist he knows uses Florida Water in their rituals. "Florida Water is an essential ingredient in spiritual work because its smell attracts the spirits," says Florencio. "The combination of the herbs and spices is very unique."

Florencia says that when he "feels the spirits coming" during a spiritual ritual, he splashes Florida Water behind his neck and on his temples to attract the good spirits. "Bad spirits will not come because the water smells so good," says Florencio, a priest in the *Loa* religion, the Dominican Republic's form of Voudon.

Brooklyn-based shaman Alex Stark says that the unique combination of herbs and the water's high alcohol content "literally drags negative vibrations out of your aura." Stark sips the cologne and sprays it on clients with his mouth for spiritual cleansing. He also claps a handful over his head after any type of spiritual work, to ensure that no "negative entities" attach to him during a ritual.

"We use it primarily to clear bad energies," says Stark. "The secret is the essential oils that are in the water, particularly lavender and bergamot, which are cleansing herbs."

Stark says that Florida Water has been used "for generations" by spiritualists in his homeland of Peru to "feed" the spirit world. They pour the water on their "power tools" "like crystal wands and

Paco opened his botanica in East Harlem more than 35 years ago. At the time, he was the head vice president of sales for Lanman and Kemp-Barclay, the New Jersey company that makes Florida Water, the citrus cologne that santeros discovered "is pleasing to the spirits" and used for cleansing of the aura "see related article". His sales duties took him around the world - to Africa, Asia and Latin America, where he began buying unusual spiritual items and herbs that he would sell in his store. The botanica caters to the Hispanic Catholic and Santeria communities, but specializes in items from Central America. Pacos Botanical is one of the few stores in the country that offers products related to the Guatemalan Saint Sansimon, a powerful indigenous doctor and healer. "Our specialty is fresh herbs," says Maria, Pacos" daughter who now runs the store with him. "We always have a large supply of green and fresh herbs for healing and spiritual protection." Maria says that a few years ago, there "was a lull" in the botanica business. But during the past year or two things have really picked up. "Every time the economy does poorly, people turn to religion. We see a lot more people now buying statues and candles," says Maria. "We are also getting a lot more Anglo-Americans coming here. It is amazing. Many Anglo-Americans who come from downtown are interested in Orisha worship, and they often know more about the Orishas than the typical Hispanic." Love potions are still the best-sellers at the botanica, Maria says. The store also stores a large selection of magic oils, baths and powders. Maria says that the botanica is unique because it is so friendly and open. "There is something for everyone here," says Maria. "We are here to help and give advice, particularly if you have never been to a botanica before."

YOGA | ESOTERIC GROUPS | WITCHCRAFT | OCCULT UNDERGROUND | BOOKS | UFOS | **BOTANICAS** | TANTRA | ASTROLOGERS & PSYCHICS |

**<<<**

magic stones" to cleanse and feed them. They also use it to "feed" the element of fire during certain rituals to "please the spirits of fire"; the water's high alcohol content makes it burn easily. In his healing work, Stark will often spray the water directly onto a client's chakra points to "deal with a specific emotional issue." During particularly difficult healing sessions, he knows of healers who will have an assistant spray the water on the back of their neck while they are conducting the healing, to keep them from picking up negative energies from the client.

"Florida Water is like aspirin ñ it serves all purposes," says Stark. "It is great for cleansing, purifying and attracting. Spirits love smells and Florida Water has the smell they like."

It is unclear whether or not Murray intentionally created Florida Water for spiritual purposes. He named the cologne after the legendary "Fountain of Youth" in Florida. The bottle's distinctive label features a print of the fabled fountain by the famous illustrator George Du Maurier, who was commissioned to draw it for the company in 1855. The company maintained its headquarters in Manhattan until 1957, when it moved to New Jersey.

Lanman and Kemp-Barclay now makes a wide range of unique soaps and scented waters, including Money Soap Jackpot, Rose Cologne and Pacholi Scented Soap. The company also makes Kananga Water, also used in the spiritualist community for attracting the spirits, but Kananga does not have the wide-ranging uses of Florida Water.

The only comparable cologne on the market used for spiritual work is Hoyt's Cologne, used in the African-American "Hoodoo" community to bring "gambling luck." However, Florida Water is a phenomena and in a class by itself, as the world's favorite spiritual cleanser.

"Florida Water is the bomb, there is no equal," says Florencio. "Doing a spiritual ritual without Florida Water is like baking a cake without sugar - Florida Water is the sugar."

# Tantra: Enlightenment Through Sex

There are many paths to enlightenment. You can meditate, pray, chant mantras and fast. But there is a group of spiritual adepts who believe the quickest, most direct way to experience the divine is through sensual experience.

The tantric philosophy originated in the Indus Valley, more than 5,000 years ago, when India was a matriarchal society. It recognized women as the highest form of godhead. One ancient tantric text calls the "vulva an altar and pubic hairs the flames on the altar." In tantra, the woman is literally a "goddess" and her lover becomes a "god." When the god and goddess unite, through intercourse, the result is transcendental bliss, balance and harmony.

The tantric adept neither fears nor rejects any experience in life. Through sexual union, the tantric adept awakens the "kundalini" life force, leading ultimately to *moksha*, liberation.

Now there is a thin line that separates a true tantric experience from a mere hand-job. There are a lot charlatans advertising "tantric massage" on the internet to capitalize on the spiritual movement. Make sure you check the lineage and spiritual practice of any self-proclaimed "tantric goddess" or "god" before forking over your money. Many occult groups, such as the OTO (Ordo Templi Orientis), also use tantric-like "sex magic" rituals in their higher degrees; for them, sex is a powerful magical tool.

A true tantric session can release amazing amounts of energy, dissolve blocks and bring positive transformation. You do not have to be beautiful to experience the bliss of tantra. Seeing every woman as a goddess can help heal us individually and collectively. Embrace your sexuality - it can bring both bliss and enlightenment.

**REVEREND GODDESS CHARMAINE**
*The Sensuous Mystic*
www.revcharmaine.com
973-471-1099
Rev. Charmaine (see feature article) says that her life mission is to unite sex and spirituality. She was ordained by the New Seminary in New York City and has been leading spiritual workshops in the area since 1992, using her background of reiki, hypnotherapy, chakra balancing and stress relief. In July 2000, she was initiated into "goddesshood" and now works primarily with tantric energies. Her individual sessions include sexual counseling, spiritual counseling, tantric energy work and massage and are

held at the Source of Life Center. Her tantric massage sessions are conducted in a candle-lit room, with wafting incense and soft music playing. She has a profound understanding of the human body and energy system. Her workshops include Tantric Massage, Sacred Erotic Dancing, Pussy Power, and Energy Orgasm with the Chakra Wave - a class that teaches "mystical erotic masturbation." Unlike many other tantric teachers, Rev. Charmaine teaches classes the way they were meant to be taught - in the nude. Most classes are co-ed and students shed their clothes at the door. Classes are surprisingly respectful and boundaries of the students are honored, though everyone leaves satisfied and uplifted. Rev. Charmaine sees herself - and all women - as an embodiment of the "goddess." Her philosophy is important and timely - particularly as humanity becomes more in touch with the goddess energy.

## SEXY SPIRITS NEW YORK
*Eden House*
*212-696-7495*
*www.sexyspirits.com*
Sexy Spirits was founded in 2001 by Anton (Richard Diaz), a student of Taoist Master Mantak Chia. Anton runs a bed and breakfast on West 55th Street called "Eden House," which caters to tantric explorers and also hosts a series of tantric and Taoist workshops. Anton, a former professional ballroom dancer, is an instructor of the Healing Tao system founded by Chia, who regularly visits Eden House to give workshops. Anton has also trained with Jack Taylor (pelvic-heart integration), Deborah Anapol (tantra, polyamory) and Patricia Taylor (expanded orgasm training). Some of the most prominent tantric teachers in the country pass through Eden House. Anton teaches an ongoing The Tao of Sex, Love and Passion class every Monday evening. Recent workshops have included Expanded Orgasm with Patricia Taylor, Polyamory and the Tantric Community with Dr. Sasha, and The Jade Goddess and Dragon Workshop with Saida.

Polyamory is when a group of individuals live together in "multiple partnered relationships," which are long-term and committed. It takes the concept of "open marriage" to a new dimension - and of course demands detachment and a spiritual discipline. At a recent Tantra Ritual for the Polyamrous, given by Dr. Sasha and Janet Lessin, seven couples rotated partners, "exchanging energy from the seven chakras" while chanting specific mantras. This powerful ritual was practiced thousands of years ago in India to bring spiritual transformation.

## CAROL TARANTOLA

*718-899-2267*
*www.tantranewyork.com*
Carol Tarantola, also known as "Carla Tara," is probably the most visible tantric teacher in New York City. She has lectured at the Open Center, New Life Expo, as well as the Learning Annex. She also gives private sessions at her "Healthy Love Center," located in Queens. Tarantola, a trained psychotherapist, believes that tantric work can release emotional blocks and, ultimately, use sexual energy as a fuel "to expand love into ecstasy and to enlightenment." The goal of tantra, she says, is to "stay present and open to each moment with full consciousness, embracing all sensations and feelings." Tarantola has studied in India and the United States with such masters as Gurudev Shri Chritrabanu, Dr. Ramamurti Mishra and Dr. Pandit Rajmani Tgunait, along with tantric masters Margo Anand and Charles Muir. She works privately with both individuals and couples. She also regularly presents day-long tantric workshops for couples and singles at her Queens center.

## THE IMPERIAL ORGY

*www.theimperialorgy.com*
The Imperial Orgy began almost by accident. The band of the same name was performing at a club in Manhattan when a female fan jumped onstage and began performing a simulated blow job on attractive lead singer Caeser Pink.

"Before I knew it, everyone out on the dance floor was on the ground making out and groping each other - it turned into a huge orgy," says Pink, a songwriter. "Right then, I knew we had something special." Pink mixes his own pagan spirituality with sexuality. "When you see everything as sacred, then worshiping your lover is the same as worshiping God," says Pink, an ordained minister with the Universal Life Church.

Pink has had a rough road to success. He grew up in a small town in Pennsylvania, which he fled after being arrested and beaten by local cops for a minor infraction while delivering pizzas. "I was different and I stood out," says Pink. "They (the cops) decided to mess with me one night." Then, after moving to New York City, he ended up homeless for a while, living in a car in the East Village.

Pink says that he eventually had a "religious

YOGA | ESOTERIC GROUPS | WITCHCRAFT | OCCULT UNDERGROUND | BOOKS | UFOS | BOTANICAS | TANTRA | ASTROLOGERS & PSYCHICS |

# Rev. Goddess Charmaine:
# The Sensuous Mystic

Reverend Goddess Charmaine has made it her life mission to reconcile sex and spirituality through tantra.

"I believe that our body is a holy temple and our sexual energy is our life force," says Charmaine, who conducts workshops and one-on-one tantric healing sessions. Charmaine is also an initiated "goddess," which she says has become her everyday consciousness.

Charmaine has not always manifested the goddess consciousness, however. At one time, she was "overweight, very negative and in an abusive relationship." She says that she hit rock-bottom one day when her ex-husband had beaten her up and she was getting ready to bail him out of jail, yet again.

"I remember looking into the mirror and wondering if I should try to cover the bruises on my neck," she says. "I looked into my eyes and I finally saw my true self - I saw infinity, the endless me." From that day on, her life changed. "I got my ex-husband out of my life and began to empower myself."

Her spiritual journey had begun. She began exercising, reading self-help books, eating better and transforming the way she thought. Then she read the book that changed her life. It was The Art of Sexual Ecstasy by Margo Anand. "For the first time, I realized how to bring consciousness into sex," she says.

Her passion was re-awakened. A series of coincidences led to work at a sexual surrogate's office, where she began intensive study in sexual therapy. She also ended up studying directly with Anand in both in New York and in California.

"Tantra is about honoring your partner's body and spirit," says Charmaine. "Physical love is only about fulfilling needs."

As a child, Charmaine had developed the ability to see aura and to tell the future. With her initiation into tantra, Charmaine says that her psychic abilities have returned.

"When I touch someone's body now I can read their sexual energy," she says. "I know if someone has a sexual block and what the origin of the block is."

Charmaine also noticed something else, as well. And other people did too. The goddess had descended on her. Her mentor Reverend Georges initiated Charmaine as a goddess during an elaborate ceremony at the Source of Life Center in Chelsea.

Charmaine says that she wants to share tantric healing with all people, not just those in the New Age community who understand tantra.

"I want to be able to heal everyone - from the professional to the blue-collar worker," she says.

Many people come to Charmaine for sexual issues - impotence, inability to find a mate and performance issues. But many others come for empowerment and a celebration of their own life energy.

"People are all hung up about sexually transmitted diseases, but I am more concerned about spiritually transmitted diseases," says Charmaine. "Sexual energy is powerful and universal. When we learn how to live with it and not repress it, our lives become transformed."

experience," which propelled him to see everything as sacred - particularly sex. Pink began studying paganism and Wicca and discovered that the orgy was actually a pagan religious festival.

"Our performances are like the Wiccan Drawing down the Moon Ritual," says Pink. "We make people break out of their inhibitions. The event is very paganistic."

Pink has developed an international following and has established a group in Salt Lake City. Pink has become somewhat of a "pan-pagan" guru to women and men, the leader of a very unique group of spiritual seekers. The group is now looking for a permanent space in Williamsburg, where most of its members live. That way, the group can have workshops and events, without worrying about hostile bouncers or sometimes-violent male concert-goers who don't deal well with the highly-charged sexual atmosphere of the performances.

"Aside from our public performances, we also get together as a group for private parties," says Pink. "This is our inner circle. This is where the real tantra and transformation takes place."

### TRANSFORM NOW
*Melissa Zwanger*
*212-769-6407*
*www.transformnow.com*
Melissa Zwanger says that her path to tantra evolved out of her own eclectic spiritual path, which includes training in Kahuna shamanism in Hawaii and Ericksonian hypnosis.

"I've always felt a need to educate people about the spiritual nature of their sexuality," says Zwanger. "Our culture splits spirituality and sexuality. On the one hand, advertising uses sex to manipulate people. But at the same time, our religious organizations make us feel shameful about our sex drive."

Zwanger says that Margo Anand and David Deida have been the greatest influences on her tantric work. Since the early 1990s, Zwanger has been giving tantric workshops in Manhattan and also conducting private sessions with singles and couples. She says that her sessions are "intuitively guided" and she provides the client with what they need at the time.

"I help people integrate the male and female aspects of themselves," she says. "Tantra is a path for achieving wholeness. I view it is an entire way of life."

Zwanger has created a tantric healing system called Integral Balance, in which she teaches clients to work with their sexual energy and use it to "become the creator their lives rather than a victim of circumstances." At the same time, clients learn to be better and more responsive lovers, release sexual blockages and gain better health as the sexual energy is allowed to flow more freely.

"Tantric work will help anyone who is interested in growing and becoming a fully empowered individual," says Zwanger. "You also don't need a partner to use tantra to realize your full-potential. Many single people come to me and benefit a great deal from the training."

## WHITE LOTUS EAST
*www.whitelotuseast.com*
Located somewhere in mid-town Manhattan, White Lotus East is a "group of tantric teachers, sex educators and counselors" who offer a whole range of services, including Bath Ceremonies, Tantric Massage, Chakra Balancing, and Tantric Philosophy. White Lotus East says that its mission is to "improve intimate relationships and sexual fulfillment," using tantric, as well as Taoist philosophy. They promise to teach the achievement of multiple orgasm and ejaculation control through tantric massage, as well as dealing with the sexual issues that hold many people back. Sessions are for both men and women.

# What's in Your Future: New York's Best Psychics, Astrologers and Palm Readers

There are times when you need guidance from beyond, when conventional means simply can't give you the information you need to make a key life decision. Some people, however, are born "gifted," and have the ability to see into the future - or at least possible patterns of the future.

New York City has one of the highest concentrations of psychics in the world. A good psychic can really get to the bottom of an issue. Many times, one session with a talented psychic can accomplish more in one session, than a year of therapy.

Not all psychics are reputable, however. There is a certain breed of psychic who has no supernatural ability other than to con people who are in need. Beware of any psychic who charges large amounts of money and demands follow-on visits. Another rule of thumb: if there is neon-sign in the window, chances are you don't want to be there.

The following are some of the best and most reputable astrologers, palm readers and psychics that I have come across in New York City. Many have trained in their art for years; others are naturally gifted. They are a diverse and eclectic collection of fascinating individuals.

In order to choose a good psychic, it is important to honor your intuition. Chemistry is really important during a reading. A psychic can give you important spiritual guidance, first aid for the soul - or simply tell you whether or not to take that new job you have been offered. It is often good to visit a good psychic or astrologer before reaching that "crisis stage," when it may be too late to avert a personal disaster. As psychic Lexa Rosean puts it, everyone should treat themselves to a regular "psychic tune-up," with someone who has the power to look into your soul.

**SHELLEY L. ACKERMAN**
*Astrologer*
*212-539-3100*
*www.karmicrelief.com*
Shelly Ackerman made her debut as a professional astrologer with a bang in 1992, when she became the first astrologer to obtain then-President Bill Clinton's exact birth time. Ackerman - who began her career as a singer, actress and comedian - used her charms to get the precise time from Clinton's mother, Virginia Kelley. The rest, they say, is history; Ackerman has become one of New York's top media astrologers. Besides her own radio show, Karmic Relief, Ackerman regularly appears as a guest on

radio and television talk shows. For the last five years, Ackerman has also been the in-house astrologer for the New York Theosophical Society and gives the enormously popular Monday night class, the Art of Astrology for Inspired Students and Creative Professionals. "I see all sorts of creative applications in the aspects and configurations of a natal chart," says Ackerman. She says that many of her clients tend to be very creative. "Most are already on a path of discovery. They are prepared to take the emotional, psychological and spiritual responsibility of what is going on in their lives," she says. Ackerman looks at a natal horoscope and immediately sees the client's potential. "As a counselor and astrologer, I get the client to believe in the possibilities of their lives," says Ackerman. "I encourage my clients to take a leap of faith and believe in themselves."

### KIM ALLEN
*Psychic, astrologer*
*718-443-3202*
*www.lovepsychic.com*
Talk show host Montel Williams dubbed Kim Allen the Love Psychic after she appeared on his show - and the name has stuck ever since. "There are many types of love," says Allen, who has been working as a psychic for 20 years. "I embrace it all - especially love for the One Most High." Allen says that her approach to psychic readings has become much more spiritual during the past few years and she is studying to become an interfaith minister. Allen says that she discovered her psychic abilities while growing up in Detroit. She says she uses tarot cards "only to get started" in her readings. The rest is all of her natural psychic abilities. Many of Allen's clients are actors and producers from Broadway. She can be found every Friday night at Seppi's Restaurant, 123 West 56th Street, Manhattan, from 7-10:30 pm. It's best to call before to make an appointment - with Allen's success rate, there are usually long lines at her table.

### NATHANIEL ALTMAN
*Palm reader, metaphysician*
*718-499-2384*
*www.healingsprings.com*
Nathaniel Altman had his first palm reading in 1969, during a semester abroad in Colombia. Famed Colombian palmist Teresa de Barberi took one look at his hand and told him that he was destined to

become a palm reader. "She became my first teacher," says Altman, who has since read more than 20,000 palms. Altman has become one of the country's top palm readers and has written five books on the science of palmistry. "I tend to focus on the psychological aspect during a reading, rather than fortune telling," says Altman. "The future can change. I may see a trend line in the hand concerning a client's health. If the client makes the necessary changes, that line itself will change." For Altman, palmistry is mostly science and a small part intuition. He says that the only way to become proficient is through experience. Altman has also written a great deal about holistic health, as well as about the power of healing springs. He gives readings in his Brooklyn home, as well as in Manhattan. "A palm reading can remind a person of who they are," says Altman. "People learn to accept themselves better as a unique individual."

## FRANK ANDREWS
*Psychic, tarot reader, palm reader*
*212-226-2194*
Frank Andrews is arguably New York City's best-known psychic. He has been a professional reader for the past 40 years and has inspired a generation of younger card readers. Andrews' psychic abilities were recognized when he was very young. He was mentored by a colorful group of spiritualists and Theosophists in New York City, most notably the renown psychic Marion Tanner, whom Andrews claims is the real Auntie Mame. Andrews also studied under Clifford Bias, the founder of the Universal Spiritualist Association, and learned how to become a medium and communicate with the deceased. Andrews' primary focus, however, is assisting people by using his psychic vision. His readings are stunningly accurate and some of his past clients include John Lennon and Princess Grace. Andrews also teaches a small group of handpicked students, sharing his years of experience. "Everyone has the ability to become psychic to some degree," says Andrews. "If you activate it every day like I do, it becomes like second nature."

## MADALYN ASLAN
*Astrologer, palm reader, medium*
*212-631-5844*
*www.madalynaslan.com*
Madalyn Aslan is an elegant and sophisticated reader who is known internationally for her predictive

| YOGA | ESOTERIC GROUPS | WITCHCRAFT | OCCULT UNDERGROUND | BOOKS | UFOS | BOTANICAS | TANTRA | **ASTROLOGERS & PSYCHICS** |

ability. Aslan split her time growing up between the United States and England and lectured at the prestigious College of Psychic Studies in London. "I have been psychic ever since I can remember," says Aslan, who was a child actress. "I began reading people at a very young age." One of her first clients was actor Rock Hudson, who appeared with Aslan in the film The Martian Chronicles (Aslan played Hudson's daughter). While living in London, Aslan honed her abilities by studying with such luminaries as the late astrologer Howard Sasportas. Aslan is the author of the first astrology book for children, What's Your Sign, as well as the recently released Madalyn Aslan's Jupiter Signs. Aslan's premise in her latest book is that you should live according to the zodiacal sign that your Jupiter is in, to reach your full potential. "In my readings, I help people clarify what they are here to do and what their potential is," says Aslan. "I make everything very practical and down-to-earth. It's cathartic, but gentle."

## BILL ATTRIDE
*Astrologer*
*212-995-0889*
Bill Attride is one of those rare astrologers able to predict "mundane" events like the stock market and political events, yet also able work with clients on their personal development and spiritual growth. Attride majored in both economics and philosophy at the New School. Attride followed the Hegelian school of philosophy at one time, however his whole world view shifted after he began studying the works of Carl Jung and the theory of archetypes. Attride is essentially a self-taught astrologer, influenced by the works of psychological astrologer Dane Rudyar and the mystical path of Theosophy. "I became interested in astrology for the same reasons I was interested in philosophy," says Attride. "Astrology shows that life does have reason and that there is a rhythm and order to the universe." Attride has developed an international following, including a large number of clients in Hollywood, attracted to Attride for his spiritual insights and practical advice. He prefers that clients see him for two initial one-hour sessions - the first to go over the birth chart and the second, a month later, to discuss specific issues. "Astrology is not about fatalism," says Attride. "The more aware you are, the more you can use your free will. When you are aware of the astrological cycles of your own life, you realize that you don't exist in chaos, but rather in a very well-ordered universe."

## NANCY AZARA
*Psychic consultant*
212-925-5777
www.nancyazara.com
Nancy Azara considers herself an artist first and foremost; she is a sculptor whose work has been featured at a number of galleries and spaces in the city. However, Azara has also become known for her psychic abilities. "While working as an artist, I noticed that I was working with the same energies and qualities of the unseen world," says Azara, from her Tribeca studio. "The art-making process brought me to a place where I was dealing directly with the psychic world." Azara has been a professional psychic for about 20 years. She begins each reading by working on a client's chakras and then works with "guided imagery" to bring a client to a place within themselves, where they can access their own personal power and healing. "My readings are about creating awareness," says Azara. "The client usually doesn't learn anything that they did not already know at a very deep level. I reinforce the wisdom they already have. It is an amazing process."

## CLAUDIA BADER
*Astrologer*
212-874-7441
Claudia Bader is a board certified art therapist and psychotherapist who combines these talents with astrology to create profound changes in people's lives. As the executive director for the Institute for Expressive Analysis, Bader is innovative in her use of astrology with art therapy. "I tend to integrate therapy into each astrology session," says Bader, whose office is on the Upper West Side. For instance, Bader can often tell what transits are happening in a client's horoscope by their artwork. "Someone who is using a lot of dark colors on the palette is most likely going through a Pluto transit," says Bader. She often has her clients draw mandalas, which can give an accurate window into their inner state. Bader published the book Love Planets in 1990 and is also certified by the National Council for Geocosmic Research (NCGR). "Astrology and art go hand-in-hand as a window into a person's soul," says Bader. "Together they are a powerful tools for transformation."

## LAURIE BAUM
*Astrologer*
888-482-7827

| YOGA | ESOTERIC GROUPS | WITCHCRAFT | OCCULT UNDERGROUND | BOOKS | UFOS | BOTANICAS | TANTRA | **ASTROLOGERS & PSYCHICS** |

www.lauriebaum.com
As a journalist, Laurie Baum was trained to be a
skeptic. So when she was sent to do a story on an
astrologer, she didn't expect much. But the accuracy
of the reading she received stunned her - to the
extent that she took a leave of absence from her job
at Business Week to study astrology in London with
famed psychological astrologer Liz Greene. This put
Baum's life in a completely different direction.
Baum returned to graduate school to become a
licensed psychotherapist and now combines psychotherapy and astrology. "It is an excellent combination," says Baum. "The horoscope is a blueprint of
the psychological make-up of a person." Baum says
that in the process of becoming an astrologer, she
has become very psychic and developed the ability
to see auras and look into the past lives of her
clients. She now splits her time between New York
and Los Angeles. Her book Astrological Secrets of
the New Millennium was a success and propelled
her into the limelight as one of the country's best
astrologers. "The sacred symbols of astrology open
pathways in the brain to allow you to access a higher
intelligence," says Baum. "You can use this information to help a client understand the cosmic reason
that they are here on the earth plane."

## ADAM BERNSTEIN
*Psychic medium, tarot reader*
*212-330-8189*
www.betweentheworlds.net
Adam Bernstein can talk to the dead - which is a
great comfort to the living. Bernstein, a Manhattan
native, discovered his mediumship abilities in the
late 1990s, while working as the resident psychic
of the New York Theosophical Society. "While doing
tarot readings, I was getting a lot of other information," says Bernstein. "I was getting messages from
loved ones of my clients who had passed on." Since
then, Bernstein has been concentrating on his
unique ability. Bernstein says that he became aware
of his psychic abilities as a child; he used to accurately predict the weather. It was during college,
however, when he began studying martial arts, that
his psychic abilities began to blossom. "I began to
see auras and energy fields," he says. "The exercises
really began to open some stuff up." He soon began
studying tarot and immersed himself in New York's
metaphysical scene, working for four years at
Enchantments in the East Village, then several years
as a reader at Quest Bookstore. He now splits his

time between Manhattan and his home in the Catskills. "Many people can begin the recovery process after getting a reading and receiving a message from a deceased relative," he says. "They realize that their loved ones are still with them, only on a different level."

## MAX BLACK
*Tarot reader and astrologer*
*212-254-2355*
Max Black is one of the top protégés of Frank Andrews. Black, a graphic artist who lives in the East Village, specializes in reading for creative types - most of his clients are young actors, models, singers and fashion designers. Black has been an astrologer for the past 11 years, however his career as psychic "increased 100-fold" after he began studying with Andrews. He calls Andrews' system "magic" and very straightforward. "The cards give such a clear message, it is truly amazing," says Black. Black does a combination of tarot and astrology in every reading. "In a reading, you don't always get great news about a person's future," says Black. "I always try to be constructive. Some readers only give the positive. My goal is to make a difference in someone's life and let them know where they need to make changes."

## REVA BOND
*Tarot reader, astrologer*
*212-971-1953*
Reva Bond achieved local fame through her regular appearances on Metro Access Psychics, as well as being the "Sports Psychic" on the Don Carlyle Show. "To this day, people will stop me when I am shopping and tell me that they saw me on television," says Bond, who is also a poet, songwriter and musician. Bond now concentrates on client readings, using a combination of astrology and tarot. Bond - who lives in the East Village - has clients all over the world. She says that she considers herself a "psychic counselor," and has been reading the tarot since she was a young girl. She also collects tarot decks - and has more than 60 decks. Her favorite deck is Aleister Crowley's Thoth deck, because it has a more "universal vision." "A good tarot reading expands people's horizons," says Bond. "They get in touch with positive energy and remove the barriers to their success."

## J.B. BROWN
*Spiritual development, tarot,*
*advanced crystal healing*

*212-473-7753*

For the past 30 years, J.B. Brown has been one of the city's most eclectic intuitive healers and readers. Formerly of Soho, Brown recently moved her healing space to Fort Green, Brooklyn. She says that she was born intuitive and aware. "When I was young, I knew exactly where I was from during my last incarnation," says Brown, who has cultivated her awareness throughout years of metaphysical studies. Brown practices a number of healing modalities, including space clearing, chakra balancing and her primary modality, Energy Transfer. "I don't like to call myself a psychic," says Brown. "I don't want to get in the way of someone's free will. It is important that people take responsibility for their own choices." A typical session with Brown could involve the use of crystals, bodywork, flower essences and psychotherapy. The Energy Transfer is a "five-session experience," which "transforms negative energy into positive energy." The hands-on sessions clear out energy "obstructions" which may hinder the life-flow of a person. "I get down to the bottom line during a session," says Brown. "Everything that happens to us also lives in our bodies. Once that energy is released, you can live your life in a new, unobstructed way."

## CONNIE BURO
*Psychic, tarot reader, energy healer*
*212-529-8205*

Connie Buro uses her psychic skills to help her clients find their "authentic soul purpose." "The goal of a reading is to help a person find their true potential and talents," says Buro, who is one of the top readers at the Association for Research and Enlightenment (A.R.E.) in Chelsea. Buro says that she cannot separate her psychic work from her own spiritual beliefs. A Brooklyn native, Buro began her spiritual path in the 1960s with involvement in Transcendental Meditation; she then spent 18 years in the Science of Mind movement. "I always felt there was more," says Buro. Then she discovered the work of Edgar Cayce and says she found her true path. Buro ended up taking an early retirement from the New York School Board and moving to the A.R.E. headquarters in Virginia Beach for a year and half to volunteer and take classes. She returned to New York as an accomplished psychic and healer and now conducts readings both at the A.R.E. offices and at her home. Her focus in her readings is to assist clients in recognizing that they are spiritual beings.

| YOGA | ESOTERIC GROUPS | WITCHCRAFT | OCCULT UNDERGROUND | BOOKS | UFOS | BOTANICAS | TANTRA | **ASTROLOGERS & PSYCHICS** |

"If someone does not like what they see when they look in the mirror, the person needs to change from within first," says Buro. "The reading gives clients all the tools they need to change."

## WILMA CARROLL
*Psychic, tarot reader, palmistry, astrology and numerology*
*212-410-1299*
Wilma Carroll uses an original divination method that blends palm and tarot card readings with astrology and numerology. Carroll began her metaphysical studies in the early 1970s, traveling to California, the Middle East, Asia, London and finally Madrid, Spain, where she spent three years. "It was an exciting time," says Carroll. "I met with the best spiritualists, Wiccans, palmists and yogis of that time, particularly in London." Returning to the New York area, she immersed herself into the New Age community, giving popular lectures on tarot and other forms of occult self-help. She quickly built a private practice as an intuitive consultant, appearing on numerous television programs, including Live with Regis and the Late Show with David Letterman. "I blend a lot of things together during my readings," says Carroll, who begins each session by examining the client's palm. Carroll has published articles in numerous magazines and is about to release a new book, The 2 Hour Tarot Tutor. Carroll conducts most of her readings from her Upper East Side apartment. She also gives educational programs on the practical uses of divination for self-analysis. "I never tell people what to do. Instead, I show them where the winds are blowing," says Carroll. "You can't control all of the external forces around you, but you can control your responses to them."

## LEONARD CASSARA
*Tarot reader*
*718-816-7316*
It was an interest in the predictions of Edgar Cayce, the "sleeping prophet," which initially got Leonard Cassara interested in the tarot. Cassara began studying tarot at the Association for Research and Enlightenment (A.R.E.) in the 1980s and now is one of the A.R.E.'s top readers. "It was Edgar Cayce's belief that, if we are made in the image of God, then we must have the attributes of God," says Cassara. "And one of those attributes is the ability to see the future." Cassara, however, does not see his readings as only telling the future. "It is soul development," he

says. "I believe that tarot has a higher purpose that can provide fundamental answers to our existence." Cassara gives regular readings at the A.R.E. center in Chelsea, and offers both half-hour and hour sessions. "Tarot readings carry with them a great deal of responsibility," says Cassara. "We need to remember that we are spiritual creatures having a physical experience here on Earth."

### RON CIRAMI
*Tarot reader*
*212-570-9738*
For Ron Cirami, a client's future is not etched in stone. As a result, Cirami - who studied under Frank Andrews - utilizes several blank cards in his deck. "When a blank card comes up, I know that the future indicated for the client is conditional," says Cirami. "The client has a choice that they have to make for the future." Cirami had been interested in the tarot for a number of years, but it was Andrews who "unlocked the keys" for him. "The tarot holds the elements of destiny and dreams of our lives," says Cirami. "It shows where we are headed and points out the areas in which we need to change." Cirami lives on the Upper East Side and works with a wide variety of professional clients.

### ROBERT COHEN
*Esoteric astrologer, channel, tarot reader*
*917-692-4651*
As a professor of mathematics, Robert Cohen really took to astrology when he was first introduced to the science in 1969. After all, astrology is nothing more than math, measuring the degrees and aspects of planets. But when Cohen picked up a deck of tarot cards, it was a completely different story - he immediately began channeling information directly from the cards. "Astrology and math are very left-brain activities," Cohen says. "But channeling and the tarot use a completely different side of the brain." Cohen uses both modalities in every reading he does. He begins first with a 40-minute channeled reading from the tarot cards. "I'm guided from a very high source," says Cohen. "It resonates exactly to where people are at." With the issues clarified, Cohen then looks at the astrological chart. Cohen's readings have been influenced a great deal by the work of Alice Bailey, who wrote Esoteric Astrology. He says that he carries a copy of the book with him at all times. Cohen lives in Greenwich Village, however teaches at the University of District of

Columbia during the week. Cohen also specializes in medical astrology, and often alerts clients to hidden illnesses they may have. "The tarot and astrology work synergistically," says Cohen. "Some people want to turn the session into a counseling session, but when I channel information, they get exactly what they need. They get predictions and they also find out what they need to be working on."

## ELLIE CRYSTAL
*Psychic, tarot reader, medium*
*718-833-4264*
*www.crystalinks.com*
Ellie Crystal had her first metaphysical experience when she was eleven years old, in the Nevada desert, where she was vacationing with her parents. It was dusk and Crystal says that she came face-to-face with a large, "diamond-shaped spaceship," which hovered over her and her family. Crystal says that it was during this supernatural experience that she met her "spirit guide," Zoroaster, and soon realized that she had the power to heal people and tell the future. "I later learned that Zoroaster played the roles of many prominent characters in the Earth's history, including Thoth, who was also Hermes Trismegistus," says Crystal, who grew up and still lives in Brooklyn. In 1984, Crystal embraced her spiritual life and went from a "middle-class Jewish housewife" to a teacher, psychologist and psychic reader. She hosted her own television show, The Metaphysical Experience and began working with other people, under the guidance of Zoroaster, also known as "Z". Her spiritual quest has taken her throughout the world and, thanks to her popular website, she has developed an international client list. Her readings include information from "Z," her own psychic information and the ability to see the "reality" behind any situation. "When I do a reading, I look at the soul of the person," say Crystal. "I address a person's soul mission and their karma. A lot of my work here on the planet is about creating balance - both in the universe and in people's lives."

## KATINA DEMETRA
*Psychic tarot reader*
*212-957-1779*
Katina Demetra developed her psychic skills growing up in Los Angeles as a hearing-impaired young girl. "I tried to hide the fact that I couldn't hear," says Demetra. "As a result I studied people very carefully, their facial expressions and body language. Instead

of hearing their words, I became to feel intuitively what people would say." Pretty soon her intuition expanded to what people were thinking as well. "The reactions I got from them were not great. I learned pretty quickly to clam up," she says. However, her interest in psychic work continued. She learned palmistry, tarot and astrology and uses all three modalities in her readings. Demetra's readings come from a profoundly spiritual place; she joined Self-Realization Fellowship (SRF) after having a vision of SRF founder Paramahansa Yogananda. Demetra's hearing impairment is difficult to notice during her in-person readings. "I only have problems on the phone, when I cannot see someone," says Demetra. She conducts her readings in her Lincoln Square-area apartment, which is decorated with photos of various spiritual masters. She begins with an examination of the palm, then a discussion of the astrological chart and finally she draws several tarot spreads to get at specific issues raised during the reading. "I connect the client with their higher self," says Demetra. "They have to embrace this part of themselves and rediscover the passion in their life, what really makes their soul sing."

### ALLISON DIAMOND
*Astrologer, tarot reader, numerologist*
*212-579-2214*
Allison Diamond uses astrology, tarot and numerology in every reading she does. She throws down 12 cards - one for each astrological house to find out where the client's issues are in the horoscope. She then looks at the numerology of the client's name and birth date. "Every bit of extra information helps," says Diamond. "It helps focus the reading." Diamond has been reading for more than 23 years and has studied with such luminaries such as Joanna Shannon and Mae R. Rudlam. Diamond takes a distinct metaphysical and spiritual approach to her readings. She is an active member of Unity Church, a metaphysical organization in Manhattan. "I like to educate people and help them find their life purpose," she says. "The reading lets the client know who they are and how to get back on their true path."

### RONNIE GALE DREYER
*Vedic astrologer*
*212-799-9187*
*www.ronniedreyer.com*
It was during a trip to India in the 1970s that Ronnie Gale Dreyer first began studying Jyotish, the Indian,

Vedic science of astrology. At the time, not many Westerners had heard of Vedic astrology. Dreyer had to meet her Indian Astrology teacher at Benares-Hindu University every evening after he finished class. "I had to wear a Sari when I met him," says Dreyer. "It wasn't very common for an American woman to be alone in India - I had to be very modest." Although Dreyer had studied Western astrology, she became hooked on the Vedic astrology for its stunning precision in predicting events. "Vedic astrology can pinpoint, in a very clear way, issues relating to health, marriage and career choices," says Dreyer. "It is an ancient system that is time-tested." Unlike Western astrology, the Vedic system offers "remedial measures" that one can take to "soften" a bad astrological aspect. Some of the measures could be as simple as wearing a specific gemstone, chanting an appropriate mantra, or volunteering at a soup kitchen. Dreyer uses the best of both systems. She also draws a Western horoscope for all of her clients to examine the progressed Moon and the outer planet transits. "The Pluto transits can be very important, which the Western chart will give," says Dreyer. Most people use Vedic astrology for the timing it gives. "Everything in life is timing," says Dreyer. "The essence of astrology is finding out your cycles in life, when to act and when not to act."

## PATRICIA EINSTEIN
*Clairvoyant, psychic tarot reader*
*212-627-3810*
For years, Patricia Einstein has been teaching others how to develop their intuitive abilities. Einstein, the author of Uncommon Sense, believes that everyone has the ability to become psychic. "Psychic readings are not just about predictions and fortune-telling," she says. "The future comes from the present. It is more important to get a deeper understanding about what is happening in your life now." Einstein generally begins a session by holding a personal object, such as a ring or watch, to "tune into a client." She says that she receives psychic impressions during the reading and may do a tarot spread in order to focus on a specific question. Einstein says that she won't read the charts of children because the personality has not formed yet. "I don't like to treat a psychic reading as a parlor game," says Einstein. "People who come for a reading are interested in gaining more awareness about themselves and their place in the world."

## THOMAS EISELE
*Psychic, tarot reader, astrologer*
*212-569-8326*

Tom Eisele's psychic abilities were not always welcome in his life. While in college, he would often leave his body just prior to falling asleep, and astrally travel through his dorm building. His answer, at the time, was to numb himself with alcohol. However, he has since learned to see his occult powers as a gift. Eisele's spiritual mentor is the late English occultist Aleister Crowley and Eisele has a personal relationship with Crowley that transcends time and space. "We share the same horoscope," Eisele says of Crowley. "When you progress Crowley's chart to the present time, it becomes the progressed chart of my own horoscope." In October 2000, Eisele conducted a ritual, and invoked "Crowley's spirit." The visions that Eisele received during the ritual were both personal and apocalyptic, and resulted in his upcoming book The Rose and the Scorpion, which were the two primary symbols shown to Eisele. A year later to the day of his vision, Eisele's ex-wife Rosa was killed in a plane crash while the Sun was in the sign of Scorpio. "It was a powerful vision, that said a great deal about occult philosophy, that there is light and darkness in all things and everything in life is cyclical," he says. Eisele's first book, Modern Magical Keys, is also about to be published. It discusses ritual and talisman-making. Eisele currently gives readings and lectures at the Association for Research and Enlightenment (A.R.E.) in Chelsea, but prefers to do "house calls" when it comes to psychic readings. "When I go into someone's home, I can immediately sense if there are other spirits there. I get a better picture of what is going on in that person's life," says Eisele. "People tend to get stuck in negative patterns, which show up in the horoscope. My goal is to free people from their old patterns and the first step is when people become more aware."

## FAHRUSHA
*Psychic, tarot reader*
*212-254-5948*
*www.fahrusha.com*

When Fahrusha does a tarot card reading, she brings with it years of esoteric study. Fahrusha began her career as a Middle Eastern dancer, though she has always had psychic abilities and gave readings in her neighborhood as a teen. Her father, who was psychic, made talismans and a device with which to "communicate with other realms." Fahrusha has been to sacred power spots around the globe, including Egypt many times. Fahrusha begins each reading by getting a mental picture of the client, even as the client is on the phone with her making an appointment. She begins the actual reading by looking at the client's palm "to get an overall view of the person," and then moves into a tarot card reading. Her clients often bring photos of people and pets, living and dead, about whom they wish to learn more. Fahrusha believes that the forces she works with are mysterious, and through understanding these forces, one can "gain a better insight into one's life." But most importantly, she tries to help people make the best possible decisions for their lives. Fahrusha conducts metaphysical research during her overseas travels. For instance, she has an affinity for cats and studies the esoteric role they played in ancient Egypt. She believes that the cats live simultaneously on more than one dimensional plane, transmitting information between realms. "The cat has always been a sacred animal in Egypt," says Fahrusha. "In a way, psychics are like the Egyptian cat - we are here in this world, yet we also exist in a completely different reality."

## CATHERINE FERGUSON
*Pet psychic, smoke reader, flower reader*
*212-445-4730; 201-433-7955*
Communicating with the animal kingdom is something that Catherine Ferguson specializes in. She can establish a telepathic relationship by looking into the animal's eyes - or simply connecting through a photograph. Sometimes she is surprised at what she learns. "During one reading I did on a dog, I learned that the dog was a teenage boy in a previous life and was very close with the present dog's owner," says Ferguson. "There are often karmic connections between animals and their owners." She trained with famed animal communicator Sally Jordan Austin and says that an animal reading can often "bring a new dimension to the relationship with a pet." Ferguson also does the unique divination techniques of "smoke readings" and "flower readings," that she learned through the First Universal Spiritualist Church. She studied with Rev. Anna Jederiewski, who taught her how to run a piece of paper over a flame and then read the pattern of the smoke on the paper. Ferguson tells the future through the "images evoked" from the smoke pattern. Her divinations that use flowers are "gentle

readings," which provide guidance and insight into life issues. "People get very supported from these types of readings," she says.

### ROSEMARY GANT
*Palm reader, tarot reader*
212-874-64903

When Rosemary Gant gives a palm reading, she doesn't only look at the palm - she also looks at the fingerprints. "It is the fingerprints that tell you what your life purpose is," says Gant. "They tell you where your greatest satisfaction is in life." Gant studied with noted palmistry teacher Richard Unger, to get a more in-depth understanding of the skin ridge patterns, and how these patterns correspond to physical and emotional issues. Gant says that the lines often will change in a person's hand, as the person's life changes. But the fingerprints always stay the same. "That is because your soul mission does not change. We are all born for a purpose, and the key of a good reading is to find this purpose," says Gant. Gant also uses tarot cards during her readings to get at current life issues. She generally likes to conduct her readings either in a client's home, or in a neutral location. "My approach is not one of fortune-telling, but one of an approach to life," says Gant, who does a lot of work in the entertainment industry. "By understanding your life purpose, you can optimize your life."

### ELLEN GOLDBERG
*Tarot, palm reader*
212-924-5816

Ellen Goldberg approaches divination from a very deep level. As a psychotherapist, she has studied Eastern and Western philosophy. "When I first began studies of the I-Ching I was amazed," says Goldberg. "I realized that there is a divine intelligence that really loves to communicate with us." Goldberg has been reading professionally for nearly 30 years and is also on the staff of the New York Open Center, where she teaches tarot. Her two-year Professional Tarot and Palm Reading Courses are among the most comprehensive in the country. Goldberg says that all of her readings are a combination of tarot and palm reading. "The first thing I do is look at the hands," says Goldberg. "It is very powerful when you integrate the two together." Goldberg says that she used her background in psychotherapy to help clients deal with any issues that may come up during the reading.

**ERIC HEAD**
*Hand analyst*
*718-472-4342*
Through a person's hand, Eric Head can find a person's life purpose. Head looks at the lines of the hand, as well as the texture of the skin, flexibility of the hand and the fingerprints. "It all adds up to who a person is," says Head. "You are carrying around your divine contract - and it is all written on your hand." Head studied with noted palmistry teacher Richard Unger and approaches each reading through a deeply metaphysical approach. Head is an associate minister at the Science of Mind Church, which promotes a positive thinking philosophy of life. Each reading takes about an hour and is personalized according to the needs of the client. Head also teaches palmistry and spiritual counseling in a ten-week course taught out of his Queens home. "A reading will give you clarity about your life and will tell you what your soul agreement is in coming into the world," says Head. "Although the lines in your hand may change according to your consciousness, the fingerprints - which give the soul destiny - never change. The reading will help your highest potential to flower."

**HEAVEN**
*Indian Vedic palm reader*
*718-224-1667*
Heaven, formerly known as Lali Kakar, learned palm reading while growing up in New Delhi, India. His style is direct and accurate. "Life is recorded in the subconscious, which is reflected in the hand," says Heaven, who moved to New York City 14 years ago. He teaches, as well as appears at numerous expos and conventions. In one weekend, he claims he can teach all the basics to give a successful palm reading. The Queens resident is also a student of self-help and psychology - his other passion is as a motivational speaker. In every reading, Heaven uses his motivational skills to help the client to achieve their destiny. "Palm reading is an excellent tool, but it takes the client to use the information wisely to improve their life," says Heaven. "And it is my job to get them to look in that direction."

**JENNA HUNT**
*Astrologer*, feng shui *consultant,*
*flower essence healer*
*212-615-6979*
Jenna Hunt specializes in bringing "practical magic" into people's lives. Using feng shui and flower

| YOGA | ESOTERIC GROUPS | WITCHCRAFT | OCCULT UNDERGROUND | BOOKS | UFOS | BOTANICAS | TANTRA | **ASTROLOGERS & PSYCHICS** |

essences, Hunt can help address challenging issues brought up during an astrological reading. "I tend to focus on people's gifts," says Hunt, who also dances professionally. "I can bring light to the shadows of someone's life." With Jupiter prominent in her own chart, Hunt has an expansive philosophy of life, seeing the positive even in difficult client circumstances. Hunt also considers herself psychic and looks for the "synchronicities" that occur with a client. "The universe is constantly communicating with us, we just need to tune into it," says Hunt. Hunt feels that using both Western astrology and feng shui is a powerful combination for self-transformation. "I always try to relate feng shui principles in my astrological readings," she says. "In certain cases, a person's issues can be resolved through the use of feng shui."

## ISADORA
*Medium, channel, tea-leaf reader*
*516-241-3589*

Isadora is a woman of mystery. This intriguing 23-year-old is one of the city's best tea-leaf readers, practicing the arcane art of looking into an empty cup of tea and divining the future. Isadora was "discovered" by astrologer Jenny Lynch while Isadora was conducting tea readings at Three Jewels Bookstore in the Bowery. "I consider myself a channel," says Isadora, who splits her time between New York and Los Angeles. "I speak to the gods and the gods speak back to me." She learned tea-leaf reading from her grandmother, a spiritualist from "down South." Isadora, who follows a Wiccan and Tibetan Buddhist spiritual path, begins each reading by "casting a circle" and conducting a prayer and meditation. She then "channels a higher power" during her tea or tarot reading. She ends each session with suggestions on what type of candles to use for healing and spiritual-growth purposes. Isadora says that she prefers to conduct readings in the city's more eclectic coffee shops. She says that many of her clients are "people who will be famous." "When someone gets a reading with me, they get in touch with their higher power," says Isadora. "Their chakras also become aligned and they get much more clarity in their lives."

## CAROL JEPSON
*Astrologer*
*212-758-4887*
*www.caroljepson-astrologer.com*

Carol Jepson has received the highest certification

from the National Council for Geocosmic Research (NCGR). Her specialty is the precise timing of events. "Many astrologers don't forecast events anymore," says Jepson. "My focus is on forecasting events, whether it be getting a new job, or meeting someone new." Jepson has also been researching, teaching and reading tarot cards for the past 30 years. Her tarot readings give her a "window" into what is happening currently in a client's life. She also trained with legendary New York medium Clifford Bias in order to develop her psychic ability. Jepson also specializes in events planning, the use of horary charts (answering questions) and investigating relocation possibilities. She can tell you when to open a business or if that move to Los Angeles is good for you. "Even the best psychics can have a bad day," says Jepson. "But astrology is a science. It always will provide you with a road map for the future."

### ANN JOHNSON
*Psychic, tarot reader, palm reader, face reader*
212-246-4975
Ann Johnson is known as the "self-help psychic." For the past 25 years, Johnson has read the auras and palms of New York's rich and famous. She developed her innate psychic ability while reading for her fellow actors about their love relationships while working as an actress on Broadway. She is one of the first New York psychics to read at corporate events. She says that is able to "tune into" a person and advise them with the answers to their questions. During a reading, Johnson will give people specific meditations, affirmations or life changes to make, so that they can follow their true life path. "I believe in emphasizing the positive," says Johnson.

### ROBERT JOHNSON
*Trance medium*
212-405-2976
www.angelspeakstoyou.com
Robert Johnson came into contact with a group of angels from the star system "Alpha Centuri" more than 35 years ago while participating in a local meditation group.His relationship with the angels grew over the years so that now he can channel them at will, he says, for the benefit of humanity. "This is not fortune-telling, this is spritual counseling," says Johnson, who give consultations in the tradition of Edgar Cayce. Johnson begins each consultation with a prayer and brief meditation, before the Alpha Centurian entities take over his body. Johnson is a

"full trance" medium, which means that he has no memory of what the angels say. "I tape every session so that I know what messages the angels have given," says Johnson. The channeled angels start each session by telling the client something important about their personal lives, and then the client is invited to ask the angels questions. "The angels will tell you about the important issues in your life, including past life issues," says Johnson. "That is the job of the angels - to bring people back home to God."

## JEFFREY KISHNER
*Astrologer*
*718-907-0847*
*www.jeffreykishner.com*
Jeffrey Kishner is relatively new on the astrological scene, however he is making his mark for his integration of psychotherapy and the horoscope. Kishner studied with noted astrology teacher John Marchesella and earned his master's degree in counseling psychology from the California Institute of Integral Studies. "I do many single-session con-sultations, but I also offer the option of long-term psychotherapy," says Kishner, who works out of his home in Park Slope, Brooklyn. "Using astrology together with psychotherapy is powerful tool which gives the therapist and client a snapshot of the client's psyche." Kishner is also a movie buff and founded the popular astrological website astrologyatthemovies.com, which features astro-logical essays about actors, actresses, movies and directors. "Life is all about cycles. Some may be bad, but there is always an end to a bad cycle," says Kishner. "Life always changes and astrology can give people hope by showing them the light at the end of the tunnel."

## JAN KOEHLER
*Tarot reader for humans and pets*
*718-720-6553*
Jan Koehler became interested in animal communi-cation after a tarot client asked her for advice on a misbehaving dog. Koehler came to the realization that she could communicate with the dog through a "telepathic communications bridge." She then began giving tarot readings to animals. "Animals often have a message that they would like to give to humans," says Koehler, who is a licensed massage therapist as well. Koehler works with fellow pet psychic Catherine Ferguson to teach a course

called: All Hearts are Equal: Our Animal Friends - Building a Communication Bridge. Much of Koehler's work revolves around people who have adopted animals from shelters. She uses tarot and her psychic abilities to determine the past experiences of each animal. "Sometimes the animal wants to tell me what happened to them, and other times they want to forget. Animals live, for the most part, in the present," says Koehler. Koehler, of course, still gives tarot readings for humans. She started to develop her psychic abilities while working as a massage therapist in the 1970s. "I noticed that whenever I touched someone, psychic information would come to me," she says. "At the same time, I began to realize that we are all connected together - and that includes the animal kingdom."

### REV. ELIZABETH ANN LEVY
*Psychic intuitive, spiritual counselor*
212-243-0579
*http://hometown.aol.com/ealrev/index.htm*
Rev. Elizabeth Ann Levy combines her psychic and intuitive ability with a spiritual focus of being an interfaith minister. Her readings include tarot, numerology, astrology and some palm reading for "guidance on relationships, career and personal growth." Rev. Levy was ordained in 1987 by The New Seminary and says that her emphasis in every reading is spiritual. "I look at an issue in someone's life to see what is behind it," says Levy. "Many times these issues can block healing and prevent a person from reaching their potential." Levy has an eclectic background and is also a Middle Eastern dancer. She also conducts scientific handwriting analysis for personality profiles and vocational aptitudes. "My readings are pragmatic and practical," says Levy. "I bring in a lot of psychic information but also bring in my spiritual side to every reading." As an interfaith minister, Rev. Levy is also available to officiate at weddings and other spiritual ceremonies.

### BART LIDOFSKY
*Tarot reader*
917-951-8278
*www.e-magick.com/tarot*
Bart Lidofsky began his tarot reading career more than 25 years ago, while a high school student studying stage magic. "I thought tarot would be a good addition to my stage routine," says Lidofsky. "I ended up reading Eden Gray's book on tarot and have been studying ever since." Lidofsky is cur-

rently one of the in-house tarot readers at Quest Bookstore on East 53rd Street and is a frequent lecturer at the New York Theosophical Society. His tarot course at the Theosophical Society is one of the more popular in the city. "I take a very corporate approach to my teaching," says Lidofsky. "By the end of the six sessions, students are able to conduct readings. I give very specific methods for memorizing the deck, as well as strategies for establishing a reading business." Lidofsky's own reading style is unique; he uses Aleister Crowley's Book of Thoth deck because its minor arcana include the elemental dignities on each card. Lidofsky also reads each tarot spread "as a whole," and does not look at each card separately. "I look at the way each card relates to the other cards in the spread," says Lidofsky, who has training as a computer systems analyst. "I look at the tarot spread as a system, rather than a group of individual pieces." Lidofsky can be found every Saturday at Quest; he offers both hour-long sessions, as well as ten-minute "quick focus" readings.

## JOHN LIGHT
*Astrologer*
*212-724-4516*
For John Light, activism and astrology go hand-in-hand. "Finding our cosmic purpose is the most important thing a person can do on the planet," says Light. "If astrology is not helping the world, then why do it?" Light began studying back in 1974 and has been a professional since 1980; he was resident astrologer at the Feather Pipe Ranch in Montana from 1982-1985, before moving to New York City in 1989. During the 1980s, Light also became active in the peace movement. Light sees his work in astrology as helping in the overall spiritual evolution of the planet. "What I do is help a person find their own potential and unique gift to the world," says Light. "Life itself is a gift and we have a responsibility to use these gifts for the betterment of all." Light's style has changed through his nearly 30 years of practice. "Some of my best readings come through reading right out of the ephemeris, without a chart." Light sees our present time as an "incredible period of transition." It could "go either way," however. "We have a choice right now. We could go Plutonian, very dark, or we could choose the path of light," he says. "Astrology is an important tool for us to create an awareness to make the right choices both personally - and collectively."

## LILY
*Palm reader, fortune teller*
*212-982-5995*

Lily is one of the best bargains in town for telling your future - that is, if you can find her. Lily can usually be found sitting on a chair near the corner of Mulberry and Bayard Streets in Chinatown, in front of the Chinatown Manpower Project. For $15 she'll read your palm, face and do up a quick astrological chart. Lily says that she learned her divination techniques in her homeland of China. If you agree to a reading, Lily will pull out a small, plastic chair for you to sit on, amid the bustling pedestrian foot traffic. She will first ask your date and time of birth, to get your "animal sign." Then, she'll grab your hand, examining the lines. She gives specific predictions about marriage and money. She also gives specific instructions to overcome bad aspects - like growing certain fingernails longer to extend the length of the finger and wearing rings on certain fingers to "activate" the planetary force. Lily says that she is usually sitting at her location most afternoons, when the weather is good. "These are very ancient Chinese practices," says Lily. "What I see in your hand and face does not lie."

## MITCHELL LEWIS
*Astrologer (medical and financial)*
*212-726-3814*
*www.mitchastro.com*

As a musician, Mitchell Lewis sees a strong connection between music and astrology. "Astrology is music - planets are the notes and aspects are the chords," says Lewis, an accomplished jazz musician who has taught music at the New School. "The Greeks knew this. But, hey, we discovered Jazz - and we have better chords now." Lewis has taken his musical skill and applied it to astrology - he is one of the best financial and medical astrologers in the city. He honed his skills on the floor of the New York Commodities Exchange, forecasting commodity prices, using astrological methods. "We had some amazing results," says Lewis. "I also began doing the charts of the traders. I started predicting when and what type of health problems they would have." Lewis has studied with such luminaries as the late Isabela Hickey from Boston. He also is still active in the arts and has recently completed a play Nostrodamus: A Man of Vision, which deals with the little-known fact that Nostrodamus was a practicing Jew. Lewis specializes in using the horoscope to pinpoint weaknesses in the body, so that the client can prevent future diseases. His readings incorporate physical, emotional and spiritual information. Lewis also teaches now at the New York Astrological Center. "The only way to change your destiny is to change your attitude," says Lewis. "There are gifts found in your astrological chart that you may not be aware of."

### LUHREN LOUP
*Seeress*
*212-348-1356*
*www.luhrenloup.com*
Luhren Loup helps people through her own unique spirituality, based upon shamanism, Wicca and Native American practices. "I'm not into straight prediction - I deal with things from a shamanic perspective," says Loup, who has trained with shaman Michael Harner, as well as the Wicca Priestess Starhawk. Loup says that she uses tarot cards in her readings and will also work with a client's dreams. "I try to get at what is in a client's psyche," says Loup. "I also help a client find their power animal - everyone has one." Loup went on a vision quest 12 years ago and, as a result of that, her own psychic abilities have grown. Loup also conducts space-clearing rituals. "My task is to teach others how to tap into psychic energies within the self that are outside the bonds of society," says Loup. "Ultimately, it's about power - how to get it and how to use it."

### MICHAEL LUTIN
*Astrologer*
*212-529-6464*
*www.michaellutin.com*
Michael Lutin is probably best known for his irreverent and entertaining astrology column in Vanity Fair and German Vogue, though his real love is working with people one-on-one. "Astrology is by far the best diagnostic tool for the issues in our lives," says Lutin. "I try to give people a perspective on their lives - as well as to give them back the power that was taken away from them in their childhood." Lutin says he became interested in astrology through the "pop art" of Roy Lichtenstein, who portrayed stereotypical characters in his drawings. "I began to notice that character was destiny," says Lutin. "People were archetypes - they were living their astrological signs." Although astrology can point out issues and probable events, Lutin says that it takes work on

the client's part to improve their lives. "If you want to change the future, you need to change what you are doing in the present," says Lutin. "This takes continuous dedication and practice. My goal is to eventually free people from the need to see me by giving them the tools to empower themselves and letting them know that their past experiences are a gift."

## JENNY LYNCH
*Astrologer*
*212-502-0732*
*www.jennylynch.com*
Jenny Lynch is on the cutting-edge of astrology. She began her astrology studies in the 1970s and has become one of the city's most fashionable and creative astrologers. Her eclectic interests have drawn her to the esoteric studies of Uranian, Renaissance and ancient astrology; she is also a master at Astro-Carto-Graphy, the art of using astrological information for relocation. "I can look at a chart and within a few minutes I know exactly what the client has to do in order to achieve their dreams," says Jenny. Many people may know Lynch from her cable TV show Star Power. Lynch also puts together special events, like the Tea Salon Readings at the T Salon (also reviewed in this section). Jenny has recently teamed up with astrologers Christopher Warnock and William Stickevers to perform Ceremonial Renaissance Astrology, in which rituals are conducted to channel certain astrological powers, based upon the ancient Arabic text the Picatrix. Jenny is also using her astrological knowledge to launch a new company, Sacred-Events.com, that arranges special events, according to the power of the planets. "A lot of ancient astrological information is now coming to light," says Jenny. "We are now able to use astrology to improve our lives and to quicken our spiritual evolution."

## JOHN MARCHESELLA
*Astrologer*
*212-255-8497*
*www.astrojohn.com*
John Marchesella is one of New York City's finest astrologers. As past president of the New York Chapter of the National Council for Geocosmic Research (NCGR), Marchesella is one of the area's leading astrologer instructors, teaching with wisdom from his years of experience. Marchesella designed the astrological curriculum for the New York Open Center and has been a speaker at a

number of professional events, like the United Astrology Congress. Marchesella uses his experience as a certified psychotherapist to give his readings and extra depth. Marchesella conducts readings out of his Chelsea apartment, concentrating on the traditional elements of the chart. "For every season, there is a purpose under heaven," says Marchesella. "Astrology indicates what season we are born into, and therefore, what purpose we serve in life, as well as revealing the meaning of the current time."

### PATRICIA MASTERS
*Clairvoyant, clairaudient*
*212-288-5467*
Patricia Masters usually shuns publicity, but was gracious enough to conduct an interview for this guide. "The people who need to find me, usually find me," says Masters, a truly gifted psychic. Masters calls her psychic ability a "gift" and says that she became aware of it as a child, growing up in Manhattan and Brooklyn. Her family encouraged her talents and would often gather around to ask her questions. Masters prefers to work with people who come to her "at a very particular time in their life, when they need direction." She takes a spiritual approach to her readings, but she is also known for a making "very clear predictions" about the future. As a preparation for her reading, she will write the name of her client on a piece of paper and meditate on the name. Her readings are deep and stunningly accurate - sometimes delving into the past life of a client. "I help a client affirm themselves, to know who they are," says Masters. "I help them know what direction to take in life."

### SHALA F. MATTINGLY
*Past Life Regressionist*
*212-307-1049*
*www.past-life.com*
Sometimes the quickest way to solve today's problems is by going back in time to a previous lifetime. Since 1981, Shala F. Mattingly has been helping clients live better in the present, by examining their past lives. "The conscious mind comprises a minute part of who we are," says Mattingly. "This is why it is necessary to go into the subconscious level of mind." Mattingly, who is originally from London, England, is certified in clinical, forensic and regressive hypnosis and is considered one of the country's foremost experts in past life regression therapy."

Most people who come to work with me know they can do better, but feel blocked by major issues that keep sabotaging them," says Mattingly. "These issues may be trapped emotions that originated in some other time and place. Once the subconscious level of mind is accessed, the origin of the problem can be found and released." For instance, Mattingly tells of a client who was unable to conceive a child. During the hypnotic regression, the client revealed that in a past life her lover killed her when he discovered she was pregnant. In her present life she married the same man, and her old subconscious fear of losing her life if she became pregnant was preventing her from conceiving. "I then worked with her to release the old memories and to forgive her husband. She was then able to become pregnant and have a child." Mattingly says, "Fear is at the root of all our problems. By releasing fear and replacing it with love, healing can take place. It is life changing!"

### DEB MCBRIDE
*Astrologer*
718-832-3129
Deb McBride has had an interest in astrology since she was five years old. "This is something I've always wanted to do - for me it is a calling," says McBride, who has been practicing professionally since 1986. McBride's style of astrology is very therapeutic; she honed her skills by studying counseling for three years with noted astrologer Michael Lutin. Her clients are primarily people who are "in a situation and want to know how and when they will get out of the situation." That situation could be anything from a bad relationship to an unfulfilling job. "The astrology chart is amazing because it can pinpoint exactly when these cycles will end." McBride lives in Park Slope, but her clients are from all over. "I specialize in helping with people who are at a crossroads in their lives," says McBride. "I am not a psychic. All of the healing that takes place in my sessions occurs because there is a dialogue going on. I make people aware of what is going on in their lives."

### MARY ELLEN MCCABE
*Astrologer*
914-478-0193
www.maryellenmccabe.com
Mary Ellen McCabe specializes in finding a person's "soul mission." "I look at the natal chart as a map of the higher self, and as a tool to actualize the soul mission of one's life," says McCabe, who uses the

configurations such as the "grand cross" and "finger of God," to determine one's destiny. McCabe began her own journey into astrology in the late 1960s, after she discovered Agni Yoga, along with the works of Alice Bailey and Rudolph Steiner. In addition to sparking an interest in astrology, McCabe also became fascinated by the sacred destiny of the United States of America, as set forth by the Founding Fathers. The result was her musical play and CD Heroes and Heroines, which uses music to tell the story of the esoteric principles behind the founding of this country. "I used astrology to explain both the founding of the country, as well as the times of major darkness, like the Civil War," says McCabe. "During the low time of this country, Saturn and Pluto were always active in the country's chart." She notes that our country currently is undergoing similar, challenging astrological aspects. McCabe says that she uses her more than 30 years of esoteric training in her readings. "I'm interested in the soul application of astrology," says McCabe. "The reading helps to clarify one's real purpose in life and to actualize one's talents."

## FAITH MCINERNEY
*Astrologer*
*212-598-0754*

Faith McInerney has the reputation of being a "nuts and bolts" astrologer - that is an astrologer who can pin down specific events and issues. McInerney uses Uranian astrology to identify the "real life issues" in one's life, like profession and finances, particularly where your money is coming from. "Uranian astrology is almost a completely different animal than traditional astrology - it is high-tech," says McInerney, who studied with Charles Emerson. "Most astrologers talk about psychological aspects of a chart, but the Uranian system focuses on material circumstances." Uranian astrology was discovered in 1914, by a German, Alfred Witte, and is a complicated system that is focused on specific prediction. "My job is to talk about what the weather will be and from what direction the wind will come from," says McInerney. She says that her best teacher has been experience; she has read thousands of horoscopes. "Astrology has demonstrated to me that the universe was created by a divine intelligence," she says. "The world moves according to a specific cycle according to the planets. The key is to understand these cycles."

## MEETINGS WITH REMARKABLE READERS

*atT Salon and Emporium*
*11 East 20th Street between 5th and 6th Avenues*
*212-538-0506*
*Wednesdays, 5:30-8pm: The Inner Circle of Readers*
*www.Jennylynch.com*
T Salon's popular Wednesday Psychic Tea draws talented psychics, tarot readers, palm readers and tea-leaf readers each week to this trendy Chelsea hideaway ñ all hand-picked by astrologer Jenny Lynch. T Salon, with its red walls and Buddhist motif, has an energizing, yet calming effect. It offers sandwiches, soups, salads, along with a wide variety of tea blends with names like Zen Blend, Tibetan Tiger, and Whispering Heaven. The evening that I wandered by, I was drawn in by a ceremonial tea-leaf reader named "Isadora" (also reviewed in this section). She grabbed me by the arm and guided me over to a side table. "Concentrate on your tea," she said as she placed a steaming cup of green leaf tea in front of me. "And think of the divine mother." After taking my hands in hers and invoking my "spirit guides," along with the eternal yogi Babaji, she turned to my tea. Her reading was stunningly accurate, as she described my love of writing, travel and accurately described the Celtic "fairies" around me. In a stream-of-consciousness monotone, she said she saw the god Odin playing a "bone" flute, told me to beware of my brother and gave me a ritual to ensure that I would have enough money to "follow my dreams." The reading was quirky, articulate and delightful. Isadora told me that she comes from Bulgarian ancestry and that tea reading came naturally to her. The Wednesday night readings at T Salon are a blessing which will provide you with insight and inspiration. The reading nights are held during certain times of the year, so check Jenny Lynch's website to find out when the next will be held.

### SAMUEL MINOND
*Dowser, psychic healer*
*718-263-3037*
*http://members.aol.com/_ht_a/samnond*
As a child, Samuel Minond could see dead people. "I would walk in a room and my deceased relatives would all be sitting there," says Minond, who grew up in Argentina. "My parents become very upset when I would mention this, so I learned not to say anything." His psychic powers grew and by the time he entered college, he learned that he could heal with his hands. He spent many years as an agricultural engineer

in Israel, "making the desert bloom." While in the desert, he began his life-long interest in "dowsing," to find water. He soon discovered that his dowsing instruments could find much more than water. "I realized that the dowsing tools can also locate illness on the body of person," says Minond. He uses the "double-fisted" dowsing approach ñ holding a pendulum in each hand, which swirl counter-clockwise when they come across a diseased part of the body. After locating the illness, Minond then goes to work with his hands, sending "divine energy" to the person. "I am a channel for the energy," Minond says. "The energy comes from God." He decided to move to New York City in 1976, to pursue his true love of healing and psychic prediction. He now lives in Queens. Minond says that he forces his clients with serious medical issues to see a doctor before they see him. "This is an ethical issue," says Minond. "You also don't have to be sick to see me. When I put my hands on you, the energy will wake you up. You will feel it. This is the proof that my system works."

### SINGH MODI
*Psychic palm reader*
*212-874-6169*
Singh Modi is a world-renowned psychic palmist who has read palms in 187 different countries of the world. Modi, who has been reading professionally since 1958, spends much of the year traveling to distant countries, reading the palms of the rich and famous and teaching this arcane science. His famous clients have included Roberta Flack, Swami Muktananda, Yogi Bhajan, Louise Hay and Joni Mitchell. Modi says he is one of the few palmists in the world who can read the palm from a person's aura. "I can see the aura around each line when I look at a person's palm," says Modi. "For some people, I don't even need to look at their hand to read their palm - I can do it from the aura of their body." Modi claims to have read the palm of Michelangelo from the "aura" of the artwork, David. From his Upper West Side apartment, Modi says that part of his purpose here is to "prepare the planet for the coming Messiah," whom he says will be a woman from the Middle East He approaches palm reading from a profoundly metaphysical background. He believes that, in a past life, he was a temple priest at the Temple of Karnak in Egypt. His lifelong dream is to reopen the School of Mysteries in Luxor, a metaphysical school that would combine the wisdom of

ancient Egypt with the wisdom of other mystery traditions. He envisions the school being on a boat on the Nile, near Luxor. "Bringing back the wisdom from Atlantis and remembering the power within the pyramids will enable us to heal the Earth, our-selves and create a living paradise," says Modi. His readings usually include discussions of health, as well as job and relationship issues. He says that he has saved many lives by pointing out potential health problems. "Just as our lives are ever changing, so are the messages in our hands," says Modi. "Palmistry is an excellent tool for growth and under-standing divine destiny."

### DIANE MUENZ
*Trance channel, healer*
*212-831-9812*
Diane Muenz has the ability to talk to the "other side," whether it be disembodied spirit guides or people who have passed away. Muenz, a former actress and performer, went to a seance in the early 1980s given by the late medium Clifford Bias. "I got hooked - it was so dramatic," says Muenz, who later studied with noted medium Alexander Murray. "I didn't go for spiritual reasons at first, however over time it became very spiritual for me." While Bias would produce "physical manifestations" of spirits, like ectoplasm and "gifts from the astral plane," Munez says that her own channeling style is much less dramatic. Muenz says that she has developed her own style that she teaches, in which she stays semi-conscious throughout the channeling session. It is through the "higher self" that the spirit world is contacted, which makes it a very safe system, she says. Muenz says that, through her channeling, she is in regular contact with Babaji, Daskalos, the "Divine Mother," and the archangel Michael. During a reading, however, beings from the "angelic realms" and even extraterrestrials can come through. During a recent reading, an up-and-coming rock musician asked Muenz to contact the spirits of several, dead, well-known musicians to ask them "how they used their energy systems to create music" (she was suc-cessful in contacting the deceased musicians and the client was happy, she says). Most clients, howev-er, come to her because they are "at a crossroads" in their lives and need some direction. "There are guides out there that can help us with our lives," says Muenz. "My own higher self is a gatherer of information. Other people's guides communicate with my higher self, so that I can bring the informa-

tion to them."

## ALEXANDER MURRAY
*Channel, psychic*
*212-724-0934*
Alexander Murray came to New York more than
35 years ago to be a musician, but he ended up
getting drawn into the city's eclectic spiritualist
scene. In the late 1960s and early 1970s he studied
with such channeling luminaries such as "Agatha"
Wojiechowsky and Clifford Bias, of the First
Universalist Spiritualist Church. His talents were
recognized and he soon found himself reading and
channeling full-time. Murray begins each session
with a "psychometry reading," in which he holds an
object that belongs to the client. He then has the
client sign their name on a piece of paper. "That
way I get a reading about the energy of the past, as
well as where they are in the present," says Murray.
Murray is also well-known for his Tuesday evening
channeling sessions, in which he publicly channels
his "spirit guides, angelic beings and other spiritual
entities." As many as 25 people cram into Murray
Upper West Side apartment to ask questions and
receive guidance from the channeled beings. "I like
people to come on a regular basis because they
begin to become very intimate with the channeled
entities - they start to recognize each being from
the spirit and voice," says Murray, who works primarily by word-of-mouth publicity. "This is not entertainment," he says. "This is for people who want to
grow spiritually and understand their lives better."

## JEAN NIEMILLER
*Psychic astrologer, tarot reader*
*212-734-9276*
For the past 30 years, Jean Niemiller has counseled
New Yorkers with her psychic abilities. "From a
very young age I have been a spiritual seeker," says
Niemiller, who works out of her office on the Upper
East Side. "For me, the psychic realm and material
realm are two-sides of the same coin. Spirituality is
a part of daily life." Niemiller began her astrological
studies in the late 1960s and gave her readings
a psychological focus after working toward her
doctorate in clinical psychology. During a reading,
Niemiller begins by looking at the natal horoscope,
then she consults the tarot to "see what a person's
situation is currently like." After years of reading,
Niemiller says that she relies less and less on
planetary transits to tell the future of a client,

and uses tarot readings more. "If you have a good understanding of a client's natal horoscope, you really don't need to rely on transits so much to understand what is likely to occur in a client's life," says Niemiller. "Honesty can change your life. If you can clearly see what the truth of your life is, your can change it much easier."

## NICOLE
*Tarot reader*
*914-946-8924*
Nicole spent more than eight years as a reader at the famed Gypsy Tea Kettle psychic readers' cafe on the Upper East Side. One of her regular clients was Don Conte, president of the New York Theosophical Society. So when the teahouse closed two years ago, Conte invited her to become a regular reader at Quest Bookstore, the bookstore of the TS. Nicole can now be found nearly every day at the bookstore, using her unique skills to enhance people's lives. Nicole grew up in France during World War II. She later moved to Los Angeles with her family. Her interest in the esoteric began when she joined the Rosicrucian Order (AMORC) in the late 1950s and also studied with tarot masters Rev. Sawcet and "Roxilana." Nicole began her reading career at the famed Bodhi Tree and Joshua Tree bookstores in the Los Angeles area. She moved to New York City in 1991. "A lot of what I do is like psychotherapy," says Nicole. "I've read for so many people that I can very quickly get to the bottom of a situation." Nicole's schedule at Quest is usually full, so it is best to make an appointment with her.

## ARLENE NIMARK
*Uranian Astrologer*
*718-377-7625*
Arlene Nimark is one of the few genuine Uranian Astrologers on the East Coast. Uranian Astrology, you say? "Put it this way, one of my clients said that regular Astrology is like an x-ray of your life - and Uranian Astrology is like an MRI," say Nimark, a Brooklyn resident. Nimark began her astrological studies in the 1970s, studying with such luminaries as Charles Emerson and Wayne Booher. Uranian Astrology was discovered in 1914, by a German named Alfred Witte, who realized - on the eve of World War I - that traditional astrology simply wasn't picking up important events (like the war). This type of astrology stresses "hard aspects" and uses a "360 degree dial" to key in on future events.

YOGA | ESOTERIC GROUPS | WITCHCRAFT | OCCULT UNDERGROUND | BOOKS | UFOS | BOTANICAS | TANTRA | **ASTROLOGERS & PSYCHICS** |

Uranian astrologers are not that common, most likely because the system is complicated to learn. But clients swear to the accuracy of its predictions. "Astrology is like a light switch in a dark room," says Nimark. "If you walk in the room with the lights out, you bump into furniture. Astrology is the light that helps you walk around pitfalls, rather than stumbling around."

### JACK OLMEDA
*Psychic clairvoyant, palm reader*
516-568-1829
As a young boy, Jack Olmeda would have vivid, lucid dreams about the people that he knew. "When I told people about the dreams, they were amazed because what I would dream, would eventually happen to them," says Olmeda, who grew up in Queens and the Bronx. Olmeda found that he had a talent to tap into the psychic world, as well as the ability to channel spirits of the deceased. While a teenager, Olmeda worked as a "trance medium," channeling the spirits of the people who had passed away, and giving information to their relatives. "After each reading, I felt very tired and drained," says Olmeda. "I just couldn't do it anymore." Olmeda took a break from psychic work, until he ended up in the hospital with a collapsed lung. Olmeda says that his "spirit guides" came through during the illness, and told him that he must "follow the path" of helping people through his psychic gifts. Olmeda says that he now conducts psychic readings using tarot cards, as well as palm reading. "I tend to read very quickly, because the information is being channeled so quickly," says Olmeda. "I encourage people to tape the sessions." Olmeda also conducts healing sessions with a reiki master and reflexologist; Olmeda uses his psychic vision to guide the two healers to areas of the client's body, which need healing energy. "A reading helps a person to control their destiny," says Olmeda. "When I predict that a negative event will occur, the client has the power to prevent his event. God gave us free will so that we can all change our destinies."

### VICTORIA O'NEILL
*Psychic consultant, tarot reader, dream analyst*
212-420-0548
Victoria O'Neill has spent much of her life with one foot in the spirit world. From a very young age, O'Neill - who grew up on St. Mark's Place in the East Village - has been in contact with spirit guides from

the astral realms. "I believe in the power of prayer," says O'Neill. "We are all connected telepathically." O'Neill is a true mystic, connected with the ascended master Saint Germain through the I Am Temple in New York City. She also has the ability to talk to the spirits of those who have passed away. "Sometimes when a client comes and sees me, the person brings with them the spirit of a deceased loved one," says O'Neill. "This does not happen in every reading, but many times the client does receive a message from the beyond." O'Neill's esoteric interests include time travel, automatic writing, UFOs, palmistry and "trumpet phenomena," where the spirits of spiritual masters "speak through" a megaphone-type instrument. O'Neill also received her ordination from the New Seminary. O'Neill usually begins each reading with tarot spread (she has been reading the tarot since she was 15 years old) and then begins to receive information from her spirit guides. She generally likes to conduct her readings at her home, which is on East 15th Street. "I have the gift of being able to see things that other people can't - like dead people," says O'Neill. "People get very comforted when they have a reading with me. They realize that their loved ones are still with them." O'Neill has an uncanny ability to pick up on psychic information; during the phone interview I conducted with her, she told me the street that I lived on, the street my brother lived on - then predicted the "blackout of 2003."

## OSTARO
*Astrologer*
*212-686-4121*
*www.ostaro.com*
You may have seen Ostaro as the "swami" in Woody Allen's Stardust Memories, or lately, as the Indian researcher in the Geico commercials. But Ostaro's real talent is as an astrologer - he has accurately predicted the breakup of the Soviet Union and foretold the elections of former President Bill Clinton and New York Governor George Pataki. Ostaro studied both astrology and the Kabbalah while in Paris in the late 1960s. Ostaro says that he practices a little-known form of Chaldean astrology - the original astrology, he says. His readings are very specific. In addition to future predictions, Ostaro also uses numerology to determine "lucky days," as well as the "places of power" in the world, where you can reach your destiny. Ostaro is a mystic who uses his occult philosophy in his accessible self-help

YOGA | ESOTERIC GROUPS | WITCHCRAFT | OCCULT UNDERGROUND | BOOKS | UFOS | BOTANICAS | TANTRA | **ASTROLOGERS & PSYCHICS** |

book, Art and Craft of Success. Ostaro keeps a spiritual focus on all his readings; he is a disciple of Paramahansa Yogananda and practices yogic healing techniques. "My readings will tell you the ways to maximize your life," says Ostaro. "My system is very powerful and accurate."

## ROGER PRATT
*Psychic tarot*
*212-677-9588*
*www.rogerpratt.com*
Roger Pratt was raised as a witch, so the supernatural comes as second nature to him. "My mother was a witch from Scotland," says Pratt, who once belonged to the Triple Star coven in Greenwich Village. "Witches generally run in families." As a very young boy growing up in the Bronx, Pratt was fascinated by the tarot and "intuitively knew what the cards meant." He began reading professionally in 1982, after years of study and reading for friends and relatives. Pratt's readings are unique because he is assisted by a "spirit guide" he calls "Madonna," who informs him about the issues of his clients. "She tells me a lot. Sometimes she talks so much that I have to almost stop the reading," says Pratt. "She won't tell me her real name. All I know is that she worked on a plantation - she's a mammy figure." Pratt worked for a number of years as an art teacher and once owned a store called Predictions, but now concentrates full-time on his readings. He says that much of what he does involves specific predictions, however most of it is counseling. "After years of doing this, I have realized that most people have come into the world with a specific purpose. There is one thing that they have always wanted to do, but might not have been able to," says Pratt. "The reading helps identify what this is and how they can do it and achieve their dreams."

## MARIA PAPAPEDROS
*Psychic*
*212-935-4441*
*www.mpapapedros.com*
Maria Papapedros become known as the "Hollywood Psychic" after she coached Demi Moore on how to be a psychic in the movie Ghost. From that time on, Papapedros has become a favorite reader of Hollywood types, and now spends half her time in the California. "I originally went as a movie consultant, but I ended up reading for the actors and directors," says Papapedros, a native of Greece. Papapedros is one

of the most sought-after psychics in New York City, and has been reading professionally since 1974. She begins each reading by holding an object of the client, such as a piece of jewelry or keys. Papapedros, however, does not believe that one's future is written in stone. "I believe that people create their own reality," says Papapedros. "I point out what is going to happen and then how to create it or change it - because you can."

## RAE RAMSEY
*Animal communicator*
*212-688-5638*
*www.ramseycommunication.com*
Rae Ramsey has been called the "UN translator" for the animal world. Since a young child growing up in Michigan, she realized that she had the unique gift of being able to telepathically communicate with the animal kingdom. She later honed her skills by studying with renowned animal communicators Don Hayman and Penelope Smith. Ramsey's style of communication is "heart-to-heart, mind-to-mind." "It is a two-way communication," says Ramsey. "I tell the owners what their animal is saying and then communicate to the animal what the owner wants the animal to know." For instance, a couple recently brought their sick hamster to them. "They wanted to have the hamster put to sleep," says Ramsey. "But the hamster didn't want to die that way and communicated to them that he wanted to go home and take his medicine." The hamster eventually recovered, and later died a peaceful death at home. Ramsey has communicated with iguanas, snakes and lizards, but the majority of her clients want her to communicate with their dogs and cats, particularly during times of "life transitions," like moving or having a baby. Ramsey does most of her consultations over the phone and, as a result, has clients throughout the world. Clients usually send a photograph of their pet so that Ramsey can establish a telepathic link. "Many people get a deeper sense of who their animals are," says Ramsey. "Often times the reading brings transformation and peace into the life of the client, as issues with their pets are resolved."

## PAULA ROBERTS
*Clairvoyant, graphologist, ghost hunter*
*212-751-7122*
*www.paularoberts.org*
Paula Roberts is a gifted psychic who gives "straightforward readings, without the gobbledygook". Born in England, Roberts has become well-

known in New York City as "The English Psychic"
and has been frequently featured on network TV
shows to discuss her work. "The bottom line is
whether or not a reader is really clairvoyant," says
Roberts. "The true clairvoyant can use a variety of
tools, or none at all, and get accurate information."
Roberts was recognized as a clairvoyant as a child,
growing up just outside London. She went into a
trance when she was five years old and began having "mediumistic" experiences. In 1971 she joined
the Spiritualist Association of Great Britain, where
her talents where developed and nurtured. She
moved to the United States in 1978 and quickly
established herself as one of the city's most accurate predictors and even had her own weekly, live,
call-in show for over 10 years in which she gave psychic readings on the air to viewers. Roberts can see
the future as well as past events in a person's life.
She also has the rare ability to sense ghostly spirits.
Unsolved Mysteries once brought her to a haunted
Philadelphia Inn (of which she knew nothing) and
she immediately described exactly where she saw
the Revolutionary soldier who has been seen there
for over a hundred years! She is also a favorite of
New York Post columnist, Cindy Adams, who has
published her annual world predictions for many
years. Roberts' specialty, however, is giving personal
readings. Her book Love Letters, the Romantic
Secrets Hidden in our Handwriting and video
Foretelling the Future, Learn the Tarot with Paula
Roberts are in current distribution. She begins each
session by quickly looking at the client's handwriting
to get insight into the person's energy levels and
personality traits. Then she opens her clairvoyant
vision to "see" the client's talents, future and past.
"I give practical information about situations (and
people) occurring over the next few years" says
Roberts. "The readings are precise and direct. I bring
people the information they need to anticipate, deal
with and enjoy their lives."

**LEXA ROSEAN**
*Tarot reader, astrologer, spell consultant*
212-529-1353
www.easyenchantments.com
When doing a reading for a client, Lexa Rosean sees
both tarot and astrology as indispensable. "For me,
the tarot is the right hand and astrology is the left
hand," says Rosean, the author of the several popular books, including The Supermarket Sorceress. A
long-time practitioner of Wicca, Rosean also assists

her clients through candles, incense, oils and magical baths. "The reading is like a diagnosis for a client," says Rosean. "The prescription, in this case, is the spell. I feel that you need to help a client, more than just telling them a certain event is going to happen to them." Rosean - a natural psychic who was born with a caul - honed her reading skills after being initiated into Wicca by Lady Rhea in 1982 and working in a local occult shop. She now does readings every Wednesdays and Fridays at Morgana's Chamber in Greenwich Village. Following the publication of her first book, she now has clients from around the world. Unlike in Europe, Rosean notes that many New Yorkers are unique because they don't come in for readings "until there is crisis and they have gotten in trouble." She suggests that people come in regularly for a "psychic checkup." "It is much easier to deal with a situation before it happens," says Rosean. "The purpose of a reading is to enlighten a person and make them more aware of themselves."

## CELESTE RUSTON
*Astrologer, numerologist*
*212-465-3295; 212-330-9126*

For years, astrologer Celeste Ruston's international clientele included some of the scions of the business and art worlds. "All they wanted to know was the timing of things, like when to buy a property and when to open a business," says Ruston. "However, my primary interest now is working with people on their relationships and direction in life." Ruston spent her childhood and formative years living in England, where she travels to regularly. It was while pursuing a degree in psychology in Europe that she developed a love of astrology. She studied with such astrological luminaries as Liz Greene, Stephen Arroyo and Michael Lutin, and has been a professional astrologer, as well as a psychologist, since 1979. Ruston sees personal relationships as the keys to creating a peaceful world. "Relationships are everything in life. How we live our lives on a day-to-day basis forms the foundation of how we heal the planet," she says. "You can't go out and help others when you are conflicted yourself." Ruston likes to spend several hours with a client during the first "master session" visit, to get to know the client through their horoscope. During follow-up sessions, she works with clients to actualize their dreams, according to the life destiny as shown in their natal chart. "The follow-on sessions is when we start creating," says Ruston. "Each of us has a unique destiny.

With the reading, we begin planning the client's life, so that they live in harmony with their life purpose."

## RUTH
*Playing card reader*
212-685-2848

Many who patronized the "Gypsy Tea Kettle," which was located on East 56th Street most likely have come across Ruth, the playing card reader. Ruth has been reading playing cards for more than 22 years - and 20 of those years have been at the Gypsy Tea Kettle. Ruth - a native of Switzerland - learned how to read cards from a real group of Gypsies who lived near her village. "In using playing cards, you have to use a great deal of intuition," says Ruth. "Everyone is psychic to a certain extent. It is a talent that needs to be exercised." Ruth says that she prefers playing cards to the tarot. "Every playing card has a meaning," says Ruth. "It can be very precise." Ruth reads every Tuesday at TRS and also does phone readings. At the Gypsy Tea Kettle, Ruth gave thousands of readings, which has honed her skill. "Most people come in worried about love or money," says Ruth. "The reading helps put your mind at ease."

## CLARA SALA
*Evolutionary astrology*
212-388-7135

As a spoken-word poet, Clara Sala has always been interested in "matters of the spirit." "My intention in both astrology and poetry to help people heal themselves," says Sala, who lives in Fort Green, Brooklyn. "Both art forms facilitate the healing of the emotional body." Sala graduated from Jeffrey Wolf Greene's intensive Evolutionary Astrology course, which focuses on the "soul's intention coming into this lifetime." Wolfe's method uniquely pinpoints the soul's talents and what experiences the soul carries from past lives. Sala's specialty is working with gender identity and sexual intimacy issues, along with the "emotional dynamics" that cause these issues. "I work a lot with childhood trauma issues and the karmic patterns of a person's life," says Sala. "Once you understand the soul's purpose for incarnating, it becomes a lot easier to make life decisions and become aware of your potential."

## JORDANA SANDS
*Psychic*
212-832-7657
www.jordanasands.com

Jordana Sands' specialty is helping her clients find their soul mates. "The problem with most women and men is that they have a specific idea of what their soul mate should be and look like," says Sands. "However, I teach my clients that they need to define themselves first before they can attract this soul mate." Sands' book How to Recognize Your Soul Mate, Across a Crowded Room, at a Boring Cocktail Party details her years of experience in bringing many of her clients to the relationships of their dreams. Sands is a clairvoyant who uses tarot, palmistry, graphology and numerology in every reading she does. She also offers a unique service called "psychic art," in which she draws the psychic impressions she receives from a client. A former actress and performer, Sands began giving psychic readings when she was 17 years old and has had a private psychic consulting practice since 1983. "I like to look at myself as a flashlight, a guide for people," says Sands. "You are what you think and I help my clients change the way they think so that they can make lasting changes in their lives."

## MATTHEW SAWICKI
*Tarot reader, crystal skryer, psychometry*
*917-434-5223*
He's young, he's hip and he's a witch. Matthew Sawicki is one of "Lady Rhea's children," and has been initiated as a Wiccan high priest. His readings blend in his occult knowledge and his intuitive sensitivity. He honed his skills by working as a tarot reader and oil blender at Enchantments in the East Village, after graduating from high school. "It was a great education. Working there opened my eyes up to so many new things," says Sawicki, who grew up in a small Pennsylvania town. Sawicki says that his Wiccan training has helped him develop his psychic skills, as well as his skills as a medium. "I've been able to communicate with the dead on more than one occasion and can hear spirits," says Sawicki. His readings, however, focus on helping people "gain clarity in their lives." While at Enchantments, he did readings for several movie stars and carved candles for a number of well-known recording artists. He found that many young people were drawn to him for readings. "I tend to get people in my own age group. I can relate to them and know where they are coming from," he says. Sawicki has since left Enchantments and now reads for private clients. Sawicki is also active in re-energizing the Minoan Brotherhood, a coven for gay male witches.

## CASSANDRA SAULTER
*Psychic, tarot reader*
*212-929-3490*
Cassandra Saulter's art is an integral part of her tarot readings. In the late 1980s, she channeled her original tarot deck, Tarot Des Artistes, an impressionistic rendering of the major arcana. She also designed a second deck, Deck of Bells. "I am an artist, first and foremost," says Saulter. "I don't advertise for clients. People find me through word of mouth." Saulter's unique reading style uses four separate decks, and she only uses the major arcana cards. Saulter first became interested in the tarot while living as an artist in Northern Italy. A close friend was doing a reading and Saulter noticed that she could understand the meaning of the cards as her friend drew them. She has been reading ever since. "When I do a reading, I become like a mirror," Saulter says. "Through the cards I open a window into a person's universe."

## MARK SELTMAN
*Palm reader, astrologer, tarot reader*
*212-777-0540*
*www.markseltman.com*
Don't ever call Mark Seltman a psychic. He says that he considers himself a scientist. Dubbed the "Mozart of palm readers," Seltman contends that palm reading is based on a science that began more than 5,000 years ago in Vedic India and has evolved throughout the centuries. Pamistry entered the modern age with the works of William Benham in the early 1900s. "At one time, palmistry was even taught in the universities of Europe," says Seltman. Seltman says that his main focus is helping his clients evolve and resolve their problems. "Some readers want to impress their clients with a lot of predictions," says Seltman. "I work on a psychological level. I want my clients to walk out of a session feeling good about themselves." Seltman's clients include corporations, individuals and he specializes in reading at parties. Seltman has made some outstanding predictions, including the fall of Enron (which he did through studying the astrological chart of the company). During his 20 years in business, Seltman has studied thousands of hands. He is considered one of the best palm readers in the country and says that someday he would like to become a spokesman for the science of palmistry. "The science of palmistry is not that difficult," Seltman says. "But teaching it in a way that people will understand, now that is the challenge."

## KATHRYN E. SPENCER
*Palm reader, tarot reader*
212-714-7068
www.mystic-media.com
From a person's palm, Kathryn E. Spencer can tell a person's destiny and potential. Spencer has been giving readings and teaching since 1985. Spencer's reading typically includes a tarot spread and looking at a client's palm, but it is in the palm where she obtains most of her information. "Whatever the cards don't tell, the palm will," says Spencer. "What I do is point out a person's talents." Spencer says that she can tell where a person works by the shape of their hands. "A person who works on Wall Street has a very distinctive hand shape," she says. Chillingly, Spencer has also studied the hands of Holocaust survivors, who also had distinctive markings on their hands. "All of them had a certain marking line next to their life line, which signified a second chance at life," she says. Spencer can be found every Thursday at Quest Bookstore on East 53 Street. Spencer also teaches a popular palmistry course at the New York Theosophical Society. At the end of the course, her students are able to do basic palm readings. "One of my goals is to keep palmistry alive and well respected," says Spencer. "Most people walk around not knowing their potential - but it is all there in their hands."

## WILLIAM STICKEVERS
*Classical Astrologer*
212-986-9739
Willam Stickevers specializes in medieval astrology and alchemy based upon the works of Bonnati, Lilly and Marsilio Ficino.In addition to reading your natal chart, Stickevers can make a magical talisman, which can bring the energy of a specific planet into your life. This arcane science is based upon the ancient Arabic book the Picatrix.For instance, if you wanted more love in your life, you could have a Venus talisman made. Stickevers studied with medieval astrology expert Robert Zoller, along with noted astrologers Jim Lewis and Alphee Lavoie. Stickevers has also made it big in Japan, and travels there several times a year to lecture and conduct readings.

## LLOYD STRAYHORN
*Numerologist, palmist, astrologer*
212-685-2848
www.numbersandyou.com
Using only your date of birth and name, Lloyd

Strayhorn can tell your life story - as well as your future. "In numerology, each letter corresponds to a number," says Strayhorn, who has been a professional numerologist for more than 30 years. "From the name I get your numbers. All numbers are ruled by the planets." From these numbers, Strayhorn can tell one's talents, skills, abilities, the types of people attracted to you and your "lucky lottery numbers." Strayhorn's unique numerology system has been detailed in his book Numbers and You, one of the most respected numerology books in print. Strayhorn can even pick up health problems from your birthdate, since "each number rules a different part of the body." Many clients swear by Strayhorn's picks for best days, weeks and years. "The lucky numbers are very important," he says. "They can help you in both love and career - which is why most people come to me." Numerology is a love and passion for Strayhorn, and he is one of the best in the field. "I learned by doing this for people," he says. "My goal is to help a person help themselves - through numbers."

## SARA TSUTSUMI
*I-Ching consultant*
*212-995-5813*

Sara Tsutsumi learned the I-Ching the traditional way - from her grandmother, who was a healer and psychic in Tsutsumi's homeland of Japan. Tsutsumi has been reading the I-Ching for clients for about 20 years. She is well-known in the Japanese community of New York for her uncanny abilities to give sound spiritual advice, but she is also getting more European and American clients. "When you want to make a decision on a job or relationship, it is good to consult the I-Ching," says Tsutsumi, who originally moved to the United States 13 years ago to pursue a degree in psychology. The I-Ching is traditionally consulted by "throwing" coins or yarrow sticks, and from the result of these tosses you get a "hexagram." The I-Ching book has the divinatory meanings of each of the 64 hexagrams. The written I-Ching can be quite vague, which is why a good I-Ching reader is needed to interpret the meanings. Tsutsumi, however, doesn't use coins or yarrow sticks during a divination. Instead, she uses a special set of beads that her grandmother gave her; Tsutsumi has been blind since birth and has memorized all of the divinatory meanings of the hexagrams. She meets clients in her Greenwich Village apartment, where she also has a thriving psychotherapy practice." "Experience is very important when using the I-Ching," she says. "When I do a reading, the I-Ching speaks through me. It is like I am not talking and someone else is talking. People end up having much more peace of mind when they leave the reading. Their anxiousness and confusion leaves them. That is why the I-Ching is such a revered oracle."

## STACEY ANNE WOLF
*Psychic, astrologer, medium*
212-330-8189
www.staceywolf.com; www.getpsychic.com
Stacey Anne Wolf has been called the "Generation X" psychic, for her uncanny predictions and her popularity with New York's young crowd. But, at one time, Wolf says that she considered herself the "reluctant psychic." "I had my first prediction when I was three," says Wolf. "The nursery school teacher was late and I told everyone it was because she broke her arm. When it turned out I was right, it really freaked my parents out." Wolf has since learned to accept her gift and has become one of New York City's hippest psychics. She has appeared as a "psychic expert" on television shows like Beyond with James Van Praagh, The View, Sally Jesse Raphael, and The Late Show with David Letterman. Wolf is no stranger to television - she is a graduate of NYU Film School and once worked as a producer for MTV. She decided to devote all of her energy to her psychic career in 1992. Wolf begins her sessions by holding her client's hands to "tune in" to their energy. She meditates deeply prior to a session and often gets information from a client's deceased relative. She may also use the tarot to "zero in" on a particular issue in a person's life. Wolf has become popular on the special events circuit and has numerous clients in the publishing, public relations and entertainment industry. "My readings remind people of who they are," says Wolf. "I help them take off the old clothing that does not fit them. Underneath they will find their true self."

## HENRY WEINGARTEN
*Financial astrologer*
212-949-7211
www.afund.com
Henry Weingarten has taken the art of financial astrology to a new level. Weingarten has been a practicing astrologer for the past 30 years and is the founder of the New York School of Astrology

and New York Astrology Center. But his passion is using astrology as a predictive tool for the stock market. "Astrology is the edge," says Weingarten, from his office on Lexington Avenue. "It allows you to make more money with less risk." Weingarten founded the Astrologer's Fund to provide financial advice for investor; his weekly newsletter Wall Street Next Week has become required reading in certain investment circles. Some of Weingarten's more prominent predictions include the 1990 Tokyo Market Crash, the beginning and end of the last recession, both wars with Iraq, the Nasdaq correction of 2000 and the decline of the Euro after its 1999 birth. Although Weingarten does consultations for select clients, his primary focus now is reaching a larger audience through his newsletter. Weingarten's office, at 370 Lexington Avenue, Suite 416 (near 40th Street), is a must-stop for serious astrologers, since it has the best collection of astrological books for sale in the city. "Astrology is not a perfect tool, but it is right more often than any other technique," says Weingarten.

## ELAINE WOODALL
*Psychic counselor*
*212-781-3600*
It was a bout with chronic fatigue syndrome more than 20 years ago that propelled Dr. Elaine Woodall from a career as an art history professor to a career as a psychic and healer. "Shortly after I healed myself from chronic fatigue, I started to develop psychic ability and people began coming to me for guidance," says Woodall. "The illness was a sign from the universe that I was living a life not consistent with my life purpose." Since then, Woodall has earned her Ph.D in psychotherapy and founded The Psycho-Spiritual Institute, which offers energy healing, meditation, psychology and past-life regression, to help clients access their "inner guidance and Higher Self." Woodall has been called a "natural healer" by the International Society for the Study of Subtle Energy and Energy Medicine (ISSSEEM). Both her psychic readings and healing sessions are held in her midtown office, near the Empire State Building. She says she works with her spirit guides and higher self to connect with the client's "primary spirit guide and higher self," to provide psychic information.
"If good things happen to you, that is great," says Woodall. "But the key to a good psychic reading is to become aware of the impending bad things, and then having the awareness to avoid these events."

# Index

### *About the Author*

Scott Harney graduated from Boston College and earned his master's degree from the Boston University Graduate School of Journalism. He spent many years as a news reporter and editor for *Journal Transcript Publications* in the Greater Boston area; he also spent several years as an editor at *Egypt Today* magazine in Cairo, Egypt.

Harney served as a diplomat at the United States Mission to the United Nations in New York City from 2000-2003. He is currently a Foreign Service Officer with the United States Department of State. He is a long-time student of mysticism and the Western Mystery Tradition.